Rob&Gris

Wishing you

the best always!

Your friend ..

M Vega

DEAL

In a deadly game of working undercover, DEA Special Agent Michael S. Vigil recounts standing face to face with treacherous drug lords who began their conversation with "If you are a federal agent we will kill you."

Michael S. Vigil

DEAL
IN A DEADLY GAME OF WORKING UNDERCOVER,
DEA SPECIAL AGENT MICHAEL VIGIL RECOUNTS
STANDING FACE TO FACE WITH TREACHEROUS DRUG
LORDS WHO BEGAN THEIR CONVERSATION WITH "IF
YOU ARE A SPECIAL AGENT WE WILL KILL YOU."

iUniverse books may be ordered through booksellers or by contacting:

iUniverse LLC
1663 Liberty Drive
Bloomington, IN 47403
www.iuniverse.com
1-800-Authors (1-800-288-4677)

ISBN: 978-1-4917-3519-0 (sc)
ISBN: 978-1-4917-3521-3 (hc)
ISBN: 978-1-4917-3520-6 (e)

Library of Congress Control Number: 2014909231

Printed in the United States of America.

iUniverse rev. date: 07/21/2014

Dedication

This book is dedicated to my parents, Alice and Sam, whose tremendous sacrifices and love made this a better world for my sisters and me. Their teachings of compassion, dedication, dignity, justice, and courage became indelible traits in my life. They provided us with the education required to succeed in a highly competitive world. They are in my daily thoughts and deep in my heart.

I also dedicate this book to my sisters, Anita and Mona, for all their love and support.

And to my niece Ursula, who has made me proud with her accomplishments and energy. She is a shining star in my life. I admire and love her unconditionally.

The book is also in loving memory of my niece Nicole, who was taken early in life.

For my grandchildren, Luke Edward and Sarah Claire Haynie, who make life worth living and whose love I will treasure forever.

To my wife, Suzanne, whose love and support have been key to my life and accomplishments.

Contents

Foreword

It is a distinct privilege to have Colombian National Police General (Ret.) Leonardo Gallego Castrillón write the foreword to my book. He is a legendary figure in the history of Colombia and the greatest general to come from the ranks of the Colombian National Police. He was responsible for many of the most significant counterdrug operations ever conducted in Colombia. His leadership and operational abilities are beyond reproach. I have always considered him a brother, and I will always treasure his friendship.

During his tenure as commander of the world renowned DANTI (Anti-Narcotics Police) he played a key role in the dismantling of the Medellin, Cali, and Valle del Norte cartels, which were the largest and most powerful in the world. He has served in other command positions to include anti-terrorism and intelligence for more than twenty-five years. General Gallego is one of the most highly decorated officers of the Colombian National Police. He holds awards and decorations from law-enforcement and military organizations of the United States and other countries around the globe.

—Michael Vigil

It was an honor to work with Mike Vigil during the most difficult and violent years in the history of Colombia. It was a time when the brutal drug-trafficking organizations posed a significant threat to my country and also the United States. Many individuals were tortured and murdered for simply denouncing the drug cartels in mere conversations with other individuals. The traffickers employed vicious killers, and they could order the death of anyone perceived as a threat to their illicit business, with less fanfare than ordering a glass of *aguardiente*. These notorious assassins charged as little as fifty US dollars for taking a human life. It was sometimes impossible to avoid these assassins, since they pursued their victims on motorcycles and maneuvered through heavy traffic until they were able to direct volleys of high-velocity bullets at their human targets. Blood flowed through the streets, and no one was safe, especially officials of the Colombian National Police and our colleagues from the Drug Enforcement Administration (DEA).

Mike was one of the most extraordinary and courageous warriors, who always led from the front and never from the rear. He was always the first one through the door on raids, which is quite a risk, since one never knows what is waiting on the other side. Mike was willing to take those risks, which could have easily gotten him killed, in order to protect others from harm. He knows the face of death full well and never once flinched, despite knowing that he could be drawing his last breath.

I worked closely with Mike, and together, we seized tons of cocaine and other illicit drugs. Additionally, we arrested thousands of drug traffickers, many of them cartel heads who were brought to justice in my country or the United States. Our struggle was horrific, and it can only be described as one with "no quarter asked for and none given." It was one of triumph and great sacrifice. We lost many of our close friends to the random and senseless violence generated by narcoterrorists. We witnessed more violence than most individuals witness in a hundred lifetimes, but we continued to pursue the drug traffickers with great vigor, despite the constant threats.

Mike was responsible for the complex operation that resulted in the capture of Juan Ramón Matta-Ballesteros in Cartagena, Colombia. Matta was a major cocaine trafficker from Honduras who was married to Nancy Vasquez, a Colombian woman from Cali. Matta was responsible for smuggling tons of cocaine into the United States each year and was also the source of supply to the most prolific and deadly traffickers operating in Mexico. He was involved in the killing of DEA Agent Kiki Camarena in Guadalajara. Mike meticulously planned and executed the operation that led to his capture. Matta offered several millions of dollars to the agents to buy his freedom, but he ultimately knew his opulent lifestyle was coming to an end.

Mike is truly a brilliant tactician, and he was able to initiate numerous multinational operations, which had significant impact on the international drug trade and facilitated the sharing of information between countries. These operations were only made possible because of the magnificent leadership skills possessed by Mike and [his] army of individuals who were willing to follow him into the fires of hell with no hesitation. During the annual International Drug Enforcement Conferences (IDEC), I watched in awe the great deference and respect given to Mike by all of the directors of national police agencies from around the world. They depended on his leadership and guidance on operational matters. The representatives from the various countries actually put aside decades and even centuries of political conflict if Mike intervened and requested their participation in large operations. He was a formidable force of great strength that inspired others in overcoming insurmountable obstacles.

Mike has always had the courage to stand alone in the face of adversity, the tenacity to never succumb to pressure, and the patience to keep fighting against all odds until the struggle is won. He refuses to accept defeat, and this defines his leadership style. His character is also defined by humility and the ability to make decisions under fire. Mike never demanded respect, but earned it in the jungles of Latin America and the dark alleys of metropolitan areas. I have heard his colleagues refer to him as a "wartime general," and he most definitely is worthy of the title. He bears the scars of many violent and protracted struggles against the treacherous drug cartels. His courage exceeded normal human boundaries, and it became psychologically intoxicating to his subordinates who, as a result, pushed themselves above and beyond the accomplishments that they believed themselves capable of reaching. Mike is a great hero in my country and in the United States. He has achieved what others cannot envision.

—General Leonardo Gallego Castrillón
Director of Colombian Anti-Narcotics Police (Ret.)

Chapter 1

If You Are a Federal Agent, We Will Kill You

Imagine a criminal foreign environment with no computers, no cell phones, and no diplomatic protection; this was Mike's world ... this was Mike's playground ... make a mistake, a miscalculation, or misread the intentions of an individual, and your life ends in a blink of an eye. Now live that life, make cases, prosecute, arrest, and produce volumes of intelligence that to this day is the history of that threat ... and you begin to see that Mike Vigil's journey into the depths of that world is something that modern law enforcement will never experience or ever see ...

—L.D. Villalobos
Chief Intelligence Officer, DEA
El Paso Intelligence Center (Ret.)

The small caravan moved swiftly on the narrow, winding road. The blazing sun beat down on the scorched Sonora Desert. Heat waves bounced off the dark, cracked asphalt in a yellow, shimmering curtain. Most of the caravan consisted of at least a dozen grizzled and hardened Mexican Federal Judicial Police (MFJP) based out of Hermosillo, Sonora. They were heavily armed with 9 mm semiautomatic handguns

1

and their weapon of choice, the .45-caliber pistol. Many of them also carried machine guns with long curved magazines packed with dozens of bullets, in case fate was not kind and the afternoon turned violent and nasty. I was leading the caravan in a truck with a large camper shell that made steering on the winding road somewhat problematic.

The truck had been seized by the MFJP at a roadblock when they found a couple of tons of marijuana hidden inside. The marijuana was destined for the lucrative consumer market in the United States, where distributors would have sold it on the streets for millions of dollars. After all, the drug trade was all about the money. Ironically, the truck would now be used against the violent Mexican drug traffickers, who were some of the most vicious and brutal in the world. Accompanying me in the truck was an informant who, a week earlier, had introduced me to a group of significant drug traffickers associated with Rafael Caro Quintero. The organization belonging to Caro Quintero was responsible for numerous brutal murders throughout Mexico.

The informant was short and heavyset, with thick, dark hair, and his eyes always reflected a blank, merciless stare. He was on the periphery of the drug trade and knew enough about the business and certain drug networks to be a valuable source of information. He realized that it was better to provide information and act as a mercenary than take the risk of going to jail or dying. Jail or premature death is the typical retirement plan for drug traffickers. Of course, he was in danger as well by acting as an informant, but to him, it was less of a risk and the DEA was paying him decent money.

The MFJP who were part of the operation were friends of mine, and I trusted them. I had quickly learned that when working dangerous undercover assignments, especially in foreign countries, I was always facing death and therefore had to be self-reliant and prepared for the unexpected. Regardless, I knew that the MFJP had little tolerance for long surveillances. Their patience had a very small window, and this was always a compelling concern when working with them on undercover operations. When their impatience was at a peak, I knew things could rapidly get out of control and I had to be prepared to deal with the worst-case scenarios. Conversely, I knew they would not compromise my identity. Without this trust, I could not have successfully continued my mission. I had learned that personal relationships were the key when working with foreign police counterparts. Professional relationships are always important, though not sufficient without a more personal camaraderie. I broke bread and drank with them on a regular basis. They trusted and protected me as one of their own. Although the MFJP did not wear uniforms, it seemed as though they all dressed in what I called the "Mexican *federale* couture": tailored leisure suits and the obligatory massive gold bracelets. Many had their names spelled out in large diamonds. For reasons I could not fathom, they typically emulated the typical drug trafficker's attire of choice.

During the previous week, the informant and I traveled to a small Mexican town called Caborca. It was a tiny village located in the northern part of the state of Sonora. The locals were primarily farmers whose fruits and vegetables were sold to US distributors, while the poorer-quality produce ended up in Mexican food stores. It was a matter of economics in which the farmers were able to sell their products at a higher price to buyers from the United States. Based on its proximity to the US border, the town had also become a staging area for illicit drugs smuggled into the United States through the California, Arizona, and New Mexico border areas. Caborca was a known stronghold of Rafael Caro Quintero, a major drug trafficker, who had a longstanding reputation for being a ruthless, homicidal psychopath.

Caro Quintero, many years later, would be responsible for abducting and killing DEA Special Agent Enrique "Kiki" Camarena. Caro had been raised in the state of Sinaloa and had been a cunning street thug as a teenager. Since he came from a very poor family, it was unlikely that an education was in his future. Many of his uncles were involved in the drug trade, and they mentored him on all facets of the business, which he took to like a duck to water. Eventually, he rose to become one of the most prolific and significant criminals in Mexico. He ordered the killings of dozens of police officials and political figures, based on nothing more than a whim.

The informant had arranged for me to meet with the traffickers at a local restaurant. It also served as a gas station for tractor-trailer rigs that hauled produce grown in the area to the US border. That afternoon, I had decided to meet and conduct initial negotiations with the drug dealers, without surveillance or backup. I knew it was extremely dangerous to go in alone, but I had no choice if I wanted the operation to be successful. Undercover work in Mexico was not for timid souls, and this was the way things were done in the late 1970s.

Shortly after we arrived, I saw a black Ford Ranger pickup truck park in front of the restaurant. Two well-dressed Mexican males stepped out. They were wearing cowboy hats and expensive ostrich boots. Their belts had large gold-and-silver belt buckles the size of Roman shields. When they entered, they immediately recognized the informant and approached our table. They looked at me suspiciously, but I always made it a point never to immediately begin negotiating a drug deal without breaking the ice through general conversation. This always put drug traffickers at ease and, for the most part, alleviated their suspicions that I was an undercover agent. We discussed my drive to Caborca and that my trip had originated in Tucson, Arizona. We also spoke of the beautiful women who came from the state of Sonora. They liked to talk about women and their conquests. This set the stage for negotiating the purchase of three tons of high-grade marijuana. I told them that rival traffickers had recently killed one of my primary suppliers and I was in need of a reliable source because I supplied several organizations in the southwestern United States. As the negotiations continued, I became aware the traffickers had the capability to furnish any quantity of marijuana that they cultivated in several northern Mexican states. They guaranteed the product was very potent and had already been compressed into kilogram packages for easier transport.

Drug traffickers in Mexico purchase marijuana grown by *campesinos* (peasant farmers), who grow it in isolated areas in order to avoid detection by the police. Once the plants are mature, the campesinos cut them with machetes and allow them to dry under the blistering sun. Many of the traffickers purchase it in bulk form and hire cheap labor to compress the plants with the leaves, seeds, and stems into kilogram bricks. The marijuana is then carefully wrapped in tape to prevent moisture from damaging it.

As we discussed the price, the traffickers explained that based on the quantity, they would let me have each kilogram for $400. I haggled a bit, even though it was not my intent to purchase the drugs. It was important to negotiate, since it would arouse their suspicions by immediately accepting their initial price. Prior to ending our discussions, we made arrangements to meet at the same location a week later to consummate the drug deal. The stage was set, and I returned to Hermosillo to coordinate the operation with the MFJP.

I met with Carlos Peniche, the MFJP *comandante* for the state of Sonora. His father was well connected within the government and had been able to obtain this position for his son. Peniche had charisma, but he was not the usual hard-core MFJP agent. Many years later, he was transferred to another state, where he killed two Mexican army officers in an argument over a prostitute, while drinking at a bar. He was convicted of murder and went to prison for many years.

A week passed quickly, and I returned to Caborca for the final phase of the operation. This time, the MFJP accompanied me and were ready for the action to begin. The informant was also with me, and so we made small talk during the trip. When our caravan entered the town, the MFJP sped past me to take positions close to the meeting site so they could conduct surveillance. I drove into the restaurant/gasoline station and parked on the side. Several tractor-trailer trucks were next to the gas pumps getting fuel for their trip to the United States, and I wondered how many were carrying illicit drugs rather than legitimate produce—or perhaps a combination of both. The restaurant itself resembled a typical small diner in the US. I could smell the pungent cilantro and *menudo* wafting from the greasy kitchen. I was hungry, but anxious to get the operation accomplished successfully and effectively. Fifteen minutes after I was seated inside, the two broadly grinning traffickers, brimming with confidence, entered, and I knew exactly what they were thinking. It was their town; they owned it and believed they had complete control of the situation. I would need to use all my skills acquired over many years of working deep undercover. These skills had become highly polished and were now instinctive. My undercover experience had allowed me to develop a sixth sense to read people quickly and anticipate situations. It was extremely dangerous work, and I didn't have the luxury of making mistakes. As an undercover agent, I had to deal with the mistakes of others during operations, think quickly, or risk getting killed.

Working in Mexico was even more difficult, since I did not have diplomatic immunity—even as a federal agent. Frequently, I had no choice other than to rely on poorly trained and equipped local police. It was more risky than maneuvering through a minefield. Although I didn't intend to truly purchase the tons of marijuana, the traffickers were expecting to see a substantial amount of US dollars before making delivery. Prior to leaving for Caborca, I had arranged large stacks of one-dollar bills, placing a one-hundred-dollar bill on each side of the bundles. At a quick glance, they appeared to be all one-hundred-dollar denominations. The bogus bundles would pass for the full amount of the transaction fee. We called this a *flash roll. I* had taped the bundles of cash to my ankles with clear packing tape, allowing me to quickly show the money but not permit the traffickers an opportunity to closely examine it.

The drug dealers sat down at my table, and we exchanged greetings. They told me everything was ready and asked if I had the money. I raised my pant legs and very quickly showed them the "flash roll." They looked at the money and smiled. Fortunately for me, they didn't ask to count it. The traffickers wanted the informant to accompany one of them to where the marijuana was hidden. The other would remain with me at the restaurant. I handed the truck keys to the trafficker, who said they would return soon. As he stood up from the table, I caught a glimpse of a .45-caliber handgun with shiny gold grips. At this point, I knew at least one of them was armed.

Once they left the restaurant, the other trafficker snarled and said, *"Si eres federale, te vamos a desplumar"*: if you are a federal agent, we will kill you.

I had no doubt, they were sincere, even for a moment. An hour went by, then another as I continued to make small talk with the trafficker sitting across from me. Another hour passed, and I was getting concerned, because the MFJP were unquestionably becoming impatient. It was beginning to get dark, which would compromise visibility, a key factor when conducting operations. Suddenly, one of the MFJP agents appeared near one of the windows and raised his hands to gesture, "What's going on?"

My first thought was *does he really expect me to respond with a trafficker sitting next to me who has already threatened to kill me?* I asked the drug dealer why there was such a long delay, and he explained the marijuana was hidden several miles from Caborca in a very isolated area. He abruptly stood and said he was going to the restroom.

As luck would have it, the restaurant didn't have an indoor facility. The only one available was outside. I also stood and said I would accompany him, since it was important to watch his every movement. As we stepped outside, one of the MFJP agents rushed in putting his 9 mm handgun on the chest of the trafficker. In an instant, the trafficker grabbed the barrel of the weapon, giving him substantial leverage. He twisted it around with the barrel now pointing at the agent. The weapon exploded with a loud boom. I remember the scene occurring in slow motion as the bullet slammed into the MFJP agent's head, causing a cloud of dark red blood to spray into the air in a fine mist. The trafficker whirled around and fired two rounds at me from a few feet away. I could feel the bullets whistle past my left ear. Two well-placed bullets to the trafficker's chest made his legs buckle and stumble backward as he gasped, moaned, and took his last breath lying on the ground. The entire episode took place in a matter of seconds.

Within minutes, the MFJP agents were beside me with weapons drawn. People in the immediate area began crossing the street to catch a glimpse of the violence that had just occurred in their quiet little village. Soon after the shooting, I could hear the piercing scream of sirens from the Cruz Roja (Red Cross) ambulances as they approached the scene. They rapidly loaded the MFJP agent and the trafficker, who appeared dead, into the ambulances and hurriedly drove away.

Half an hour later, the truck driven by the second trafficker turned the corner and approached the restaurant cautiously. No doubt, he had seen the MFJP with their machine guns and the large crowd that had gathered and realized something had gone very wrong. He rapidly accelerated the truck, which fishtailed, causing the camper shell to hit one of the tractor-trailer rigs being fueled. The MFJP gave chase, but as it swerved into a sharp turn, he jumped out and disappeared into the night. Fortunately, he hadn't killed the informant, but had viciously struck him on the head with the butt of his handgun. The marijuana, worth several millions of dollars, was seized, and we left Caborca as soon as we could, since the traffickers could mount an ambush or counter attack. It was a violent night, leaving everyone completely exhausted. Loss of life was always a strong possibility on every operation we conducted, but it was a reality we lived with each day.

Chapter 2

Dragnet and *The Untouchables*

I met Mike late in my career at DEA, but I feel as though I have known him far longer than the actual years reflect. He has the ability to forge relationships across many cultures and to accomplish objectives under difficult, if not impossible, situations. Mike is a professional who is widely respected for his dedication to the counterdrug effort and for his fidelity to unwavering principles. It was an honor to have worked with him.

—William J. Snipes
DEA Regional Director, East Asia (Ret.)

I was born and raised in northern New Mexico in the small village of Espanola. I was the oldest of three children. My sisters, Anita and Mona, followed me by two and three years respectively.

The Espanola Valley, known as the San Juan Valley to the early Spaniards, is also known as the first European-founded capital of the *New World*. The Spanish conquistador, Juan de Onate, arrived in the Espanola Valley on July 11, 1598, where the Chama and Rio Grande Rivers join together. He established the capital and settlement in an area already inhabited by the indigenous descendants of the Anasazi

9

tribe. Naturally, this commingling of peoples with diverse traditions caused grievous conflict between the Spaniards and Native Americans. Espanola was later founded in 1879–80 with the introduction of the Denver and Rio Grande Western Railroad. The now-famous railroad that predominantly ran through the Rocky Mountain region created an extension of its narrow gauge into northern New Mexico. The line would be established along the Rio Grande River and later become known as the Chili Line.

Life was very simple and uncomplicated in the 1950s. We didn't have a lot of material possessions, but we appreciated the value of things most people took for granted. Neither my sisters nor I had the sense of entitlement that is so prevalent today. My father, Sam, was a decent and hardworking man. He worked for many years as a successful automobile salesman. Alice, my mother, worked occasionally as a substitute teacher and was well liked by all her students. Looking back in time, I remember the love and kindness my parents showered on us. They frequently sacrificed to provide us with advantages they had not enjoyed in life. They taught us the value of a strong work ethic, integrity, and most important, the courage to do the right thing. Their ancestors came from Spain into Mexico and eventually into the United States, bringing with them a rich culture and history. We lived in a home typical of the Southwest, filled with the food, smells, and sounds of New Mexico. We spoke only Spanish, and when I entered first grade at the public school, I had a rude awakening. I stood out from the mostly English-speaking children and was punished when I spoke Spanish, a commonly implemented practice at that time. But like most Hispanic youngsters, I learned English quickly, aided by television and books.

My father was a true war hero and answered his country's call to arms during the beginning of World War II. After completing basic training in the army, he was stationed in the Philippines. He served in a coastal artillery unit, and after the Philippines fell to the Japanese army, he and thousands of US and Philippine soldiers were subjected to the infamous Bataan Death March. My father spoke infrequently of this tragic event in his life. He always remembered carrying other POWs, sick with malaria or dysentery, who could barely stand and would have fallen behind. The Japanese soldiers would undoubtedly have bayoneted or shot these men if he and others had not helped them. He also remembered how Japanese soldiers mercilessly killed hundreds of POWs by running over them with vehicles, including tanks, and beheading them with swords. Prisoners were mistreated and denied their very basic needs of food and water during this horrific and brutal chapter of the war. This abject cruelty to fellow human beings is a scar on humanity that will never heal.

Later, my father and other POWs were transported from the Philippines aboard antiquated, barely seaworthy Japanese freighters and fishing boats appropriately called *hell ships*. He was crammed into one of the holds of a decrepit ship with hundreds of other POWs. The starving, bedraggled men were huddled so tightly they couldn't move and could scarcely breathe. The stench was unbearable, because many sick soldiers lost control of their bowels and were mercilessly deprived of the solace of medicine and toilets. Many of these men were dying from disease, wounds, and want. As small buckets of rice and water were lowered, the desperate, starving soldiers fought for the meager rations, spilling most of it. My father said the POWs who perished were handed up to the Japanese soldiers and merely thrown overboard. These insults were not the only horrors endured by many of our valiant POWs.

Allied submarines and aircraft not aware the hell ships flying the Japanese flag were transporting POWs sank many of them. My father safely made it to Osaka, Japan, and was interred at the Tsuruga POW camp for almost three and a half years, until the end of the war. He was truly a hero in so many ways and was highly decorated, receiving the Bronze Star. His brother, Ramón, in the Eighty-Second Airborne, was assigned to the European theater of operations during World War II. He parachuted behind enemy lines during the Normandy invasion and was wounded during intensive combat action. He was later sent to Belgium and killed during the final German offensive known as the Battle of the

Bulge. He was twenty-three years old. My uncle received the Purple Heart with an oak-leaf cluster and two Bronze Stars. The Vigil brothers are both represented on the Española Wall of Honor, which pays tribute to local war heroes.

Although my parents did not have a formal education beyond high school, they recognized the value of a college education. They sacrificed in numerous ways to ensure an education for their children, understanding it was the door to success. But they did not forbid TV. As a young boy, I hurried home from school to watch *The Untouchables* and *Dragnet*. These early police shows began to attract my interest in law enforcement. Like many other adolescents, I decided to pursue a career in law enforcement very early on in life. I knew it would be dangerous, but at the same time it seemed no other profession would be as interesting.

After graduating from Española High School, I decided to attend New Mexico State University (NMSU) in Las Cruces, one of the few universities in the country with a four-year program in criminology/police science. On the first day at NMSU, all freshmen were segregated into different areas, depending on their chosen field of study. I was instructed to report to the large theater located in the middle of the university campus. On a large screen, a projector highlighted the major fields of study, including criminology/police science. The moderator began to announce the names of professors who students should accompany, depending on the desired degree. He eventually yelled out, "Everyone interested in criminology/police science, please follow Professor Edward Farris!" Only about seven of us stood, while many in the crowd booed. Keep in mind, the time frame of the late 1960s–early 1970s was the heyday of the counterculture movement, and drug use had become prevalent throughout the United States. Those same seven students who entered the program with me were the only ones in my classes during my freshman and sophomore years.

One of my roommates at NMSU was Alvan Romero, who later became a special agent with the Internal Revenue Service. He is now one of the premier experts in money laundering and threat finance in the United States and has been involved in high-profile investigations. Moreover, Alvan has worked on undercover operations throughout the country that resulted in successful prosecutions. He is a certified public accountant and currently the director of the New Mexico Tax Fraud Investigations Division, which he personally created. Alvan also provides training to the Colombian judiciary and national police, and we have remained friends since our college days.

I had two professors; besides Edward Farris, a tough, ex–Los Angeles police officer, there was also Richard Lease, who had retired from law enforcement in Tucson, Arizona. They taught me many important lessons and principles that would prove invaluable later in life. I am indebted to them and personally want to thank them for all their efforts and the education they provided to so many students.

After I graduated from NMSU with honors, I began to submit job applications to several law-enforcement agencies, both federal and state. One of them was the Bureau of Narcotics and Dangerous Drugs (BNDD). I was intrigued by how they enforced US drug laws, but more important, by their undercover work. BNDD not only investigated complex drug-trafficking organizations, but also used agents to penetrate them. In my mind, undercover work was an ultimate type of chess game. The challenge against ruthless and violent international drug dealers was fascinating. It was an alluring occupation that would provide the most unique and dangerous challenges. A year later, I received a letter offering me a position with the new *super* anti-drug agency called the Drug Enforcement Administration.

The DEA came into existence on July 1, 1973, under then President Richard Nixon's Reorganization Plan No. 2, which among other things, created the new agency and placed it under the US Department of Justice. The BNDD, Office of Drug Abuse Law Enforcement (ODALE), US Customs anti-drug sections, and other federal agencies were merged to form the DEA. Richard Nixon mandated an "all-out war on the drug menace." He added,

"Right now, the federal government is fighting the war on drug abuse under a distinct handicap, for its efforts are those of a loosely confederated alliance facing a resourceful, elusive, worldwide enemy. Certainly, the coldblooded underworld networks that funnel narcotics from suppliers all over the world are no respecters of the bureaucratic dividing lines that now complicate our Anti-drug efforts."

Before starting special-agent training in Washington, DC, I reported to the DEA office in Albuquerque on December 9, 1973, where I worked for several weeks. My first day on the job, I was introduced to Special Agent in Charge (SAC) William Proffer, who could be described with one word, gruff. I quickly learned this was nothing more than a façade and he was truly a decent man who took care of his employees. Additionally, I became acquainted with many veteran agents, one of whom, Bob Candelaria, was a fellow native New Mexican and a talented undercover agent. If fate allowed me, I would return to Albuquerque and partner with him. Weeks later, I traveled to Washington, DC, to undergo training.

This was a great adventure for someone who grew up in a very small town and had never been exposed to a large city. The DEA headquarters building was located at 1405 I Street NW, which also housed the training facilities. It was in DC's red-light district on a street lined with strip clubs, peep shows, and prostitutes who stood wearing their "work clothes" in doorways or strolled up and down the sidewalks. I can still recall entering the DEA building for the first time and seeing a bar located just off its lobby area. This was the famous Golden Eagle, where DEA personnel congregated and met after work to "tip back a few." In a hilarious twist of events, the DEA administrator later tried to close it, but the owner got revenge by turning it into a club featuring belly dancing. It was surreal getting off the elevator in the lobby to hear Middle Eastern music and the sound of clinking metal from the gyrating dancers' skirts.

I became part of DEA class 2, which consisted of thirty special agent trainees. On the first day, the class coordinator made it a point to tell everyone that, historically, a large percentage of the trainees would not meet the rigorous training standards and would "wash out." We felt the pressure immediately! Older candidates coming from other agencies during the merger were particularly unnerved. As the youngest in the class, I felt the stress as well. Fortunately, I had conditioned myself mentally and physically to successfully complete the training. There was no way in hell I'd return home as a failure. I was in top physical condition and had the ability to understand and remember the class material and lectures. Washing out was not an option. I concentrated on overcoming each and every challenge thrown in my path.

All special-agent trainees were housed at the Sonesta Hotel on Thomas Circle, located a few blocks from the DEA headquarters. Two trainees occupied each room, and my roommate was formerly with the US Customs Service. He was tall, thin, very quiet, and introverted. He was easy to get along with primarily because we didn't spend much time in our rooms.

Our training was very intense with both classroom and practical exercises. These scenarios allowed us to practice undercover work, arrest tactics, surveillance, weapons, raids, evidence collection, and other *tools* of the trade. We also had considerable physical training in a small, narrow gymnasium next to the headquarters building that appeared to be a bank from the outside. An indoor pistol range was located on the second floor, and our lungs were constantly polluted with gunpowder residue. The pungent smell hung dark and heavy in the air during long firearms training periods in the poorly ventilated range. The DEA firearms instructors were exceptional and patient with those of us who had never previously used weapons. Practice makes perfect, and we became good marksmen who understood the rules of engagement and use of lethal force.

As we went through the extensive training, many students, as predicted, began to "wash out." Too often, the person who had been sitting next to me in class the day before was simply gone. Naturally, our anxiety grew, wondering who would disappear next, but the challenge only strengthened my resolve. On the last week of training, another two students were terminated, but most of us were able to breathe a sigh of relief that we were almost done with the grueling training. During the last few days, we were shown our official DEA credentials and gold badges, which gave a great sense of pride to become part of this bold and dynamic agency. We were given our assignments, and I was fortunate enough to be returning to Albuquerque. I left the DEA training academy twenty pounds lighter and in exceptional physical condition.

DEA was a wise career choice. A single-mission agency, its mandate was to combat drug trafficking worldwide, the only agency with a charter for working both domestically and foreign. DEA was created to

1. develop an agency to coordinate federal anti-drug efforts with the many state and local agencies across the United States and with foreign anti-drug law-enforcement agencies;
2. develop accountability and prevent corruption by having a single administrator in charge of federal drug law enforcement;
3. consolidate all drug enforcement efforts within one premier agency; and
4. maximize efforts in federal investigations and prosecutions and diminish rivalries.

In the very beginning, many of the objectives set forth for the fledging agency were circumvented by internal rivalries, particularly US Customs and the BNDD. They came from very different cultures and didn't particularly care for one another. Prior to the merger, Customs moved swiftly to promote their personnel, effectively moving them "up the career ladder." Consequently, the former US Customs personnel were put in charge of several DEA offices, which created unnecessary friction in the new agency. It would take many years for the conflict to be resolved and was a slow painful birth for the DEA, but it gradually settled into the task at hand.

Chapter 3

A Very Dangerous Game

Mike Vigil is one of the great silent warriors who, through personal sacrifice and over thirty years of professional service, has kept our loved ones safe from narcoterrorists. Mike's personal example of service, within the DEA and with colleagues across international, national, state, and local agencies, is a model of what "government service" means. If more were like Mike, we would be better off.

—Andre Hollis
Former Defense Department Assistant Secretary
of Defense for Counternarcotics

When I reported to work at the Albuquerque office, I was immediately thrust into the *belly of the beast*, working dangerous undercover assignments. I could look the part of whatever role was required, spoke perfect Spanish, and possessed the needed intestinal fortitude. When working high-level traffickers, I wore expensive sports jackets, Italian loafers, and four rings studded with large diamonds, two on each hand. Around my neck was a long rope-style gold chain sporting a ram's head with round, faceted ruby eyes. With lower-tiered dealers, my long hair and street clothes made it easy for me to slide in and out of their criminal circles.

Agents from the local Alcohol, Tobacco, and Firearms (ATF) office came to the office one day and said they had an informant who was providing information on several well-known and prominent drug dealers operating in the area. The ATF agents wanted to work the case with us, and that was fine, since we had a good relationship. They would furnish the informant and conduct the surveillance, and I would do the undercover work. It was the beginning of a lasting partnership. The informant was able to introduce me to numerous heroin dealers, which enabled me to make many undercover purchases of heroin. Mexican brown heroin was prevalent in the US Southwest, including New Mexico. It wasn't as refined as Southeast and Central Asian heroin, but it was just as addictive and lethal. The purity level at the time ranged from 30-60 percent, and the street-level product was usually around 3–6 percent, after being diluted with lactose and packaged in condoms, plastic bags, or aluminum foil.

The heroin traffickers in New Mexico were seasoned criminals, and many had already served time in prison for drug offenses. On one occasion, I went to the South Valley region of Albuquerque with an informant to purchase heroin at an old *cantina* known as a drug-distribution point. We parked in front, where I noticed a local dealer standing outside the bar. It was obvious he had been drinking heavily, but he asked if we wanted "anything." I answered that yes, we wanted a quantity of heroin and, for no reason, he turned belligerent and negotiations deteriorated. His machismo and bravado fueled by alcohol, led him to pull a huge knife with serrated edges from his pocket and point it directly at me. I was carrying a .38-caliber revolver tucked in my waistband and would have killed him had he moved towards me. I refused to be intimidated and stood my ground. He finally got into his car and left. Dealing with sober drug dealers necessitates courage and intelligence; when alcohol is introduced into the negotiating process, it becomes even more dangerous and unpredictable.

On another occasion, I was introduced to Frank Charles, a local, large-scale heroin dealer. Charles was a stocky, Hispanic male with dark skin and thick, curly hair, who walked with a confident swagger. He was also a heroin addict, which made my undercover role even more difficult. A short time later, I was able to purchase quantities of Mexican brown heroin from him. During the first purchase, Charles drove up in his Ford truck and suspiciously glared at me. He opened the window, handed me a large plastic bag containing the heroin, and after receiving the money, he sped away. After several purchases, I asked him for half a kilogram. Charles said that he'd have to meet with his sources of supply, but would contact me later that week. Eventually, he called and asked me to come to his house that Friday night with money for the heroin. His sources were willing to do business based on the fact that he had vouched for me.

We coordinated with the Albuquerque police and brought them into the investigation, since they were part of our task force. We made detailed plans for surveillance and the anticipated arrests of Charles and his suppliers. The bust signal would be opening the trunk of my vehicle, once the heroin was delivered. I drove to Charles's residence, where I parked my car so it could easily be seen by surveillance units. Charles answered my knock on the door and invited me into his living room. He pulled out a small bag from which he removed a syringe, spoon, and a long, thick strip of elastic rubber. He also took out a small, glassine envelope, poured some heroin into the spoon, and mixed it with water. Reaching down to his feet, he pulled some cotton from his white tube socks, rolled it up in a little ball, and placed it into the heroin solution to filter any impurities. He used a cigarette lighter to heat the bottom of the spoon, causing the heroin to dissolve in the water. Then he put the needle into the wad of cotton and pulled the plunger of the syringe drawing in the heroin. After wrapping the rubber strip around his left arm above the elbow, he injected the heroin deep into a vein. Charles handed me the syringe and some of the heroin. "You should shoot up; this is good shit." I sat back in my chair and told him I wasn't a user and was in the business strictly for the money. As a federal agent, I was prohibited from using drugs that would not only have jeopardized the investigation, but my life as well. This was a night I would need to be on my toes and make quick, logical decisions. Things could easily get out of hand and become extremely dangerous now that I was negotiating with someone on a heroin high.

We sat together making small talk about the money involved in dealing drugs. An hour later, Charles received a telephone call, and when he finished the cryptic conversation, he said everything was ready. We left his house and walked to another, almost directly across the street. As we entered, a tall, Hispanic male standing by the door holding a pump-action shotgun gave me a menacing and suspicious stare.

My mind raced with adrenaline and began developing strategies for every possible contingency which might occur that night. I was now engaged in a dangerous game and needed to be four moves ahead of them or I'd be the first casualty of the night. The man with the shotgun kept looking out the front window, obviously ready to use the weapon in the event police raided the house. There were several other armed individuals inside who were also providing security for the pending drug deal.

In these situations, I was able to maintain a sense of calm and think rationally, which would ensure my safety as well as the safety of the other agents. Several of the traffickers, including Charles, sat with me in one of the rooms towards the back of the house. They asked if I had brought the money, and I assured them it was in a safe place. They demanded I get it and bring it in. This was bad. Situations like this could result in a *rip-off* or put me in the middle of a potential shootout. The agents entering the house didn't know about the heavily armed traffickers, which would place them in grave danger. The moment reached critical mass with tensions running fast and furious. Thinking quickly, I told the traffickers it would be ludicrous for me to bring the money into a house full of armed men, especially during an initial transaction. I let them know I wasn't about to put myself in danger, since I could be walking into a rip-off and was unarmed. I did have a weapon, but that was my trump card.

After haggling, I convinced several of them to go with me to my car where we would do the transaction, giving me the upper hand. It was a very dark night, and as I opened the trunk pretending to retrieve the money, my only hope was that surveillance agents would be able to see the arrest signal. If they didn't, I was sure a gun battle would ensue, and my concern then was how many of them could I bring down before they killed me. Seconds after the trunk went up, I could hear the screeching of tires and several cars roared up the street. Many of the drug dealers threw their weapons in the front yards of nearby houses. I warned the surveillance agents there were other armed men inside with shotguns. When they breached the house, the other traffickers had fled leaving their weapons on the floor. The operation was a success, and we arrested several significant heroin traffickers including Charles and his suppliers.

Working undercover is an art and only one of many tools at the disposal of drug agents in collecting information and evidence on criminal investigations. It is not for the timid. You must think clearly and make quick adjustments to your plans, because drug deals are extremely unpredictable and traffickers constantly change the situation to protect themselves. These unstable interactions are very dangerous and can unexpectedly turn violent. Agents must spend time and energy meticulously developing operational plans. At the same time, the traffickers are not sitting idle. They are also taking precautions to protect their interests. Each side approaches the other with a good deal of distrust and not an insignificant degree of paranoia. In the DEA, only a small percentage of agents work covert operations, but quite frankly, I thoroughly enjoyed the challenge. When I worked undercover assignments, I would literally expunge the fact I was a federal agent from my mind and undergo a complete transformation. I acted and thought like a drug trafficker. I spoke their language, adopted their *coterie* habits, and cloaked myself in the same street cunning. Undercover operatives must be superb actors or they'll forfeit more than an Oscar.

With each undercover operation, I learned more about the art of deception, body language, and persuasion. William Walker, a DEA agent and a member of the Senior Executive Service, the highest rank in the federal government, commented on the skills I had acquired as an undercover agent:

"Mike's many years of successful undercover operations, including long-term, deep penetration of sophisticated and highly structured drug-trafficking organizations predisposed to violence, endowed him with the power to quickly detect malicious intent in an individual [or individuals] in order to protect [himself] and others. Mike's incredible observation skills; his capacity to focus, absorb, and instantly recognize the most subtle of cues, such as an ever so slight nervous twitch, a faint change in a person's breathing, pulse, facial expression, or an eye movement during undercover negotiations was the difference between life and death.

Mike's ability to accurately assess (read) people and immediately discern harmful intentions became a second nature that enabled Mike to mitigate risks preventing tragedy. The essence of his astonishing body language and deception-recognition technique lies in his appreciation of the tiniest of details, and having his eyes and ears open, and fine-tuned to receiving information at all times, never failing to register and appropriately assign what he saw and heard precisely to the situation Mike found himself in. Thankfully, his well-developed sensors became investigative instincts and a life-saving gift that Mike acquired along his remarkable journey."

It's true, after many years of undercover work, I developed a sixth sense and learned how to read individuals quickly and pick up signals. This allowed me to survive many dangerous moments in which I could easily have been killed. One's gifts of gab and *guts* are the most significant weapons when working against some of the most vicious criminals in the world. One slip of the tongue or allowing one's mask to slip, showing fear, can quickly end with loss of life, quite likely one's own. On occasions, when acting in an undercover role, I would use a Kel unit, a technical device better known as a *wire* to record negotiations with drug dealers. The units transmitted the conversations to other agents, who listened for signs of danger and recorded them for use as evidence. I disliked using them. Wires were unreliable, and sometimes the batteries that powered the unit would become overheated and leak acid. During one operation, I wore a wire whose batteries began to leak and burned my stomach with caustic acid. I could smell my flesh burning, and the pain was unbearable. I barely kept my composure, as painful as it was, for what seemed like hours knowing that being shot would have been considerably worse. My options were miserably limited, because I was in the company of several armed traffickers. After what felt like an eternity, the negotiations ended, and I ran to the nearest restroom and tore the wire off. I had severe burns, but they were certainly less lethal than bullet holes. After that incident, I only wore a wire in extremely critical situations.

Though undercover work is deadly serious, there are always humorous stories. I recall going to a heroin dealer's house in the southern part of Albuquerque, but he wasn't home. I had already made several purchases of heroin from him, and I wanted to make one more buy to have an airtight, prosecutable case. As I drove away, I noticed a small truck following me. The driver kept flashing his lights and beeping the horn. I pulled over to the shoulder of the road, and a large, stocky Hispanic man dressed in blue jeans and a white polo shirt approached my car. He was quick to tell me he knew I was buying heroin from his neighbor. Being quite the entrepreneur, he earnestly assured me he had a higher-grade heroin, and I should buy from him. This was a drug dealer desperate to put himself behind bars. But how could I resist his salesmanship? I made several heroin purchases from him, which eventually landed him in jail. He was shocked and dismayed when he learned I was a DEA agent. Cases like this helped me maintain my sense of humor and balance.

One early morning, during a bright New Mexico summer day, Bob Candelaria and I received a telephone call from an informant saying he knew a trafficker who was distributing kilogram quantities of high-grade methamphetamine. Apparently, he was eager to sell a pound of the drug because he needed the money. We told the informant to tell the trafficker he had potential buyers and to bring him to the parking lot of our office located at the First National bank building on San Mateo and Central. A few hours later, the informant called saying he and the drug dealer were in the parking lot. The building was a high-rise where we occupied one of the top floors. Our office had two entryways: one in the back for DEA personnel and another in front for visitors. The front door had a large wooden plaque with the DEA logo inscribed with the words "Drug Enforcement Administration."

We took the elevator to the ground floor and spotted the informant, who was accompanied by a tall, thin, white male with blond, stringy hair. He was dressed in very flamboyant clothes. His pants were bright purple, and he wore a psychedelic green, calypso shirt. He said, "Hi, I understand you're interested in some speed." We told him that was correct and asked if the "stuff was pure." He assured us it was and had recently been manufactured at a laboratory located on the outskirts of Albuquerque. We told him we worked for a nonprofit organization that found jobs for minorities, and we could do the drug deal in our offices. He was agreeable and said, "I have no problem with that." Most law-enforcement agents have a well-developed sense of humor; Bob and I were no exception. In preparation for the undercover operation, we made arrangements with another agent to help us with our plan.

As we walked to the building from the parking lot, I called the agent alerting him we were on the way up. His role was to hold the front door in such a way that the DEA logo wouldn't be visible as we walked out of the elevators to go through the back door. Everything went according to plan. We entered the office and literally walked across the entire floor with the dealer and took him to one of the interview rooms. He never noticed the wanted posters on the walls and other agents with weapons in their waistbands.

The room was sterile, with the exception of a desk and several chairs. He sat at the desk and pulled out a large, clear plastic bag containing white crystal powder. I visually examined it and asked if I could "check it out."

He replied, "No problem, man."

I took the bag from his hands and left the room. I did a quick, drug field test consisting of a small vial containing a chemical reagent that would provide a presumptive indication if the powder was methamphetamine. Within seconds, the liquid turned dark orange, giving a positive reaction. I returned to the interview room and placed my DEA badge on the table in front of the drug dealer.

He stared at it for several seconds and then looked at me, then back at the badge. He finally exclaimed, "That's great! Where can I get one of these?"

Bob and I almost died laughing. We had to explain he was under arrest and had the distinction of being the first trafficker to conduct an actual drug transaction inside a DEA office. He was in shock for hours, with the most bewildered look on his face. He didn't hold a grudge, however, and later became an informant who assisted in several important investigations. As a result of his cooperation, he didn't serve time in prison.

During my assignment in Albuquerque, I had the privilege of working with many *warriors* who stepped into the arena every day, never knowing if they would make it home in the evening. Their gallantry, courage, and camaraderie made them the elite in clandestine counterdrug operations. Names such as Robert Candelaria, Sam Herrera, Ruben Prieto, Mike Parra (task force agent), Dave Weiser, and Les Tuell come to mind. Shared common dangers forge indestructible friendships, much as the finest steel is forged by fire. These friendships are the greatest accomplishments one can have.

Chapter 4

Facing the Feared

Mike Vigil is an extremely intelligent and courageous law-enforcement executive, who has made a huge impact on the global war on drugs and crime as a street agent and as a top-level DEA leader. Mike is a valued expert on narco-terrorism and drug cartels operating in Colombia and Mexico. People worldwide can thank him for putting some of the most dangerous and violent drug dealers and killers behind bars, where they belong.

—Sylvester Jones
Assistant Director United States Marshals Service

In the mid-1970s, the DEA initiated a large-scale anti-heroin program called Operation Heroin B. Centered in the southwestern United States, it focused on the brown heroin flooding the US at that time. The heroin produced in Mexico has only one market—the United States. The US is the largest consumer of illicit drugs in the world. The basic economic theory of supply-and-demand governs the drug trade. As long as the demand exists, someone will supply. The drug trade spawns other related crimes, violence, and death on a massive scale. It unravels the social fabric of entire nations, especially countries in the process of developing into full-fledged democracies. The heroin targeted under Operation Heroin B was produced in what we called *kitchen labs* because Mexican chemists used common utensils (pots and pans) and items found in any kitchen. The *chemists* were certainly not formally trained in chemistry—most had no education at all. Frequently, they learned from experienced *chemists* who were similarly mentored by others in the elaborate process of converting raw opium into heroin hydrochloride.

During Operation Heroin B, I was sent to our regional office in Denver to work on the largest and most significant heroin trafficker operating in the western United States at that time. This kingpin was considered among the top-ten domestic heroin dealers in the country. He had already served time in prison and was very cunning and extremely ruthless. He'd been in prison for distributing heroin through his extensive and highly structured organization, whose tentacles extended into parts of Mexico. During the execution of a search warrant at his residence several years earlier by local and federal agents, a large amount of heroin was seized that had been in the process of being diluted and packaged for wholesale distribution. He was convicted in state court and sent to prison for several years. During his incarceration, he was given respect by other inmates; after all, he was a famous heroin kingpin! When he wanted to use the prison phone, the other prisoners standing in line acquiesced to him and immediately stepped aside. No one dared complain or challenge him.

His name was James Orlando Quintana and even other ruthless drug traffickers feared his reputation and power. Quintana was highly intelligent and charismatic. He could have been a successful CEO or leader in a legitimate enterprise but chose to defy the system and break any laws that prevented him from reaching his egocentric goals. His deviance would eventually lead to a tragic end. At the onset of the federal investigation on Quintana, the DEA Denver office identified a potential informant who was serving a prison sentence. He didn't have direct access to Quintana, but he could make undercover introductions to lower level dealers who worked for Quintana and his principal lieutenant, Henry Gutierrez. The rest would be up to me and I would have to weave my way through this violent organization to get to Gutierrez and ultimately

Quintana. We made arrangements to have the informant paroled out of prison for short periods of time and were ultimately responsible for ensuring he would not escape. This meant I had to conduct a large-scale covert operation and also keep a close watch on the informant. The situation became more complicated and pushed me to the top of my game.

During the initial stages of the investigation, the informant introduced me to Sonny Murillo. A streetwise heroin dealer, he was highly distrustful of anyone he didn't know. Tall and shaggy haired, he sported an Emiliano Zapata style mustache. He spoke slowly, was very cunning and had a lengthy criminal record. He appeared to analyze my every word and body movement. He was also a trusted member of Quintana's organization. I had assumed the role of a drug dealer based out of Taos, New Mexico. Selecting a cover story was critical, and I always chose one that made it difficult for the traffickers I was dealing with to check. Years later, the advances in social media and access to Internet database systems made it extremely difficult to remain in the shadows as an undercover agent. The danger increased tenfold.

While working undercover, I had to be careful of every move and couldn't afford to make mistakes. It was a game in which the winner could walk away and sometimes the loser would not. I was very convincing when negotiating with traffickers. Verbal sleight of hand worked in my favor, because they would readily accept the role I was playing or they wouldn't do business with me.

Eventually, I convinced Murillo to conduct a *hand-to-hand* heroin deal. With that initial buy successfully consummated, I was able to make several larger purchases of heroin. I couldn't, however, get him to introduce me to higher-ranking members in the organization. Why should he? Obviously, he was making money from me and didn't want to give my business to someone else. Another tactic and strategy was needed to get beyond Murillo.

The opportunity came in the person of Isaac Ruybalid, a principal lieutenant and enforcer for Quintana and Gutierrez. One evening, surveillance agents followed him as he traveled to a local Denver bar located on West Colfax. I was in my hotel room getting ready for a date and received a telephone call advising me of the situation. It was decided I would attempt a *cold hit* on Ruybalid. That meant I would approach him without the use of an informant to make an introduction. This would be incredibly difficult, but upon arrival at the tavern I could decide on how to proceed. I called my date and cancelled—so much for having a social life. I drove for about an hour in heavy traffic before arriving. I didn't immediately see Ruybalid as I entered and decided to sit at the crowded bar. I played the high-roller by ordering drinks for everyone, giving the appearance that each person in the establishment knew me.

After several patrons left, I caught a glimpse of Ruybalid sitting at the other end. He was excessively thin, and when he smiled, it looked as if his face were going to break. He wore an expensive shirt with a gold chain around his neck to complete the look. We stared at each other for a few seconds, and he thanked me for the drinks. Ruybalid had also served time in prison, and it was there he had met Quintana and Gutierrez. He had become one of their inner circle, and they trusted him. They had also tutored him on becoming a high-level heroin trafficker and how to avoid getting caught. He was loyal to Quintana and Gutierrez and was willing to follow their orders, regardless of the consequences.

We began to chat, and after a few minutes, I asked him if he knew of another location that had more "action." He assured me he did and that he planned to leave soon for a lively nightclub on the other side of Denver. He asked if I wanted to follow him. I readily accepted, since this would give me the opportunity to speak with him alone. Twenty minutes later, we left the bar. Once on the road, I contacted surveillance units on a handheld radio I kept under the seat of my car and gave them our destination. I couldn't have a regular radio system, since it would be highly visible. It was my only means of communication with other DEA agents.

At the club, I bought him drink after drink. Ruybalid, characteristic of all drug dealers, began to ask questions about what I did for a living. I was coy and told him I was engaged in a dangerous business in New

Mexico. It tweaked his curiosity, and he continued to inquire. I finally told him I sold heroin and explained that, in recent weeks, I'd been purchasing heroin from Murillo. He smiled and boasted that Murillo worked for him and the heroin actually came from him and his partners. He let me know they were the largest heroin dealers in the area and imported it from Culiacán, Sinaloa, Mexico. Culiacán is the equivalent of Sicily to the mafia. It has spawned the vast majority of the most significant drug traffickers in Mexico. So now that we were friendly, we exchanged cell phone numbers and made arrangements to meet in a few days.

In the interim, I rented an undercover apartment in Denver under a fictitious name and returned to Albuquerque. While back home, I decided to get an undercover driver's license with the alias I was using in the investigation. Several days later, I returned to Denver and called Ruybalid, who wanted to come to my apartment. When he arrived, he carefully walked through looking for a sign that would disprove my cover story. I had already scattered a few *Sports Illustrated* and *Playboy* magazines on the coffee table and put a few cheap Walmart art prints on the walls. There were clothes throughout the apartment, dishes in the sink, and juice and frozen pizza in the "bachelor's refrigerator" to make it appear I was living there. When he became more at ease, we talked about the large quantity of heroin I wanted to buy. He said he had to be careful, and naturally, his partners would have to thoroughly check me out. We left the apartment and went to my undercover car parked in a lot behind the apartment complex. As we sat in the vehicle, a Denver police patrol car pulled up alongside, and the officer quickly approached us. He asked for our driver's licenses, and I remember thinking it had been extremely fortuitous in obtaining the fictitious driver's license while in New Mexico. If I hadn't anticipated a need, the entire operation would have been placed in jeopardy. When the officer handed the licenses through the window, Ruybalid grabbed them and closely looked at mine. He saw the name and state matched my story. In an undercover role, I learned you made your own luck.

Negotiations progressed with Ruybalid, who explained his partners would have to approve the heroin transaction before he could move forward. He would make arrangements for me to meet with them. I already knew he was speaking of Quintana and Gutierrez. I was also aware they were very violent and had polished their criminal activities while in prison. Meeting with the bosses of this ruthless heroin trafficking organization was imperative for the success of the operation. I would have to be very resourceful when I met with these coldblooded drug lords. I knew drug traffickers could be dangerously shrewd and treacherous—never underestimate the enemy. I began to mentally prepare for the meeting. Preparation was not something I took lightly, since the stakes were entirely too high for mistakes. Several discussions later, Ruybalid told me a meeting had been arranged with his partners at the bar where I had originally met him.

Plans were made at the DEA office for a surveillance team to be at the bar prior to my arrival. Later that evening, I met with Ruybalid, who assured me his partners were on their way. The bar was elbow to elbow with people, and the booming noises vibrated off my eardrums. The loud voices of a crowd who had already consumed too much alcohol were a frenzied staccato. The constant clink of beer glasses was also an annoying distraction, but we continued to talk.

Ruybalid had a very high regard for his partners and spoke of them with great reverence. He boasted, "They control things in Denver, Colorado, and many other states."

I could see that Ruybalid was willing to give his life and take the lives of others to protect his masters. I could not expect hesitation on his part to use violence as a means to an end, which was not good news.

Several drinks later, Ruybalid made a few calls and disappeared for a few minutes while I sat at the bar. He reappeared and asked me to accompany him to the back of the tavern. Already sitting at a table were Quintana and Gutierrez, whom I recognized from mug shots I had seen while preparing for the investigation. A beautiful, young Hispanic woman with long, brown hair and a very short miniskirt was sitting on

Quintana's lap, but was dismissed when I approached the table. Ruybalid introduced me to Quintana and Gutierrez, who remained silent. Both of them shook my hand, but I knew they were extremely suspicious. Gutierrez deferred to Quintana who wasted no time in questioning me about drug dealers operating in New Mexico. "Do you know Toasie?" he asked?

As part of my cover, I had told Ruybalid that I was from Taos, New Mexico, which he had passed to Quintana. I didn't acknowledge any of the names mentioned by Quintana, because he could have been inventing them as a means to trap me. Furthermore, if they existed and I acknowledged knowing them, Quintana would undoubtedly call them to check on me. What I gave him were a couple of names of heroin dealers he would recognize and, more importantly, were dead, making it impossible for him to check and disprove my cover story. We connected quickly, because Quintana had been born and raised in Las Vegas, New Mexico. This is a small city in the northern part of the state an hour's drive from its capital, Santa Fe. Quintana was exceptionally intelligent and had a great personality. After an hour, he and Gutierrez indicated they were leaving. I could tell they had bought my cover story and I had answered all their questions satisfactorily. We shook hands, and they slipped through a back door. Money and power speak loudly; two gorgeous women were hanging all over them when they left. Ruybalid went outside also and returned a short time later with a wide grin on his face and told me they had given him authorization to sell me the heroin.

We remained at the bar and Ruybalid bragged how prominent Quintana and Gutierrez were in the heroin trade. It is safe to say, if someone talks enough they'll divulge valuable information, which he did as he continued to drink rum. Ruybalid mentioned that the Pontiac Grand Prix owned by Gutierrez was used to smuggle large quantities of heroin from Mexico. He also told me their primary source of supply was located in Culiacán, Sinaloa. It made sense, since the Mexican state of Sinaloa was the heartland of Mexican drug trafficking. Ruybalid said Quintana had recently sent Gutierrez to Mexico to make a large heroin purchase. The heroin had been weighed immediately after being processed at a clandestine lab and was still wet, thereby adding to the weight. Once the heroin dried, the weight was much less. Unfortunately, it had already been purchased and smuggled across the US–Mexico border. Quintana was rather upset with Gutierrez about this error in judgment.

I began to purchase large amounts of heroin from Ruybalid, who conducted the transactions in an odd manner. Normally, I would meet him at a bar and he'd drive me to a location where the heroin had been placed, usually on the side of the road. He would point at the heroin, and I would pay him. He would leave me at my car, and I would drive back to the location in order to retrieve it. His understanding of the drug laws was sorely inadequate. He mistakenly believed that he could avoid criminal liability by not handing the heroin directly to me. That was a huge mistake on his part. Surveillance determined an accomplice, later identified as Edward Joseph Zamora, would place the heroin at locations designated by Ruybalid. Zamora would watch it from a safe distance until I retrieved it. He would ensure no one else stumbled onto the heroin and also watch for surveillance by law enforcement.

I made arrangements to purchase another quantity of heroin and again met with Ruybalid at a bar. I got into his car and we drove to a residential area where he eventually parked on the side of the road. He left the vehicle, and I watched him searching the area. He told me the heroin was to have been left at that location but couldn't find it. Minutes later, Zamora drove alongside and spoke with Ruybalid for several minutes. When Ruybalid returned, he had the heroin, which he handed to me. All of his plotting to avoid a hand-to-hand transaction had come to a swift end. Not that it mattered at that point, but they obviously hadn't heard about conspiracy laws. Ruybalid told me Zamora had left the heroin on the side of the road and had been watching it from the nearby ravine. A couple of young boys on their bicycles had wandered by, noticed the package on the ground and grabbed it, not having a clue it was a lethal drug. Zamora apparently charged across the ravine and chased the boys until he recovered it. Regrettably for Zamora, he had now implicated himself in the criminal conspiracy.

One night, Quintana and Gutierrez were at a local lounge with some of their criminal associates. Sometime during the evening, a man named Moses Trujillo entered the lounge and began arguing with Quintana. I knew Trujillo and had already purchased heroin from him. He was a documented associate of Quintana and Gutierrez. The argument escalated and Trujillo, obviously not a good shot, removed a handgun concealed in his waist and shot Quintana in the leg and fled. Ruybalid told me he and other members of the organization had spent all night searching for Trujillo so they could kill him. Several weeks later, Quintana hired someone to lure Trujillo to a location where an assassin would be waiting. As Trujillo entered a secluded alley, he was shot in the head and killed instantly. He never saw it coming. The assassin, according to Ruybalid, was paid in heroin. As with most structured and complex criminal organizations, the upper hierarchy insulates itself from any criminal liability by passing orders to a trusted few, and they in turn, pass them on to others who actually commit the crime. The organization headed by Quintana was no different. He shielded himself well, and it would be extremely difficult to covertly penetrate the organization to his level. Although I had met him, there was little chance he would deal with me directly, since he left that to his subordinates. He had henchmen who were cheap, plentiful, and could take the fall. I had to think of a way to draw him out. Something innovative that would lure him from the shadows. During my first meeting with Quintana, I noticed he was wearing several diamond rings that he used as a visible symbol of his power, wealth, and status. As an undercover agent, one is trained to be highly observant and, above all, use ingenuity.

In a planning session with other DEA agents, we decided to attempt to trade diamonds for heroin in order to have Quintana and Gutierrez deal directly with me. A couple of the agents knew a local Denver jeweler who agreed to loan us several diamond rings. Meanwhile, I had told Ruybalid I was also committing armed robberies of jewelry stores in New

Mexico. I boasted that a recent robbery had just netted me a large haul of diamond rings and asked if Quintana and Gutierrez might be interested in exchanging heroin for jewelry. He replied he would check with them and let me know as soon as possible. At that point, I mentioned I would be returning to Denver within a few days and would see him then.

I waited several days before making contact with him. He said his partners were very interested in seeing the rings, so arrangements were made to meet in the parking lot of a restaurant near the downtown area. Ruybalid was waiting for me as I entered the parking area, and we drove to Gutierrez's home.

The house was in an affluent area and impressive. We parked in the driveway, and Quintana and Gutierrez got into the back seat. I handed them a bag with several diamond rings with the price tags on them. Quintana immediately suggested I should get rid of them because jewelry could easily be traced and pointed to the serial numbers on the tags. He and Gutierrez were less than impressed with the rings, because the diamonds weren't large and showy. As with everything else, guns, beautiful women, and obscene amounts of money … they were determined to impress. Quintana liked the gold mountings of the rings, stating *"Estos están chignon"* (these are damn nice). Thinking quickly, I told them I also had very large loose diamonds that were in New Mexico and would make arrangements to bring them to Denver within a few days. This served to facilitate other meetings with Quintana and Gutierrez.

After Ruybalid left me at my car, I went to the DEA office and met with other agents involved in the investigation. Don Farabaugh, the group supervisor, and I decided to walk to the jewelry store in downtown Denver to return the rings. On the way there, I looked up and saw Quintana and Gutierrez walking towards us. I quickly slipped into a music shop hoping they hadn't seen me. Talk about bad timing! Don was standing at the doorway looking at me with a perplexed look on his face. He hadn't seen them, and I frantically waved him off. If they saw me with Don, they would immediately become suspicious, which would have resulted in me suffering the same fate as Trujillo. Seconds later, Quintana and Gutierrez entered the store as I pretended to be looking at some albums.

They appeared not to have noticed Don, because they acted friendly. We walked out of the store and stood talking about the diamonds. Quintana moved his hand against the large store window and scratched it with his large diamond ring. He reiterated he preferred large diamonds and was looking forward to seeing the other stones. Quintana was not very tall, but knew he had power, which he wore as an integral part of his persona. Wealth he had accumulated during his long tenure as a drug dealer brought power, but it was just as transitory as an overcoat. It could be taken from him the minute he slipped. Gutierrez never interrupted him and always followed his lead. He was also short, but obnoxiously cocky and overconfident. After they left, I breathed a sigh of relief that I had seen them first and reacted quickly. Our unexpected meeting could have turned into a disaster and came much too close for my comfort.

A week later, I called Ruybalid on his cell phone and told him I had the larger diamonds Quintana and Gutierrez wanted to look at. The next day, he called to say a meeting was scheduled for the following morning, and we should meet at a local shopping center before seeing his partners. As prearranged, we met and drove to the residence belonging to Quintana's parents. Quintana answered the door, and we immediately went into the backyard. Many of Quintana's family were in the house, but they left us alone and didn't talk to me. During these negotiations, I had reluctantly agreed to wear a wire in order to allow surveillance agents to monitor and record the conversation. The old house had a back alley that extended through the entire block, so surveillance agents were able to park a recreational vehicle directly behind the house.

After a few minutes of small talk, I handed the diamonds to Quintana who produced a jeweler's loop from his pants pocket to examine them. He was impressed and made a comment they were clean (no flaws). Little by little, I began to maneuver Quintana towards the alley so surveillance could obtain incriminating video of the undercover negotiations. The video, combined with the audio recordings, would tie Quintana and Gutierrez to the ongoing conspiracy investigation. We discussed the price of heroin, and he said he would give me a large quantity of heroin for the diamonds. I would also have to pay him an additional $10,000 in cash apart from the diamonds. As we negotiated, he began to incriminate himself more and more. He was putting the nails in his coffin, one at a time.

We agreed that Ruybalid would meet me later that evening and deliver the heroin. I gave the diamonds to Quintana, who accepted them as a down payment. I left with Ruybalid and made arrangements to meet him at another bar. I was elated I had finally been able to infiltrate the upper hierarchy of this complex criminal organization. Accompanied by several surveillance agents, I drove to the designated area several hours later. A short time after I arrived, Ruybalid drove into the lot. As I entered his car, he handed me a large brown paper bag containing the heroin, and I gave him the $10,000. He was visibly nervous. Sweat formed on his face, and he stumbled over some of his words. He kept surveying the area and eventually saw one of the surveillance units parked across the street. He pointed at the vehicle, but I told him it could be anyone and he was seeing ghosts, so he began to count the money. He assured me Quintana had liked the diamonds and taken them to a local jeweler to have them appraised. Quintana had kept all of them; except for one he gave to Gutierrez.

It was clear Ruybalid could not relax and kept losing track of how much money he had counted and had to keep starting over. When he finally finished and I stepped out of his car with the heroin, he tore out of the lot. I grabbed my handheld radio and told the surveillance agent that Ruybalid had spotted him and instructed him not to engage in any further surveillance that evening. We had more than enough personnel conducting surveillance, and I couldn't afford to have him see that vehicle again. He was already nervous, and this would have only confirmed his suspicion.

The transaction was complete, and I was confident Quintana and Gutierrez would be heading back to prison, despite their vow never to return. Other surveillance units followed Ruybalid to Gutierrez's house. Quintana was seen arriving twenty minutes later—I'm sure to discuss the drug transaction and divide the money. The ruse with the diamonds worked very well. My philosophy was if one strategy didn't work, it was imperative to improvise and quickly develop another one. This concept not only applied to covert operations but to all other aspects of life.

Undercover work required special skills to think, anticipate, and react quickly to any situation. It was exciting, and I thrived doing it. It provided a great adrenaline rush, but one that could be extremely dangerous. At some point, I realized I began to crave it. Ironically, it became addictive over time and I began to take more risks by doing deals with traffickers in dangerous locations advantageous to them to get the same adrenaline high. As an undercover agent, I had to be extremely careful to temper this, realizing it could eventually get me killed.

After completing the heroin purchase, I contacted Ruybalid several days later and boasted I had made a lot of money selling the heroin to several of my customers. I also told him I wanted to purchase a larger quantity. He explained he would be undergoing surgery relatively soon, but suggested we meet at a local restaurant in the meantime. A few hours later, we met in the parking lot of a family restaurant in east Denver. As we negotiated, I showed him the paper bag filled with bundles of cash in the trunk of my car. He looked at it and said Quintana had commented how he would make more money by having other customers like me. He explained he would attempt to do the transaction, but was scheduled for surgery later that day. I waited at the restaurant for quite some time, but Ruybalid never showed. I assumed he had gone into surgery and the heroin transaction wouldn't happen that day.

Back at the DEA office, we collectively decided enough evidence existed for a successful federal prosecution. Arrangements were made to execute the arrests of Quintana, Gutierrez, Ruybalid, and many others, so we conducted raids using state and local agencies later in the week.

The arrests took place with no resistance or hostile action. After all arrests were made, I walked into the office where Quintana and Ruybalid were being held, and I introduced myself as a special agent of the DEA. Knowing my true identity at this point wasn't a problem since they would see me when I testified against them in court. They were completely shocked and almost fell off their chairs.

Now, I had to prepare all the evidence and deal with presenting it to a federal grand jury. A large bail was set for Quintana, but he easily paid it and was released pending trial. Naturally, as he had said, he had no intention of returning to prison and quickly fled, becoming a hunted fugitive. The other defendants, with the exception of Ruybalid, who also fled, either pled guilty or went to trial and were convicted of conspiracy and heroin-distributions charges. They all received long prison sentences.

Over a year went by, and we weren't getting any leads on the whereabouts of Quintana. We thought he might have fled to Mexico where he had extensive contacts and friends. However, most fugitives will eventually make contact with their families. They become lonely and want to be in touch with loved ones, and Quintana was not an exception. He called his family and telephone toll records that we subpoenaed from the telephone company reflected several calls from Fresno, California.

I contacted our office in San Francisco and was fortunate to get Special Agent Rodney Alvarez. Rodney was an outstanding agent and investigator. He and I later became very good friends. He did an incredible job in locating and eventually capturing Quintana at an apartment where he was living with his girlfriend. He had dyed his hair a startling orange color that made him stand out in a crowd, which was an odd way of maintaining a low profile.

During his drug trafficking trial many years before on state drug trafficking charges, Quintana had attempted to hire the prominent and famed attorney F. Lee Bailey, who later became O. J. Simpson's criminal defense attorney. Quintana wasn't pleased with Bailey's firm, because they had advised him the state charges and evidence were too strong and it would be best to negotiate for a plea bargain. Instead, and as expected,

Quintana, hired the two most prominent defense attorneys in Denver to represent him on the federal charges.

The trial finally got underway, and I was obviously the principal witness. My preparation for the trial was long and tedious, since it involved an investigation that had lasted over a year. The audiotapes had to be translated and transcripts had to be prepared that would be presented as evidence. I had to review hundreds of investigative reports in order to refresh my memory on the undercover negotiations, dates, times, and locations. I was on the witness stand being grilled by Quintana's defense attorneys for several days.

They cross-examined me, in excruciating detail, on every aspect of the investigation, but I was well prepared, and they were unable to put a dent in my testimony. I remember Quintana sitting in the courtroom wearing a semitransparent white shirt, which revealed a large tattoo of Jesus Christ covering his back. It is inexplicable to me how some drug dealers believe themselves to be devout Catholics, yet are more than willing to poison and murder fellow human beings for profit and power and justify these obviously incongruent beliefs. Quintana was found guilty on all counts, including conspiracy and distribution of heroin, but this was not the end of his legacy. Nonetheless, it was the beginning of his demise.

Years later, Denver County deputy sheriffs were transporting Quintana to the federal penitentiary located in Leavenworth, Kansas. He had been in Denver on matters related to his ongoing legal appeals. The deputies and Quintana flew into the Kansas City International airport in Kansas City, Missouri, which is about eleven miles from Leavenworth. After renting a car, they began the short drive to the maximum-security prison.

Without warning, a sedan with four men armed with shotguns forced their vehicle off the road in an isolated area. The men, who were wearing masks and disguises, pointed the weapons at the officers and threatened to "blow their fucking heads off." Apparently, they were going to kill the deputies, but Quintana ordered them not to because they had treated him with respect. The four men and Quintana left the area, driving the rental car that contained the deputies' revolvers, police manuals, and some personal belongings.

The deputies reported the driver of the getaway car, whom they identified as Louis Newton, was wearing heavy women's makeup on his face. It was also learned that Quintana's men used a red rotating light, similar to those used on unmarked police cars, in the escape.

The drug dealer's daring escape hit the front pages of several major newspapers throughout the Southwest, including the *Albuquerque Journal*. The federal judge and lead prosecutor were immediately provided with a security detail, because they feared reprisals from Quintana and his henchman. The US Marshals' search for Quintana led them to a residence in Kansas City that Newton had rented. Although they had an arrest warrant, the marshals obtained a warrant authorizing the search of Newton's house. Together, the marshals with local police support surrounded the residence. Armored personnel carriers were used, and it began to look like a full-scale military operation. Negotiations began with Quintana via telephone for the peaceful surrender of all occupants in the house. Quintana, reminiscent of James Cagney in the old gangster movies, announced, "It's your job to get me out." The US Marshals and police believed from their surveillance that a woman and four men were inside with Quintana.

After nearly twenty-one hours, a woman and two men surrendered, including Newton. The officers were still under the impression Quintana and one other individual remained inside. They also learned from Newton of the existence of weapons and explosives in the house. When it became apparent Quintana was not going to surrender, an assault was conducted. Once they entered the house, they observed various weapons lying in the open including a machine gun and several Molotov cocktails. Quintana's body was found in the hallway with a pistol lying nearby. He didn't want to return to prison and committed suicide. The search also resulted in the seizure of several boxes of ammunition, three revolvers, a shotgun, a red rotating light, a programmable radio scanner tuned to police frequencies, police manuals, a police badge not belonging to the deputies, and a shoulder holster. No one else was found. A local newspaper reported the following details:

The Daily Register: Drug Dealer Found Dead.

James Orlando Quintana, a fugitive described as "the largest drug dealer in the western United States," was found dead last night by police who entered a home after a nearly twenty-one hour standoff. Quintana was found lying face down in a hallway with five or six weapons nearby. Police did not say how Quintana died.

Police had surrounded the house about 11 p.m. Saturday and used bullhorns to communicate with the 41-year-old Quintana, who escaped from a Denver Deputy in Kansas City last week while traveling to a federal penitentiary.

Police hurled tear gas into the house about 7:25 p.m. CDT yesterday and entered it at 8:25 p.m. Quintana's body was found about 8:50 p.m., Burns said. Quintana had been dead about three or four hours, Burns said. U.S Marshall Lee Koury said Quintana claimed to have a bomb, but said authorities had no way of proving this. Quintana had been in the house a couple of days, and police had negotiated with him through the night, Treece said. Treece said Quintana's last words were: "It's your job to get me out."

Burns said police decided to storm the house because "a major portion of the community was being tied up." Other factors were that Quintana had made suicide threats and the possibility he had a bomb, Burns said.

Treece also said three people in the home with Quintana surrendered yesterday morning. They were identified as Louis Marvin Newton, Patricia Catalina

Manzanares, and Lloyd John Tafoya, all of Denver, Colorado. Manzanares handed authorities $27,000.00, mostly in small bills, when she gave herself up, Koury said. He declined to speculate where the money came from or if it was connected to drugs. However, he said authorities believe there were drugs in the house.

Authorities said four men helped Quintana escape last Wednesday near Kansas City International airport. Treece said negotiations continued sporadically with Quintana, who told officers that he had talked with his mother and his lawyer and was considering killing himself. Burns said Quintana told authorities he was considering suicide because of the lives he had destroyed by selling heroin. Treece said Quintana was irrational at times and might have been taking drugs.

Ruybalid was eventually located and arrested. Not bothering going to trial, he pled guilty to all charges. He would be returning to prison without his mentor and protector. I will always wonder what Quintana could have accomplished had he chosen a different, legitimate path.

Chapter 5

Do Whatever It Takes

DEA Special Agent Michael S. Vigil's unprecedented achievements and accomplishments in the international war on drugs and terrorism resulted in some of the most innovative tactics to the way transnational organized crime is identified, investigated, and immobilized. Mike is an exceptional strategist that revolutionized and implemented complex multinational strategies which led to the capture of some of the most ruthless and violent drug lords in Mexico and South America. He also created global initiatives that facilitated the exchange of information, which continue to function today. I had the honor of working together with Mike in Mexico City, and he is a visionary leader who is highly respected internationally.

—Davy Aguilera
Bureau of Alcohol, Tobacco,
Firearms, and Explosives (ATF)
Assistant Special Agent in Charge (Ret.)

The DEA regional office in Denver had significant intelligence from both human and technical sources of illegal drug activities through Nogales, Arizona. This border city had become a major gateway for drugs such as cocaine, heroin, and marijuana. Mexican drug-trafficking organizations using the established port of entry in Nogales were also exploiting isolated areas nearby to funnel large quantities of drugs to distributors in cities throughout the US. The traffickers knew the US Customs and Border Protection Service lacked the manpower and resources to cover the border area or search every vehicle and pedestrian entering the country. Not even 20 percent of those entering are searched, making the odds overwhelmingly in the traffickers' favor. They smuggled drugs in tractor-trailer rigs commingled with legitimate cargo, including produce and furniture. They drove four-wheel-drive vehicles across remote areas of the border, and if a law-enforcement presence was detected, they simply drove back into Mexico. They built secret compartments in their vehicles; some cars had hidden compartments located between the trunk and the rear seat. These compartments had hydraulic lifts, which were activated by placing a quarter on two electrodes in the center console and then pressing down on the brake. Traffickers were very innovative in making sure their illegal drugs made it safely across the border.

Individuals were also hired to body-carry the drugs across the pedestrian lanes. The drugs were taped to the chest, arms, or legs with masking tape, and on occasion, body cavities were used. Some couriers stuffed prophylactics with heroin and swallowed them. This is an extremely dangerous practice because, if the condoms burst, the couriers would die of an overdose unless they received immediate medical attention.

Isolated areas along the fence were also used to backpack drugs into the US. The drug traffickers hired people to act as spotters conducting surveillance at the port of entry. These spotters determined which lanes were least likely to refer a vehicle to a secondary search area. The spotters used bulky, 1970s radios and later cumbersome cell phones. to pass the information to the traffickers, which was highly effective, because it reduced the probability of getting caught. Millions of vehicles and individuals cross the border each year, and they know it's operationally impossible to search them all. Unfortunately, the odds are in their favor—much better odds than you'd find in a gambling casino, but then, most traffickers have a keen sense of probability.

The DEA regional office discussed the need to send what they termed, "the best undercover agents" to the DEA office in Nogales to maximize the impact on the flow of drugs into the US. Nogales, Arizona is approximately sixty miles south of Tucson and is separated from Nogales, Sonora, Mexico, by nothing more than a fence. Robert Candelaria and I were selected for this assignment and received transfer papers, which included funding authorization. The transfer wasn't a significant issue for me since I wasn't married and only had to deal with a few pieces of furniture. Bob, on the other hand, had a large family, consisting of eight boys, and an entire household to contend with in the move. Frankly, I was excited about the new assignment, since it would involve work in Mexico.

Our orders were to develop a working relationship with the Mexican government and conduct joint operations. We knew from the beginning this was going to be a challenge, because the office in Nogales was comprised entirely of ex-Customs personnel with a different *perspective* on how things should be handled. For the most part, their idea of making a case was to respond to the port of entry when Customs inspectors made a seizure and take custody of the defendants and the drugs for processing. These were called referral cases, but this was not why Bob and I had been transferred there. The office knew why we were coming and we expected to get little cooperation. They didn't want to look bad, and so egos would definitely play a role in our ability to carry out our responsibilities

On arrival, Bob and I both purchased desert-style homes in a small residential area called Rio Rico, about ten miles north of Nogales. The area was fairly desolate and was a typical small border town. Comments by local natives indicated the residents could be divided into either law enforcement or drug traffickers. On the other side of the border was Nogales, Sonora, which was very similar to its namesake on the US side. It seemed as if someone had just dropped a fence and separated the town in half. Shortly after we got settled, Bob and I began to establish a wide network of informants. We hit the ground running and rapidly made numerous arrests getting many of these defendants to cooperate. We developed a significant pool of informants on both sides of the border.

We also began to cultivate relationships with the MFJP who had an office in an old building in the center of Nogales, Sonora. Apart from their agents, they had several federal prosecutors. We developed a close friendship with the MFJP comandante, Pepe Sordia, who had been a federale for most of his adult life. He liked vintage cars and had a beautiful classic Thunderbird, which he had restored and drove only on special occasions. Pepe dressed immaculately and had a penchant for expensive, ostrich cowboy boots. He frequently invited us to barbeques in isolated areas on the outskirts of town.

The MFJP brought mariachi bands and had them play while we ate and drank. One of their favorite songs was "El Rey" ("The King"), which was composed and sung by José Alfredo Jimenez. Jimenez had been a bartender in the Mexican state of Guanajuato and later became famous for his *corridos* (ballads), which were about gun battles, lost loves, and violence. These were things that Jimenez had seen while bartending and later incorporated into his songs. The words of "El Rey" were "With money or without money, I do what I want. I have neither a throne or a queen, or anyone who understands me, but I am still the king and my word is the law." This was quite fitting for the MFJP, who had the power of life and death and were kings of their world.

From the beginning, Bob and I ran into obstacles engineered by many of the other agents. We learned from several informants that when they called the office attempting to speak with us, they were told we were not available and advised not to call again. This type of behavior by fellow agents appalled me. Additionally, we were seldom authorized the funding to pay our informants or make undercover buys. That group was determined that we would not outperform them and make them look ineffective. However, these efforts to sabotage our investigations changed with the arrival of Bill Ortiz, who took over the office. Bill had worked in Guadalajara, Mexico, and understood the importance of working with the MFJP. We were now free to move forward and create a viable strategy that included our counterparts.

Working on the Mexican border was a unique experience. The Mexican drug traffickers had many decades of smuggling experience. They had established pipelines into the United States for marijuana and heroin produced in their country. The production of opium in Mexico has existed since the last quarter of the nineteenth century in the northwestern state of Sinaloa. Chinese immigrants brought to Mexico to help build a railway system created the opium trade there. They carried the poppy seed from China and began growing the plant for the sticky raw opium they were accustomed to smoking. The word *gomero* was created specifically for those who cultivated and trafficked opium.

The opium produced in Sinaloa, a state that is highly agricultural, could be traced along the same route as the Pacific railroad. Many years later, the highest concentrations of opium-poppy cultivation also included the northwestern states of Chihuahua and Durango. These three states formed the "Golden Triangle" of Mexico. Criminal entrepreneurs in Mexico recognized the value of opium and realized they could create a market in the US if they converted it into heroin hydrochloride. They were aware the so-called French Connection had already made inroads into the US market, and they wanted a piece of it. Additionally, they realized their close proximity to the US and the almost two-thousand-mile stretch of common border would be advantageous. As a bonus, many of the heroin traffickers had family members already in the US who could assist in distributing the drug. For them, it was a win-win situation with huge fortunes to be made with little effort.

The proliferation of marijuana use in the 1960s created another opportunity for quick wealth and a new breed of Mexican drug traffickers who were more arrogant and willing to use violence to expand their empires. The killing of police officers was a sign that times were changing for the worse. The Mexican drug trade was an equal-opportunity employer, and drug traffickers came from all levels of society: wealthy families, the middle class, and peasants. Many created dynasties and passed their knowledge and skills to other generations, which created more resilient cartels. Further complicating the drug situation in both Mexico and the US were Colombian cocaine traffickers, who were more sophisticated and organized. They were definitely more violent and formed an alliance with Mexican traffickers. The Colombians wanted to use the existing pipelines the Mexicans had created for marijuana and heroin to funnel their cocaine. Cultural factors and a common language also fostered success and would have significant ramifications for the US and Mexico.

While assigned to Nogales, I often crossed into Mexico in an undercover capacity to negotiate with very streetwise and dangerous drug traffickers. Most of them were usually armed and didn't hesitate to shoot it out with the police. I was usually alone, and my only weapons were the gift of gab, determination, and confidence in my ability to deal with situations that might arise during the undercover operations. More often than not, I usually had no one to provide operational security and, literally, took my chances. I relied on that sixth sense I had developed through hundreds of covert operations. It continued to serve me and helped ensure my survival.

Undercover work is not for everyone and takes a special type of person to put himself at risk with some of the most ruthless criminals in the world. It is even more difficult working undercover in foreign countries such as Mexico. It's Russian roulette with the odds always against you. Undercover agents are the true warrior caste of the DEA. It is a daring, dangerous, and bold undertaking. It pits one against some of the most hardened criminals in the world, who make Al Qaeda look like choirboys. They hire *stew makers*, who make the bodies of their victims disappear by dissolving them in acid. Mercilessly, they hang their enemies as decorations from bridges, pile dozens of dismembered bodies near major highways, and brutally use sledgehammers to smash heads like they were ripe pumpkins. Part of their criminal culture includes murder, and they will not, for a moment, hesitate to eliminate anyone who might pose a threat.

The competition between Mexican drug traffickers was intense as well, as they fought for their share of the market. I remember negotiating with traffickers on the streets of Nogales, Sonora, and while engaged in discussions with one group of drug dealers, other traffickers would approach and offer me better prices and bigger quantities. They had seen me before in the company of several traffickers and believed I was a drug dealer *"del otro lado de la frontera"* (from the other side of the border). Complicating matters and intensifying the danger were individuals who posed as drug dealers and would engage in ripping off traffickers for their money. This obviously posed a serious threat when working undercover.

On one occasion, I was involved in intense negotiations with a very significant trafficker on a busy street in Nogales, when another trafficker approached me. He moved close and said, *"Señor,* I need to talk to you. I just received a large shipment of heroin you might be interested in."

I stopped, turned to him, and said, "Listen, go have a cup of coffee, and I'll meet you in five minutes."

After finishing my conversation with the first trafficker, I met with the man who identified himself as Fernando. He shook my hand and boldly announced he had some good *"chiva"* (heroin). Enthusiastically, he indicated he was in possession of several kilos of heroin, which had just arrived from Culiacán, Sinaloa. Fernando appeared to be successful at what he did and wore expensive gold rings on his fingers and a Rolex watch. We took a cab to his house out in the middle of nowhere. From the outside, it looked like a concrete bunker with a high fence surrounding it. He seemed to be hyperactive and spoke rapidly with the chatter of a machinegun. Negotiations for the purchase of two kilograms of heroin began in earnest.

I told Fernando I wanted him to deliver the heroin across the border and stated *"Está muy peligrozo para ser la tranza en Mexico"* (it is too dangerous to do the transaction in Mexico). I didn't waiver despite Fernando's entreaties to do the deal at his house.

Eventually, he capitulated and in a frustrated voice said, *"Está bien"* (okay).

Long and contentious bartering yielded a price per kilogram of $32,000 for a total of $64,000. Each kilo, if sold at the street level, would net at least $300,000. The profits derived from illicit drugs are attractive and what clearly motivate many to enter the business.

We agreed he would cross the heroin through the pedestrian port of entry at 10:00 a.m. the next morning. A grocery store was located a few hundred feet from the border on the US side and would be the designated meeting area. It was on a small hill and provided a great vantage point to see who was approaching the port of entry from the Mexican side. The next morning, I drove to the Safeway and parked in the rear lot. The surveillance units took positions nearby. They wouldn't be noticed since the store had a robust business with customers driving in and out continuously. We had arranged that opening my trunk would be the bust signal. I'd tell the traffickers the money was there, which wouldn't arouse their suspicion.

It was important to establish arrest signals, so surveillance agents knew the drugs had been delivered; otherwise the cavalry would be too early or too late. Neither option was a good idea.

I saw Fernando approaching the port of entry with a woman who turned out to be his wife. I was leaning against a railing and smiled. He made a gesture indicating she would be crossing. Her very loose-fitting dress and a large shawl obviously concealed the bulk created by the heroin. Fernando's wife easily crossed the border, and I approached her.

She said, *"Tengo la mercancía"* (I have the merchandise).

We walked to the parking area, and she appeared to be apprehensive. She kept turning her head in all directions, looking for potential dangers. We approached my car, and once inside, she reached into her dress and pulled out several large bags of brown heroin that had been strapped to her legs with masking tape. I made a cursory examination of the heroin and then told her I would get the money from the trunk of the car. The trunk went up, and a few seconds later, several cars came screeching into the parking lot. The agents jumped out of their vehicles yelling orders with weapons drawn to make the arrest. Because Fernando hadn't seen the commotion, I can only imagine what went through his mind when his wife did not return. Several days later, he too was arrested by the MFJP, who found a few more kilograms of heroin at his residence.

My work in Nogales during the 1970s, was very different than things are today. I crossed into Mexico to meet with informants and conducted undercover operations without coordinating with the Mexican government until the drug delivery was scheduled and arrests would take place. This served two purposes: one, the investigation would not be compromised, and two, the MFJP officers were not well trained in conducting static or moving surveillances. The international boundary did not impede our efforts, and the DEA culture at the time was "do whatever it takes." This type of procedure was common practice in my day.

I always made it a point to arrange drug transactions in public places, because it minimized the potential for a drug rip-off or being kidnapped and held for ransom. El Trocadero was a restaurant on the southern outskirts of town, which I used on a regular basis to conduct undercover negotiations and arrange for drug deliveries. I loved the *milanesa* (breaded veal)—the servings were generous, and it was the best I'd ever had anywhere. The dish came with roasted jalapeno peppers that complemented its flavor and became one of life's little pleasures.

During a one-month period, I used the restaurant at least six times to carry out heroin deals. The routine was that I would order the milanesa while meeting with drug traffickers, finish eating, and then give the arrest signal. The MFJP would storm in military style with machine guns ready and waving handguns in the air. They also pretended to arrest me to protect the informants who had made the initial introductions. After the third or fourth time, the restaurant staff began to recognize me. They knew what was coming when they saw me walk through the door. The staff stood in a corner and actually waited for the MFJP to come charging in to arrest me along with the traffickers we had targeted for that operation. They probably thought I was a drug kingpin who was being arrested and just as quickly paying bribes for my release. No doubt they must have been equally perplexed about why I kept conducting drug deals at their restaurant. It really was hilarious, and the MFJP got a kick out of it.

An informant in Mexico called one day and said he had arranged a meeting with a significant heroin trafficker who had several kilograms and was seeking a buyer. A meeting date and place was set for the large Catholic Church in Nogales, Sonora. I walked across the border to meet with him outside the church. He explained the heroin trafficker was already waiting inside. He was nervous, and I attempted to calm him by telling him I would plan the operation so he wouldn't be present during the arrests. He relaxed a little, but I noticed beads of perspiration on his brow.

We walked into the virtually empty church and met with a well-dressed, polished man accompanied by an attractive woman who he introduced as his wife. The heroin trafficker told me he had three kilograms of pure heroin and could supply me with any quantity in the future. He said, *"La mercancía viene directamente de un laboratorio en Sinaloa"* (the merchandise comes directly from a laboratory in Sinaloa). He also said, *"Voy a querer ver la plata antes de entregar la mercancía"* (I will have to see the money before delivering the merchandise).

During the negotiations, he was very calm, and I could tell he had conducted this type of business hundreds of times. His wife remained quiet but listened to our every word. As we concluded our meeting, I wondered what the Vatican would say if they knew a drug deal was being negotiated in one of their churches. At the same time, the trafficker might have believed he would be protected by patron saints in this holy place.

In order to buy time to coordinate the operation with the MFJP, I told him it would take a couple of days to get the money. He agreed and indicated it was not a problem. It took a day to coordinate with the MFJP and also prepare a *flash roll* that would be used to show the trafficker.

I didn't want to take the money into Mexico for obvious reasons. It suddenly occurred to me that I should persuade him to cross the border to see the money. More importantly, I would have the MFJP comandante come into the US and participate. His undercover role was to act as my associate and display the money. This allowed the trafficker to see the comandante and create an illusion of trust that would be critical once the operation shifted back into Mexico. In essence, it gave me the advantage of having the comandante with me during the enforcement phase and on site to make the arrests and minimize the potential for violence. To my knowledge, this would be the first time an MFJP agent had ever worked undercover on US soil.

According to plan, the trafficker crossed into Nogales, Arizona, through the pedestrian port of entry, and we met in a small park near the main shopping area. The comandante waited in my car until I signaled him to approach us with the money. He did a great job and opened the briefcase filled with stacks of money. (A DEA Special Agent in Charge had the ability to approve flash rolls up to $500,000, but headquarters would have to authorize a larger amount. On occasion, we used money belonging to other agencies, but it depended on the situation and circumstances involved.) The trafficker flipped through the packs of hundred-dollar bills and stated, "*Está bien, nos vemos al otro lado, pero si son federales, los vamos a matar*" (okay, we will see each other on the other side [Mexico], but if you are federal agents, we will kill you).

It was time to roll the dice. No matter how well I planned these types of operations, there were always uncontrollable variables I had to deal with as they developed. That evening, I met with the comandante and his agents to plan the operation and arrange for the drug delivery to take place in an alley close to the international fence. Some of the MFJP agents would be on foot and others in vehicles to quickly surround the area and be able to seal off escape routes.

I contacted the trafficker and made arrangements for the delivery, agreeing to meet in a few hours. He was always very serious and sounded even more somber on the telephone. Just as we planned these operations, the traffickers also conducted their planning and strategy on drug deals. Everything was on the line where life and, at a minimum, freedom, were at stake. Hours later, the comandante and I were at the designated site, which appeared to be deserted. I had an empty briefcase, since it was never my intention to bring the money into Mexico. The trafficker and his wife were waiting in an expensive late-model sedan. She was holding a small infant in her arms. As we approached, the trafficker asked, *"Tiene la plata?"* (do you have the money)? I lifted the briefcase in the air and waved it. He smiled, which looked more like a snarl and reached for it. I pulled it away and asked to see the heroin. He frowned and glared. He motioned to his wife who placed the infant on the seat and began to remove the small blankets covering the child. The baby was used to conceal the heroin contained in large plastic bags. What kind of people would use their own baby to conduct a drug deal and place its life in danger? It sickened me that these traffickers were so callous and uncaring as to risk the life of their own child. The arrest took place without incident since the comandante was with me, which eliminated him running up to the car giving the trafficker time to draw the handgun concealed under his jacket. The wife began to cry as she was taken into custody, and her husband refused to look at her. The baby was taken by child protective services and later given to the mother's sister.

Subsequently, the DEA office forwarded a communiqué to headquarters detailing the operation and the use of the MFJP comandante in an undercover capacity in the US. I was unsure how they would react to having a foreign agent engaged in an undercover operation in the United States. The next day, we received a Teletype from DEA Administrator Peter Bensinger with great accolades on the innovative tactic used in the operation. Bensinger, in my opinion, was definitely the best administrator in the history of the DEA. He lobbied to obtain adequate budgets for the agency and fully supported personnel in the field. A true leader, he treated everyone with respect and dignity.

Being a bachelor, I ate out a lot. I often went to a restaurant in Nogales, Sonora, called the La Caverna, located in a large, natural cavern, which had once served as a jail. Legend had it that the famous Apache warrior, Geronimo, was held there in captivity. One evening, I went alone and had dinner. As I left the restaurant and walked outside, I encountered a major drug trafficker known for being violent and having murdered informants and other drug traffickers. (It was not uncommon for drug traffickers I arrested in Arizona to post bond and quickly flee back to Mexico. At the time, Mexico would not extradite its citizens to the US, despite the severity of the criminal charge.) Months earlier, I had arrested this man in Arizona on drug charges, and he later became a fugitive. He saw me and started to approach. I quickly put my hand on my .38 Smith and Wesson handgun tucked in my waistband. He immediately raised his hands to signify that he meant no harm. We stood there side by side for several minutes as he asked about one of the US attorneys who was handling his case.

He said, "Como está ese hijo de puta?" (How is that son of a whore?) We were in no-man's-land, and we both knew it. We talked for a few minutes and then shook hands, and I walked slowly back into the US. He was killed two weeks later. His body had been riddled with at least sixty bullets from a machine gun and was unceremoniously thrown on the side of the road near the bullring on the edge of town.

During my work with the MFJP in Nogales, Sonora, I had an investigation involving a significant trafficker based in Santa Ana, Sonora, about an hour's drive south of the US/Mexico border. An informant residing in Mexico called to tell me he knew a trafficker involved in the distribution of large quantities of pure heroin. He agreed to arrange a meeting for me but needed to be careful because the trafficker was known as a *matador* (a killer). By the sound of his shaky voice, I knew the informant was nervous. Despite the risk, he would introduce me to the trafficker, because he needed the money.

I instructed him to say I was a drug dealer operating in Tucson, Arizona, who was distributing large amounts of heroin to several southwestern US states. I also told him to tell the trafficker one of my suppliers had been arrested and I needed a reliable source for my multi-kilogram quantities of high-grade heroin. Days later, the informant called and told me the trafficker was interested in meeting. I figured it was opportune to roll the dice again and told him to arrange for the purchase of a couple of kilograms of heroin.

In order to pay our informants, we had to fully document them through a personal-history form—photographs, fingerprints, and a signature exemplar. After being documented, they were assigned a number that would be used in all subsequent documents, including investigative reports and debriefings. Each time they were paid, they had to sign a document that was witnessed by two agents. Informants came from all levels of society, including bankers, politicians, criminals, doctors, and attorneys, to name a few. In fact, even my tailor, who made beautiful Italian-cut suits, provided information. Another was a prominent state attorney general who I often met for dinner and drinks. Some did it as a civic responsibility, others for money, some for revenge, and many to eliminate competition. I went over the cover story he would use in arranging the introduction.

On a hot Friday morning, I coordinated the operation with the MFJP, who quickly mobilized a group of about fifteen agents, all heavily armed with handguns and AK-47s with the curved magazines. The weapons in Mexico were referred to as *cuerno de chivo* (horn of the goat), because the curved magazine resembled a ram's horn. It was a weapon of choice for both the MFJP and the drug dealers. We all loaded into several MFJP vehicles and began moving quickly south to Santa Ana. We came up to the twenty-six kilometer Mexican Customs and Immigration checkpoint. It was an old, dilapidated structure with crumbling walls. We drove up as Mexican officials were searching other vehicles for contraband, primarily electrical appliances from the US, as well as weapons. They also checked for stolen US vehicles, also a lucrative business for many criminal groups. As we stopped at the checkpoint, one of the immigration officials, wearing a green uniform, approached the vehicle I was in and asked for my passport. When working in an undercover capacity, I never carried documents with my true identity. I told him, *"No tengo mi pasaporte"* (I don't have my passport). He stated, *"Entonces, no puede pasar"* (Then, you cannot pass).

The MFJP comandante who was accompanying us became irate and berated the immigration official by telling him, *"No importa; está con nosotros"* (it does not matter; he is with us). Unfortunately, the officer made the mistake of forcing the issue, and the comandante gave the order to have him arrested. MFJP agents poured out of their trucks and forcibly knocked the immigration official onto the ground and handcuffed his arms behind his back. They lifted him and threw him into the back of one of their trucks that had a camper shell. For several minutes, the truck rocked back and forth violently as the immigration officer was getting pounded. Other MFJP officials pointed AK-47s at the other Customs and Immigration officers at the checkpoint, who froze for the duration of the incident, knowing only too well the consequences of confronting the MFJP.

We continued on our way with the scuffed immigration officer now under arrest. On the outskirts of Santa Ana, the comandante made a call to General Mendiolea, the director general of the MFJP, to report the incident involving the immigration official. The comandante told the general the immigration official had been obstinate and was impeding one of their operations. General Mendiolea instructed the comandante to hire a local medical doctor and "motivate" him to write a statement "confirming" the immigration officer was intoxicated. Based on the orders, the MFJP agents located a doctor who examined the official and was coerced into writing a report confirming his intoxication. Who knows when the officer had last drunk alcohol, but he was certainly sober on that particular day. Within the hour, MFJP agents had placed him in a local jail until formal charges could be filed.

We arrived at an old hotel located in the central part of Santa Ana where I had made arrangements to speak with the informant before we met with the trafficker. He said everything was ready. However, the trafficker was now expressing apprehension in meeting someone he didn't know well. The informant had vigorously vouched for me, but fear was etched on his face. He was well aware of the risks and that his life was on the line. He was also worried about being killed in crossfire between the traffickers and the MFJP if something went awry. Realistically, these were legitimate concerns.

We rented two rooms at the hotel. I would use one to meet and negotiate with the trafficker, and the MFJP would use the other to conduct surveillance. It took no more than a couple of minutes to coordinate the arrest signal, which was to raise the trunk of the car parked outside my room in plain sight of the MFJP. We all took our positions. I had the informant call the trafficker and give him our location, and in less than an hour, there was a knock on the door.

Standing at the doorway was a large, heavyset man who introduced himself as José. He walked swiftly into the room and sat down at the foot of the bed. He was relaxed, but wary and asked me several questions. José was interested in corroborating the story the informant had provided him. Again, careful coordination with the informant was critical, and the current situation proved it. José asked where I was from and where I would be distributing the heroin. He also made it a point to say we would not leave the area alive if the deal went wrong. He stated, "*Yo se que hay algunos agentes de la DEA que trabajan encubiertos en Mexico*" (I know that there are some DEA agents who work undercover in Mexico).

We negotiated for two kilograms of heroin that José indicated were pure. I showed him $100,000 in US currency, and he thumbed through the bills. He agreed he would count the money when he returned with the heroin. He left the room promising he would be back in less than an hour. I waited a few minutes and then went outside to put the money in the trunk of my car and then walked back inside to the lobby. The MFJP comandante followed, and we met briefly in the restroom to discuss the meeting.

I returned to the room where the informant and I waited for José to return. Because I'd be leaving the room to give the arrest signal, I turned off the water to the toilet and flushed the remaining water. I didn't want to chance him flushing the heroin as soon as he saw the MFJP. An hour later, I saw José approaching through the courtyard carrying a small stool. After I let him in, he began peering nervously through the curtains. He handed me the stool and explained the heroin was hidden underneath the cushion. I peeled off the leather and found two-kilogram packages tightly wrapped in white tape. José said he had a heroin laboratory that produced about fifty kilograms of heroin each week. Apparently, he had access to a lot of opium, because it took ten kilograms of opium to make one kilogram of heroin. I told him the money for the heroin was in the trunk of my car where I had placed it for security purposes after he had left. I calmly said it would only take a minute to retrieve it. After he nodded. I left the room and opened the trunk, which was the signal.

Seconds later, the MFJP charged out of their room and into mine with handguns drawn. Some agents also carried AK-47s. They rushed in and told José he was under arrest. I sprinted back to the room and grabbed the informant by the arm and pulled him out because I knew the MFJP would be *interrogating* José with carbonated water. Their method was to place a cloth over the person's face and then soak it with carbonated water from bottles of Tehuacan, causing suffocation. We now call it "water boarding" in the US. Most suspects would quickly provide information rather than prolong the process. José was no exception, and he gave the MFJP information that resulted in the seizure of an additional kilogram of heroin. The quantity and purity levels of the seized heroin when adulterated for street sales would have yielded millions of dollars.

I often worked with the senior Mexican attorney general's (PGR) prosecutor in Nogales, Arizona. His name was Pedro Mireles Malpica, and he closely resembled Ebenezer Scrooge in the Charles Dickens novel, *A Christmas Carol*. He was very old, tall and gaunt, and did not suffer fools gladly. On one occasion while at his office, a Mexican reporter was in the reception area speaking loudly with the secretary. He was acting belligerent, insisting that he be allowed to see Mireles Malpica. The prosecutor heard the commotion and called the reporter into his office and carefully looked at him, top to bottom, and told him he looked like a *"pinche payaso"* (fucking clown) and that he should return to his hotel and change clothes. The severely berated reporter left with his dignity in shreds, and I seriously doubt he ever returned. On his belt, Malpica carried a .45-caliber semiautomatic handgun and five fully loaded magazines. He also carried a wicked-looking knife. It was difficult to believe his lanky frame could carry all that weight. I had a good relationship with Mireles Malpica that resulted in his trust and confidence in me.

During one discussion, we talked about the kidnapping of one of his prosecutors by drug traffickers. This incident had prompted a large operation in the area. Several MFJP agents were brought in from Mexico City and started massive raids and house searches. After five days, the prosecutor was released, but the bodies of many drug traffickers began appearing in dark alleys and on roadsides leading out of Nogales, Sonora. It was a message to the drug-trafficking community that was heard loud and clear. They understood his language. Mireles Malpica explained, "If the traffickers kill one of us, then we will kill forty of them in order to teach them they cannot do this—they will pay, and pay heavily for their actions."

That is exactly how *justice* was conducted in those days. It was a very harsh system, but they understood they had to fight fire with fire. The MFJP had few resources and therefore acted with brute force in addressing crime. Mireles Malpica was eventually transferred to Torreon, Coahuila, and I never saw him again.

Drug-trafficking in Mexico can be traced to the early twentieth century when legislation in the United States and many countries worldwide began to prohibit the manufacture, distribution, and use of alcohol and psychotropic drugs. During this time, Mexico was only in the developmental stages of becoming a significant source country for marijuana and heroin. Mexican drug networks were unsophisticated and involved in the production and distribution of low-grade marijuana, whose active ingredient, known as THC, was only slightly over one percent. *Sinsemilla* (without seed) marijuana had not yet entered the drug landscape. Opium and heroin were primarily produced in the tri-state area of Durango, Chihuahua, and Sinaloa. Drug traffickers moved the drugs across the border in isolated areas by vehicle or individuals who were referred to as *mules*. They also took advantage of the volume of vehicles and pedestrians that crossed the border each day into the US through the various ports of entry in San Diego, Nogales, El Paso, Laredo, and others. Most of the Mexican drug smugglers at the time were not as violent as they are today. While criminal organizations were usually family enterprises, drug trafficking was definitely an equal-opportunity employer, and traffickers came from all socioeconomic groups—the wealthy and middle class, but primarily from those well below the poverty level. To many, it was their ticket out of a choking poverty that existed in poor, rural areas and isolated mountain villages.

The Mexican trafficking organizations were loose knit and somewhat unstructured, but on occasion, cooperated with one another by sharing drug routes and protection and combining drug loads when one organization needed more to complete a load. Violence occurred in the form of vendettas, but never at the unprecedented levels seen today. They followed the same model of early Italian organized crime, where the so-called Mustache Petes kept a low profile and only used violence when absolutely necessary. They did not provoke the police, including those on their payroll. They believed violence only brought unwanted attention and the trafficking of drugs was like any other criminal enterprise: it generated enormous profits. Through time, the Mexican trafficking organizations began to expand and gain more power as a result of the changes in the global drug market and enforcement efforts that redirected transit zone movement.

In the 1970s, the emergence of the counterculture movement and the dismantling of the French heroin connection caused a vacuum, and Mexican traffickers were more than willing to fill the void. At the same time, the consumption of cocaine in the US helped create some of the most formidable drug-trafficking organizations in Colombia. The Colombians began forming alliances with other Andean Ridge traffickers, principally in Bolivia, Peru, and Ecuador, who provided them with coca paste or the more-processed cocaine base. This product was shipped to Colombia where large labs in jungle areas converted it into its final form, *cocaine* hydrochloride. The Colombians, once the conversion process was accomplished, transported it to the northern coastal areas of Cartagena, Santa Marta, Barranquilla, Rio Hacha, and others, where it was loaded onto maritime ships or aircraft destined for the southern coast of Florida by way of the Caribbean Sea.

Based on intelligence assessments that were being developed, the US began to ramp up their interdiction efforts in the Caribbean, which eventually dealt the Colombian traffickers significant losses of cocaine, personnel, and conveyances. This, unfortunately, created a *balloon effect*, forcing the Colombians to seek other, more viable, and safer routes. It was given this name, because as you squeeze a balloon, it bellows out in the area not squeezed. The same is true with the drug trade. As interdiction efforts squeezed drug traffickers in the Caribbean, routes were redirected to areas away from the interdiction pressure. Mexico was a logical alternative. Mexican traffickers had already established networks into the United States for marijuana and heroin. As a result, the Colombian drug networks began to rely on these pipelines into the US.

Those networks were simple and effective. Today, drug-trafficking organizations are large, highly structured, flexible groups, and because of unprecedented technological advances, they now have a global reach. They easily communicate and share information, transfer and launder illicit profits, monitor law-enforcement activity, and ensure quick and effective deliveries of drugs and contraband with tremendous agility. Additionally, drug-trafficking organizations and terrorists operate in a borderless world. Unlike law-enforcement agencies, they are not bound or impeded by borders and issues of sovereignty. This has allowed them to challenge the political and economic infrastructures of countries around the world by using the same technologies, financial capabilities, communications, and organizational models.

For decades, Mexico had a highly centralized political structure that played a role in determining political corruption. The iron grip of the controlling Mexian political party, PRI, had methodically developed a monopoly within Mexico on the control and use of the country's security forces, both police and military, with ultimate domination of all Mexican states. With this, came endemic corruption and bribes allowing drug trafficking to flourish. Astronomical amounts of money funneled into private and political accounts can sway any decision. Many are of the opinion that countries, drug-trafficking organizations, and transnational criminal networks are not distinct operational modules, but are somewhat interactive.

For example, the now abolished Dirección Federal de Seguridad (Federal Security Directorate), better known by its acronym DFS, was responsible for Mexican domestic security from 1947 to 1987. It was created during the same year as the CIA and was to serve basically the same function, but strictly limited to a domestic role like the FBI. In reality, the PRI used the DFS as an instrument to collect damaging information on political-party rivals, which could be used against them through the efficient use of national media sources, particularly during political campaigns. The DFS had great power and little oversight. Frankly, they were an unchecked political hurricane with the same strength and ability to exact the same carnage.

In the 1980s, the Mexican drug-trafficking organizations began to develop a significant nexus to the DFS, which was then headed by José Antonio Zorrilla Perez. This relationship resulted in the protection of many powerful drug-trafficking organizations operating throughout the country. Many drug traffickers carried DFS badges and credentials, which they displayed with arrogance and a sense of impunity. Those responsible for the abduction and murder of DEA agent Enrique "Kiki" Camarena, including Miguel Angel Félix Gallardo, Juan Ramón Mata Ballesteros, Ernesto Fonseca, and Rafael Caro Quintero, all carried DFS badges. I personally knew many of the DFS agents, and in my opinion, they were literally some of the most powerful individuals in the country.

One of the DFS zone commanders I met with on numerous occasions was Daniel Acuña Figueroa, who was responsible for many of the northern Mexican states. He frequently provided me with information on certain drug-trafficking organizations; however, I was well aware he was being selective on which networks he wanted me to target.

One day over lunch, he pulled out a huge ingot of pure gold and began examining it. He said a local jeweler was going to make a bracelet for him. He alluded to the fact he had taken it during a raid conducted at a trafficker's residence. I assumed he had several other gold ingots and this one was nothing more than a sample. I often encountered Acuña, Chow Lopez, and other DFS personnel in different cities in Mexico having meetings in many of the better hotels. One thing's for sure, they weren't planning any efforts against the criminal organizations that created mayhem in their country. Acuña and another DFS commander, Chow Lopez, were later arrested for "illicit enrichment."

The following article appeared in the *Los Angeles Times*:

Mexico Accuses 2 Former Security Chiefs Over Amassed Wealth; 427 Agents Fired

In a lengthy statement issued this week, the Ministry of Government acknowledged that two DFS agents who were captured with a drug traffic boss have been jailed on charges of working for the suspected criminal. Another DFS agent is being held for his suspected involvement in protecting a huge marijuana farm in Chihuahua state that was raided by authorities last November.

Most of the 427 discharged agents were removed because they did not meet the proper requirements, according to the government. The latest blow to the prestige of the DFS came with the disclosure Wednesday that Rafael Chao Lopez and Daniel Acuna, both of whom are former Zone Commanders of the directorate, are under investigation for "inexplicable enrichment."

The charges were lodged against them by the office of the controller of the federal government, a Cabinet-level agency created by President Miguel de la Madrid to implement his heralded "moral renovation" program, the results of which have been disappointing to many. The two ex-commanders are believed to be the first figures against which De la Madrid has used legislation written by former President José Lopez Portillo designed to make it tougher for public officials to steal.

Mexico's entry into the cocaine market in the 1970s and 1980s created a huge level of prosperity, power, and political connections. Drug-trafficking organizations in Mexico quickly developed into sophisticated consortiums structured like many *Fortune* 500 companies. They had a clear line of authority and a transparent chain of command. They also had specialized branches that handled money laundering, transportation, precursor chemicals, manufacture, distribution, security, and violent components, which eliminated rival traffickers, police, politicians, and informants. The heads of these organizations, through only a few trusted individuals, disseminated orders and instructions using a cellular organizational structure to effectively insulate themselves from any criminal liability.

With the immobilization of many Colombian drug-trafficking organizations in the late 1980s and 1990s, Mexico became a more significant hub for international drug trafficking. Due in large part to expansive political protection, competition among Mexican organizations was very limited and geographical areas of operation were clearly delineated. This era of relative harmony between drug-trafficking organizations was made possible because of arrangements with corrupt government officials who designated lucrative areas and imposed informal rules to be followed by these illicit enterprises. The level of competition and extreme conflict between the major drug-trafficking organizations began to intensify in the late 1990s, because of the restructuring of Mexico's federal law-enforcement agencies, the increase in political pluralism, and the impact on drug-trafficking organizations through law-enforcement efforts. Throughout the 1990s, the eventual move towards pluralism at state and municipal levels began to develop a more diverse and different political landscape.

The PRI, in 1997, lost its total control of the lower house of the federal legislature. Later, in 2000, Vicente Fox, a member of the National Action Party (PAN), was elected president. The citizens of Mexico were tired of decades of corruption and political impunity, and they wanted change. This political change increased the need to facilitate transparency, rule of law, and a stronger, coordinated effort against drug trafficking and organized crime. In some cases, the disrupted political connections created a situation whereby *different* criminal organizations were now favored.

It should be mentioned that none of Mexico's political parties have been immune to corruption and graft. Regardless, there has been a more-concerted effort to weed out corruption at the federal level. US and Mexican law-enforcement efforts had significant, but also unforeseen consequences on the Mexican drug-trafficking organizations. Numerous bilateral efforts and the sharing of information, arrests, and prosecutions of significant drug traffickers has served to immobilize many international networks.

The primary objective of Mexican traffickers is to smuggle their drugs across the border and into US consumer markets, which are unsurpassed in wealth, diversity, and voraciousness. It is the largest illicit-drug-consumer country in the world. The use of drugs is a feature of all the more-affluent societies, but the United States is the ultimate Disneyland for international criminals.

This challenge became much more difficult in the 1990s as a result of additional resources put in place along the US/Mexico border, but more so in the aftermath of the September 11, 2001 terrorist attacks in New York. Strengthened border security made it more challenging for the Mexican drug traffickers to reach consumer markets in the US. The traffickers were forced to seek more innovative tactics and improve their smuggling methods, including the building of tunnels and the use of maritime ships. As a result, Mexican drug-trafficking organizations suffered setbacks that changed the balance of power and created infighting and fractionalization within.

In 2002, Ramón Arellano Félix was mortally wounded in a gun battle with local police in Mazatlán. He was the violent chief enforcer of the Arellano Félix organization based in Tijuana, Baja California Norte. A source reported that Ramón, standing on a street in downtown Tijuana with several of his *sicarios* (hit men), asked them, "Quien tiene lios con alguien, para matarlos?" (Who has problems with someone, so we can kill them?) He enjoyed killing so much, he was addicted to murder. The patriarch of the Arellano Félix organization, Benjamin, was arrested in the southern state of Puebla a month after Ramón was killed. In 2003, the arrest of Osiel Cardenas and his top lieutenant, Adan Medrano Rodriguez, had a significant impact on the Gulf drug-trafficking organization. Also, Ricardo García Urquiza, a top-ranking leader of the Juarez organization, was arrested in 2005.

As a consequence, the most-significant drug-trafficking organizations became involved in a major and violent struggle against each other for control of the drug trade. The crippled Tijuana and Gulf (Gulf of Mexico) cartels went to war with the Juarez and Sinaloa networks that formed the so-called Federation. At the same time, new criminal organizations emerged at this critical juncture, i.e., the Beltran Leyva organization, which separated from the Sinaloa group, and the La Familia Michoacana (LFM), who brazenly entered the struggle, expanding both the violence and the restructured alliances. As the LFM gained power, the violence in Michoacán peaked in this strategic location for the cultivation of marijuana and as a staging area for cocaine from South America. The LFM lacked access to the *plazas*, or border gateways into the US, and fought to establish alliances with other stronger drug-trafficking organizations to solidify their power base.

As the groups fractionalized, a new phenomenon began to occur: they began to engage in the crimes of kidnapping, extortion, and theft. In the past, these were crimes they showed no interest in because of low profit margins in comparison to the drug trade. As disruptions to the drug-trafficking organizations occurred, so did the intensity of the competition and conflict, which contributed to more violence. From the beginning of the Fox administration, drug-trafficking organizations began to increase their levels of violence. From 2001 to 2004, the rise in murders attributed to drug traffickers rose modestly from 1,080 to 1,304. In 2005 to 2006, the numbers increased to 1,776 and 2,221, respectively, when central Mexican states such as Michoacán and Guerrero experienced an unprecedented level of violence. As expected, a short time later, the larger share of killings shifted to the northern border areas. In 2007, a significant percentage of the 2,300 drug-related murders occurred in Baja California, Sonora, and Chihuahua. A dramatic increase in murders was documented in 2008, and the number was now exceeding 5,000. Much of the violence was now located in the state of Chihuahua and particularly in the border city of Juarez, just south of El Paso, Texas.

Chapter 6

Just Another Day on the Job

In the international world of law enforcement, relationships are not easily established or maintained. Mike Vigil, through his skills, abilities, expertise, and determination proved to be a master of building rapport with international partners around the world. At a time when agencies battled each other as well as battling the criminal element, Mike Vigil was so respected amongst his peers that he set the standard for cooperation and not competition. One of Mike's greatest strengths was his diversification amongst various different cultures. He could relate and interact with national & international leaders as well as the lowest level of society, giving him the ability to successfully navigate politically, operationally, and tactically.

—Alonzo Peña, Deputy Director Immigration and Customs Enforcement (Ret.)

After two years in Nogales, Arizona, I applied for a position at the DEA office in Hermosillo, Sonora, Mexico. Most of my work had been in Mexico, so it was logical for me to be assigned to one of our offices located there. In the DEA, when applying for positions outside the United States, you must compete with others interested in the same foreign assignment. At the time, there were several offices in Mexico—Mexico City, Merida, Guadalajara, Monterey, Mazatlán, and Hermosillo. The main office was in Mexico City, located at the US Embassy.

Having already done some undercover work for the office in Hermosillo, I was immediately selected for the position. The office was small, with three agents and a secretary. The area of operations for the office was expansive and included the states of Chihuahua, Sonora, and Baja California Norte. The office in Mazatlán covered the southern Baja state. All were critical areas, since they were significant drug-smuggling corridors into the United States.

Hermosillo, is a city located centrally in the northwestern Mexican state of Sonora. It is the capital and main economic center for the state and region. and located on a plain in the Sonoran Desert which is flat and grassy and backdropped by serrated mountain peaks. By car it will take you about three hours to reach Nogales, Arizona, from Hermosillo.

On my arrival there, I initially stayed at the Valle Grande hotel near the northern outskirts of the city. While assigned to Nogales, Arizona, I had used it to do an undercover operation. The rooms were clean, and it had a nice restaurant and bar. It was definitely the best hotel in the city, and it would only be temporary until I could find a more suitable place. Not wasting any time, I made arrangements, through an informant, to meet with drug traffickers from the state of Sinaloa. They were large-scale dealers who engaged in the manufacture and distribution of high-quality heroin. During the initial undercover negotiations, I was surprised to see that one of them was a woman in her forties, who was very attractive, with fair skin and long, dark hair. Her expensive clothes accentuated her curvy figure, and her fingers and wrists were laden with expensive jewelry. A tall, heavyset man with short-cropped hair and a thin mustache accompanied her. He also wore designer clothes and had the traditional drug trafficker *esclava* (bracelet) studded with large diamonds on his right wrist. The gold bracelet immediately caught my eye.

It was immediately obvious the woman was the dominant personality and did most of the negotiating, giving orders to her companion. She was intelligent and educated in the way she spoke and was definitely not a novice to the drug trade. She attempted to determine whether I was also a legitimate drug trafficker. The questions came rapidly, one leading to another. She wanted to know where I was from and what other traffickers I was familiar with in Mexico. Additionally, she wanted to know how I would smuggle the heroin into the US. As she spoke, it was clear she used her beauty to manipulate men. She let her hand drop to her skirt and very lightly lifted it higher and higher to show her shapely legs. Apart from wanting to sell heroin, she was attempting to seduce me.

She had three kilograms of pure heroin and would let me have them for $180,000 US. She calculated if it were destined for street sale, the heroin could be diluted to make forty-eight kilograms, generating millions of dollars in profit. She definitely knew her business. As we continued the negotiations for at least an hour, she passed her hand over my leg, making it difficult for me to concentrate on business. Eventually, we reached an agreement and arranged to meet later that afternoon. She and her associate left.

I also left the hotel and met with the DEA agents and MFJP personnel who were conducting surveillance. We determined it would be best to arrest the two in the back parking lot of the hotel and avoid putting innocent people in the line of fire, because it was always possible a shootout could occur during the arrests. The removal of my sunglasses would be the arrest signal, which would let surveillance agents know that the heroin was in the possession of the traffickers.

As had been prearranged, I again met with the traffickers at the restaurant. The woman was carrying a very large, red purse. In a dimly lit lounge, we enjoyed a few margaritas with a small plate of lime wedges and thin slices of sweet coconut. The waiter also brought some stale tortilla chips and watery salsa. She wrote her telephone number on a table napkin and suggested I call her later that evening after the transaction was completed so we could have dinner. She had no idea she would be dining on miserable prison food in jail for a long time.

I asked if she had brought the heroin, and she pointed to the purse that she had placed under the table. She asked, *"Todo está listo de tu parte?"* (Is everything ready on your part?) I replied, *"Todo está bien. Vamos a mi habitatión donde tengo la plata"* (Everything is fine. Let's go to my room where I have the money).

Her escort was a little hesitant, but she immediately overruled him and agreed to go to my room to finalize the drug deal. Before leaving the restaurant, I opened her bag to ensure she had brought the heroin. Inside, I counted three large bricklike packages wrapped in brown tape. As we walked out, she continued to brush up against me giving me one signal after another.

When we entered the parking lot, I removed my sunglasses, and the MFJP came running in from all sides with AK-47s in hand. They threw the man and woman on the ground and placed the barrels of their weapons on their heads. They also grabbed me in a headlock, pretending to arrest me in order to protect the informant. The two traffickers were placed in separate cars, which sped away, tires screeching.

The interrogation of the two traffickers resulted in the arrests of additional individuals in the state of Sinaloa. The MFJP were so pleased they took me out to dinner and bought me a huge steak accompanied by large amounts of celebratory tequila as well. The celebration went on into the early morning hours of the next day. Truth be known, it made me wonder if drinking with the MFJP wasn't more dangerous than dodging bullets.

Although the designated area of responsibility for the Hermosillo office consisted of Sonora, Chihuahua, and Baja California Norte, I often worked in other areas, particularly in Sinaloa. What Cali and Medellin are to Colombian drug traffickers, Sinaloa is to the drug lords of Mexico. Nestled between the Pacific Ocean and the Sierra Madre mountains, its fertile fields produce vast amounts of marijuana and heroin destined for US markets. Many of the drug lords live in mansions in the hills of Culiacán, the state capital. The city even has a patron saint of drug smuggling—the legendary bandit Jesus Malverde, whose image is seen gling from the gold necklaces of many drug traffickers. According to legend, Malverde was a thief who robbed the rich and gave to the poor. Malverde's chapel is in downtown Culiacán in a glass-brick building just across the street from the government palace. The chapel walls are crowded with plaques bearing the names of known drug-trafficking families or pictures of men and their trucks, all paying tribute for "safe passage" from Sinaloa to Los Angeles and other points north.

■ ■ ■ ■

I was always available to my informants, day or night. Whatever their motives, mine remained the same—to put as many drug dealers behind bars as possible. One late night, I received a call from an informant saying he had arranged a meeting with someone who was part of a large organization involved in the distribution of heroin. That was a Tuesday. The meeting had been scheduled for Thursday, so planning the operation had to happen without delay.

I met with the MFJP comandante in Hermosillo and explained the situation. He would send his *jefe de grupo* (group leader) to arrange support from the MFJP office in Los Mochis. The comandante also arranged air transportation with the Mexican army. On Wednesday, I met with the MFJP group leader at the Hermosillo International airport. We found the Mexican army pilot, a short, heavyset man with strong, Indian features who showed us the airplane that would be used to transport us to Los Mochis. It was an old Cessna single engine, which had undoubtedly been seized. I was fully aware such aircraft are not well maintained and the Mexican government does not adhere to maintenance schedules or strict certifications of airworthiness. It was a crapshoot getting into Mexican aircraft, but I had no choice at that point.

We departed in the early afternoon, and twenty minutes into the flight, we slammed into a monstrous thunderstorm. The airplane began thrashing back and forth, so much that our heads continuously hit the ceiling. There were no seatbelts. The MFJP group leader screamed as the storm intensified, and the pilot fought to hold on to the controls.

The pilot's face was contorted, and he was drenched in sweat. He was navigating through the center of the storm, and frankly, I thought we weren't going to get through this alive. I've flown through storms in small aircraft before, but never like this one. The storm began to dissipate about ten miles out of Los Mochis, and we were able to land safely. When we all climbed out of the aircraft, our feet on solid ground felt very good. At the airport, we were met by a large group of MFJP agents who were heavily armed and divided between two black Suburbans. I briefed them in a nearby, gray sheet-metal hangar on our operational plan in detail as they listened intently. It was just another day on the job.

I contacted the informant who had arranged the meeting at the Holiday Inn, located on a large hill in the northern part of the city. The traffickers didn't know what I looked like, and they didn't expect me to arrive until the next day. In preparation, I again rented two rooms at the hotel; one would be used for the undercover negotiations, the other for the MFJP who would be conducting surveillance. We also placed transmitters in my room, so they could monitor the conversations and provide a quick response in the event things went wrong.

The next day, the informant arrived at my room with two men and knocked. I slowly opened the door, checked the hallway for activity and let them in the room. I introduced myself using a fictitious name. The older of the two men quickly moved the conversation into negotiations for the heroin. I learned he was only involved because he wanted to make a small commission on the drug deal. The other man, wearing white rattlesnake boots and a cowboy hat, said he had several kilograms of pure heroin.

I explained to him that I was interested in buying two kilos, which he agreed to let me have for $45,000 each. He wanted to see the money before bringing the heroin to the hotel. I didn't have any money, not even enough to use as a flash roll. I reversed the argument, telling him the money was in a safe location and would not be brought to the room until the heroin had been delivered and I had fully examined it. I made it clear that he had the advantage being from the area and it was the first time I had dealt with him. It was nothing more than common business sense, and I was avoiding any potential for a rip-off.

After haggling, he finally accepted my terms and agreed to return in a couple of hours. He also explained he would have some of his *pistoleros* (gunmen) in the immediate area during the transaction and warned they would kill me if I turned out to be a federal agent. He left the older man behind to keep an eye on things. To prevent him from seeing the MFJP at the hotel, I had the informant put him in a third hotel room in another part of the hotel. We would effectively isolate him from any further involvement in the operation.

I asked several MFJP agents to conduct surveillance in the parking lot of the hotel to identify others involved in the drug deal. Like clockwork that afternoon, the trafficker arrived at the room with two other men who also wore Western clothes and expensive cowboy boots made from the exotic skins of reptiles. What worried me were the highly visible Colt .45 semiautomatic handguns sticking out of their waistbands. The grips were made of gold with a large image of the Virgin Mary. Again, how amazingly ironic it was that Mexican drug traffickers would use the weapons to murder people, yet optimistically believe Catholic saints etched onto their weapons would shield them.

The trafficker stated, *"Es preferible hacer el negocio en otro lugar"* (it is preferable to conduct the business in another location). I explained if they didn't want to do it there, the deal was over.

The man with the white rattlesnake boots conceded and ordered one of the others to bring the two kilograms to the room. Everything was coming to a head, and in the event the MFJP did not move quickly or effectively, I would have to potentially take out three armed men. My mind clicked off different scenarios that might occur and rapidly developed contingency plans. I knew if a gun battle took place, I would have to fire the first rounds, otherwise my chances for survival were zero. So my weapon was fully cocked, and the safety was off. It was concealed in my waistband near my lower back and would be easy for me to quickly bring into action. I had also unlocked the door to the adjoining room where the MFJP were located, so they could quickly enter my room once the signal was given.

Twenty minutes later, the trafficker who had gone to retrieve the heroin knocked on the door. He cautiously entered the room with a large shopping bag in his hand and handed it to me. I saw two kilogram packages wrapped tightly in the usual brown tape. I used a knife to cut open one of the packages and put a small amount on one of the hotel notepads I found in the drawer of the only table in the room. I excused myself and went into the restroom where I did a field test. This is done using small, elongated glass tubes that contain a clear liquid; they come as part of a large kit containing tests for other drugs such as marijuana, cocaine, and methamphetamine. The tubes easily break in half, and I normally used a small object, such as paper clip, to put a tiny amount of the drug into the liquid. It is a presumptive test only, but accurate in most cases. This time, the chemical rapidly turned a purple color—the indication for heroin.

When I came out of the restroom, one of the traffickers was standing by the door with his hand on his weapon. He appeared wary and very nervous. In a loud voice, and standing close to one of the transmitters, I agreed the quality of the heroin was satisfactory. A split-second later, the MFJP charged into the room brandishing a dozen AK-47s and arrested everyone before they had an opportunity to react. The sight of wild-looking men yelling obscenities and waving Soviet assault rifles can make anyone think twice about drawing their weapons. It would literally be what we refer to as "suicide by police."

The traffickers were disarmed and then pushed to the floor by blows from the stocks of the AK-47s. After the situation calmed down, the informant reminded me the older man was still waiting in another section of the hotel. I spoke to the MFJP comandante, and we agreed not to arrest him, since he wasn't someone who made a significant living from the drug trade and was already about eighty years old. We wanted to scare him, though, and teach him a lesson. We went to his room and knocked loudly on the door and yelled, "Policía Federál!" Within seconds, we heard the glass doors on the other side of room slide open. We counted to five and opened the door with a key I had kept. We saw the old man run down a steep hill with the speed and grace of a gazelle, and out of sight.

■ ■ ■ ■

Working in Mexico was very different from working in the United States. The primary Mexican agency for combating drugs was the MFJP, which had a reputation for being corrupt. The temptations were high, and combined with low salaries (about $600 US per month), it was easy for them to succumb to graft and corruption. Unfortunately, there was also exposure to corruption at the highest levels of the Mexican government, where politicians used their offices to quickly become megamillionaires. The attitude of the MFJP was simple: if our superiors are becoming wealthy by taking money, why shouldn't we do the same? Corruption in Mexico was endemic. It had a trickle-down effect that made the problem insidious and exceptionally complex, and the MFJP would invariably pass a certain percentage of money back up the chain of command.

While in Hermosillo, I became aware the MFJP was collecting money from several sources, one of which was the drug-trafficking community. Another source was Mexican Aduana (Customs), which allowed a significant amount of commercial goods to enter Mexico without having to pay established tariffs. The bribes collected by Mexican Customs were enormous. There was an informal agreement with the MFJP in which Customs gave them a percentage of the bribes they collected. This agreement, on occasion, broke down between the two agencies, because the MFJP demanded a larger share of the money. Customs refused, so the MFJP—always creative and proactive—quickly established their own checkpoint a few miles south of the twenty-six-kilometer inspection point.

The MFJP began to search all vehicles, and if they found items that required the payment of importation duties, the individuals were asked to provide appropriate documentation. More often than not, they had not paid the legal fees and admitted to bribing Customs personnel. The MFJP would then drive them to the checkpoint and ask them to point out the agents they had bribed. These agents would be quickly placed under arrest by the MFJP and driven to Hermosillo where federal prosecutors charged them with corruption. Within twenty-four hours, Customs capitulated and began giving the MFJP the percentage of bribe money they demanded, to avoid further problems.

I identified cadres of MFJP personnel I could trust and work with on counterdrug operations. I knew they were more operationally oriented as opposed to having investigative skills. The DEA would conduct the investigations and then, at a later stage, involve the MFJP when arrests and seizures were to take place. I also knew the key to working with the MFJP, and to maximizing my efforts, was to develop personal relationships. This meant late dinners and a few shots of tequila. I also invited them to my house for barbeques and special events.

Many DEA agents never understood that by limiting their relationships with the Mexican federales to strictly professional ones, they significantly diminished their ability to accomplish very much in Mexico. The MFJP were not very responsive to working with agents who only came to them when they needed something and then wouldn't appear again for months. I had outstanding rapport with them at all levels and was able to work together on many successful operations. These close personal relationships provided much more support and critical collaboration than if they had been merely professional. Obviously, I was aware of the limitations. They would help me dismantle certain drug-trafficking networks but leave others untouched because these were paying large bribes.

Coordination and working relationships between Mexican law enforcement and the military were almost nonexistent. They didn't trust each other, and the Mexican military did not play the expanded role in counterdrug efforts they do today. For the most part, they were relegated to conducting manual eradication efforts against marijuana and opium-poppy cultivation, particularly in the northern Mexican states. Although the military is not without its problems of corruption, they were then and are still one of the most respected institutions in the government. However, neither the Mexican military nor the MFJP adhered to human-rights practices, and in their opinion, the counterdrug efforts were simply a "no-quarter-given, no-quarter-received" war of attrition.

The operations in Mexico were complex and many times involved both the police and the military. I worked with the Mexican army in the rugged Sierra Madre mountains of Sinaloa, where we conducted search-and-destroy operations against clandestine heroin laboratories. The work was exhausting, and the mountains were very steep and hard to climb. The extreme heat and humidity made it hard to breathe, and the constant dive-bombing of insects was even worse. We were usually in the field for over a week, with a depleted water supply and inability to replenish it. Unfortunately, we had to rely on what was available, so I always had iodine tablets for purification.

The instructions directed you to dissolve the tablets in water and wait twenty minutes, but when you're suffering from severe dehydration, that doesn't work. I was drinking from small, stagnant pools along the trail with water green from algae and who knew what bacteria in it, but at that point, I didn't care. I gulped the horrible water and swallowed the tablets, chased by more water hoping this unorthodox application would work. On a positive note, we destroyed several labs and found several opium-poppy fields hidden in ravines and under the canopies of large trees and vegetation. The opium poppies were strategically planted near mountain streams where the growers ran large, black hoses for water to irrigate the fields using gravity to bring the flow efficiently into the illicit crops.

During one particular mission, we stopped at an isolated house, close to a large stream. It was vacant, so the contingent of thirty soldiers who accompanied me decided to appropriate it as temporary quarters. It was late at night and dangerous to be in unfamiliar terrain, especially in total darkness. Around midnight, we heard horses approaching the house, prompting the soldiers to quickly assume defensive positions. A man and a woman in their early forties, with a small caravan of mules in tow, found themselves surrounded by the soldiers and ordered to lie on the ground. A search of the bundles heaped on the backs of the mules revealed a large quantity of opium. The soldiers took the couple to the stream and interrogated them by dunking them in the water. In less than twenty minutes, they admitted to being *gomeros* and provided information on the traffickers who would be purchasing the opium from them for conversion into heroin. Early the next day, as we were preparing to leave, the soldiers took everything they could from the dilapidated house. I saw one of them carrying a large mattress on his back.

The high-poverty areas of Mexico are breeding grounds for drug traffickers. There is a pervasive feeling of despair, because jobs and opportunities are rare and most people can't afford an education. For many, the only way to survive is to enter the drug trade. Older and more established drug traffickers are visible poster boys for the good life. These desperately impoverished areas have produced some of the most powerful drug lords in the world. Despite having no education, they are streetwise, cunning, and aggressive.

Through necessity, these drug lords learn leadership, management, and organizational skills that they quickly master to survive. They also hire experts in logistics, money laundering, legal matters, and security to augment their education in developing a structured approach for their illegal activities. Not having a formal education doesn't make them any less intelligent, and they master the ability to adapt to changing environments. They also learn to compartmentalize information, and only those with a *need to know* are privy to specific and sensitive data. This limits the potential for informants within drug-trafficking organizations to disclose damaging information to law-enforcement agencies. They also have one distinct advantage over legitimate companies: they use violence to intimidate members of their organizations and government officials. Their enormous wealth buys protection on both sides of the border.

In Hermosillo, I worked with many MFJP agents. Some were good and others were corrupt, making no effort to even hide it. One of the comandantes assigned to Hermosillo was Armando Martinez Salgado, "El Vampiro" (the vampire). He was given this nickname because he resembled Christopher Lee, the actor who played Count Dracula in the movies of the 1970s. Martinez was obstinate and not interested in working bilateral drug investigations. He was interested in collecting money for his personal self-enrichment and to pay off his superiors in order to maintain his position in a highly lucrative geographical area.

On one occasion, I was invited to a barbeque at the MFJP office, where they were roasting a large pig. I was the only American there. When I arrived, some of the Mexican agents had already been drinking heavily. Martinez was dressed in his usual brown leisure suit, making him look like a vampire stuck in the 1970s. He wasn't well liked by his men, since he had no leadership skills and treated them poorly. In the early afternoon, as the festivities continued, Martinez began to abuse and berate one of his agents. The argument became more heated, and finally, the agent punched Martinez in the face. The altercation was immediately diffused, but Martinez hurried to his office and called his bosses in Mexico City to report the incident.

As one would expect, the story was spun in such as a way that would favor El Vampiro. When Martinez walked out of his office, he announced with obvious pleasure he had orders to arrest the offending agent, who had already left and gone home. Martinez ordered two of his agents to accompany him to the agent's home in order to take him into custody. I knew this situation could turn ugly and violent given the culture of machismo within the ranks of the MFJP, so I decided to follow them in my car to prevent a tragic incident.

We arrived at a large apartment complex on the southern end of Hermosillo, where Martinez jumped out of his black SUV with a Colt .45 pistol in hand. He stood at the front door of the apartment and began screaming for the agent to come out. He was so angry that saliva was running down the sides of his mouth like a rabid dog. The agent refused, which proved to be a smart move, since I am convinced that Martinez would have killed him. Martinez started firing his weapon into the ground, totally impervious to the fact innocent people in the area could have been struck by the ricocheting bullets. Before it got worse, I pulled him to the rear of his vehicle and persuaded him to let me talk with the agent inside and get him to surrender peacefully. Martinez agreed to stop shooting.

I went to the door of the agent's apartment and spoke with him for a few minutes. He had a young wife and a baby with him, and I told him they were in danger if the situation escalated. He realized his predicament and decided coming out was the only option that would ensure the safety of his family. He surrendered and was later fired from the MFJP, proving they were sometimes just as brutal and violent as the drug traffickers they fought.

Years later, Martinez resigned from the MFJP to take a position as the chief of the anti-kidnapping squad for the state of Morelos. Jorge Carrillo Olea, then governor for Morelos, hired him, knowing full well he was corrupt. Carrillo had previously been an army general and later became Mexico's Drug Czar. He was a diminutive man who appeared to suffer from a Napoleon complex but moved in the right political circles and was a member of the dominant PRI political party. His political aspirations were high, but his greed overshadowed everything else.

During the tenure of Martinez, many allegations surfaced that the anti-kidnapping squad was protecting the kidnapping groups terrorizing Morelos. One afternoon, the Federal Highway Police in the state of Guerrero, which borders Morelos, observed three men parked on the side of the road acting suspiciously. The two police officers approached and identified Martinez and two of his subordinates. Inside the bed of the truck they found the tortured and lifeless body of a seventeen-year-old boy, later identified as a member of a kidnapping gang. The gang member had apparently died during a brutal interrogation involving torture. His face was a bloody pulp and unrecognizable. His eyes had a blank stare to some unknown place. Every inch of the body was covered with large, deep-purple bruises, and his clothes were covered in a mixture of dirt and caked blood. Also found inside the truck were five ski masks, adhesive tape, and blood-soaked bandages.

Apparently, Martinez and his men were preparing to dump the body in a ditch alongside the road. When asked for an explanation, he informed the arresting officers he was on a secret mission, the details of which he was not allowed to divulge to anyone. The incident provoked an investigation of the entire Morelos anti-kidnapping squad. The unit had thirty-eight members, and by the time fifteen of them had been questioned, the remaining twenty-three had left the area and become fugitives. Numerous witnesses in highly publicized cases had identified Martinez as being their abductor; he was further implicated in over forty kidnappings for ransom. Also exposed were many other state officials, the chief of the state police, the state attorney general, and several others who were convicted and sent to prison. The State Congress of Morelos also later impeached Carrillo as the governor.

■ ■ ■ ■

In the early days of drug trafficking in Mexico, a few names became legendary and were the paragons that attracted others to the illegal trade. They ran their drug business like feudal barons and were quick to use violence to reach their goals and maintain discipline within their organizations. At the same time, they acted as benefactors to many, which provided them loyalty from within the community. As a result, they were protected from governmental actions and warned of possible danger. The traffickers provided more to the poor than the government did, which created a convoluted situation. They were perceived as Robin Hoods who stole from the rich and gave to the poor. The beneficiaries of drug money failed to see the violence and death produced by those who distributed drugs and only concerned themselves with the fact that someone was providing them with assistance in their hour of need.

One of the early prominent traffickers was Manual Salcido Uzueta, who was born in the small town of San Juan, Sinaloa. His mother named him Cochi Loco (Crazy Pig), because as a child he was hyperactive and ran in and out of the house like a wild piglet. As a teenager, he began selling marijuana and heroin but later became a gunman for many of the local drug dealers. Salcido gained a reputation for being a brutal killer who enjoyed torturing his victims before ending their lives with a bullet to the head. He liked beating his enemies within an inch of their lives with his fists or blunt objects, and then he'd shave the flesh, a little at a time, from their bones with a sharp knife like a professional butcher. He disposed of the bodies in fifty-five-gallon drums of acid and said he was making *pozole*, a meat and hominy stew. Later, he associated with famous drug lords such as Miguel Félix Gallardo, Rafael Caro Quintero, and Ernesto Fonseca—leaders of the Guadalajara Cartel—and became a trusted lieutenant. He established his base of operations in the Pacific coastal city of Mazatlán, Sinaloa. With the huge drug profits he was raking in, he began buying hotels, restaurants, movie theaters, and stylish nightclubs. In Guadalajara, he opened car dealerships and factories and purchased large homes and ranches. As he gained notoriety by increasing the levels of violence, he ran afoul of the law and became a fugitive.

The inhabitants of the village of Coquimatlán, Colima, recall a stranger who moved into the area and began to purchase large plots of land. He was tall, fair skinned, and blue eyed, with a mustache. The man introduced himself as Pedro Orozco García. He told everyone who would ask that he was a successful engineer who had several construction companies in Guadalajara. He purchased a ranch he named Jayamita and built a simple two-story house. The second-floor master bedroom had a very large window that went all the way around the room, providing a panoramic view. On the other side of the room was a very narrow staircase that could only be navigated by one person at a time. Visitors to the house thought this was rather odd, but overlooked it since they liked Don Pedro. He was known for his lavish parties and on occasion hosted the mayor of Coquimatlán and the governor of Colima. He wined and dined hundreds of people and frequently provided horse shows in which he rode his white horse, El Colimote, who performed tricks during town events and parades.

The townspeople respected him. He showered the needy children with presents and donated large sums of money for public works, and for this, the governor of Colima bestowed "Don Pedro" with the distinguished title of "Benefactor of the State of Colima." A few years later, during one of his weekly trips to Guadalajara, his driver, an ex-state judicial police officer by the name of Obeso, was driving the white Dodge Ram Charger with Don Pedro and his twenty-year-old daughter, Monica. At a red light on Avenida Obsidiana, in the wealthy residential section of Victoria, two cars intercepted them and blocked their path. Two men on motorcycles also approached the vehicle. A total of eight men descended and pointed their AK-47s and Israeli Galil assault rifles at the white Dodge. In desperation, Don Pedro attempted to detonate a hand grenade, but he was killed before pulling the pin. He was shot over eighty-five times, and his daughter was shot fifteen times but managed to survive. Obeso was also a casualty with over thirty bullet impacts to his body. The killing was meant to send a very personal signal to rival drug organizations..

The murders were never solved and were undoubtedly a vendetta with a rival drug ring. The citizens of Colima were shocked to find out their benevolent benefactor was none other than the feared and ruthless *Cochi Loco*. Salcido was buried in San Juan with his favorite AK-47, fancy cowboy boots, and ostentatious jewelry. His funeral was attended by many of the major drug kingpins in Mexico.

■ ■ ■ ■

Pedro Avilés Pérez was another major first-generation Mexican drug trafficker. He learned the trade working for other, larger traffickers operating in his home state of Sinaloa. As with most early traffickers, his organization was not as sophisticated or structured as those that would follow. They were loose-knit organizations that had not yet mastered the art of money laundering, logistics, or intelligence collection used to avoid being captured and prosecuted. His operations were more reliant on the ability to corrupt public officials and less on structure and organization. Avilés tutored the top lieutenants working for him.

As with any business, those who followed refined and evolved their operations and hired others with the necessary skills to help them grow their criminal empires. They also used individuals as straw purchasers with no criminal records to buy properties and assets. Avilés mentored other traffickers who later became drug lords themselves and surpassed the drug-trafficking capabilities and ruthlessness of their mentor—cartel leaders such as Ernesto Fonseca and Rafael Caro Quintero.

Avilés pioneered the use of single-engine aircraft to smuggle drugs across the US/Mexico border. When traveling in Mexico, he always had a large security escort and normally traveled on unimproved side roads to avoid detection. He was a dangerous man who came from a culture of trafficker machismo. He was quick with the gun, and if cornered, acted with the ferocity of a wounded animal.

One morning, he was traveling on an isolated and winding road in his home state of Sinaloa. Unbeknownst to him, the MFJP had established a *retén* (roadblock) on that same road. Avilés failed to have a long-range reconnaissance team ahead of his convoy that would have given him ample time to avoid the checkpoint, but instead, abruptly came to the roadblock. When the MFJP approached his vehicles, he and his men began firing their automatic AK-47s. Bullets pierced vehicles, human bodies, and lifted small clouds of dust from the hard-packed dirt. Screams and cries of pain could be heard above the explosion of machine guns.

A friend of mine from the MFJP was involved in the shooting and stated Avilés jumped out of his vehicle wielding a gold-handled .45-caliber Colt handgun. He shot wildly as he approached my friend, who had a high-powered shotgun and lay flat on the ground. He fired the shotgun at close range and saw the criminal's head explode sending bone fragments and pieces of bloody flesh flying in all directions. This reign of terror by Avilés had come to a violent and predictable end.

■ ■ ■ ■

Arturo Beltran Leyva was another pioneer of the drug trade in Mexico. As with most major Mexican traffickers, he was born in the state of Sinaloa. He was the head of a cartel, which included his brothers Carlos, Alfredo, and Hector. The organization was a poly-drug-distribution network responsible for smuggling cocaine, marijuana, heroin, and methamphetamine into the US. It engaged in money laundering, extortion, kidnapping, murder, and weapons-smuggling as well. The Beltran Leyva organization had killed numerous Mexican law-enforcement personnel who opposed their illegal activities. Arturo patterned himself after traditional organized crime boss Carlo Gambino by insulating himself from criminal liability. He used trusted lieutenants, passing orders to those who would perform the dangerous aspects of the organization. He was cunning and used corruption and intimidation to protect the day-to-day operations of his large drug-distribution network.

By the skillful funneling of drug money, he was able to bribe and penetrate the Mexican political and judicial institutions. He also had corrupt police officials on his payroll who provided him information on operations or investigations directed against his organization. Initially, the Beltrans were aligned with the Sinaloa Cartel headed by Joaquín "El Chapo" Guzmán Loera, but later began working with the Zetas. The separation from the Sinaloa Cartel occurred when the Mexican military captured Alfredo "El Mochomo" Beltran Leyva, which was attributed to the betrayal of Guzmán Loera.

Mexican marines conducted a raid on a luxurious home located in a gated community in Ahuatepec, Morelos, which borders Cuernavaca. Arturo Beltran was having an early Christmas party and had hired famous singers to perform that evening. During the assault, the naval personnel came under fire but prevailed by killing several of the gunmen. Unfortunately, Beltran was able to make his escape in the ensuing chaos. The Mexican navy arrested over eleven bodyguards and seized almost $300,000 in US currency, sixteen assault rifles, several handguns, and over two thousand rounds of ammunition. Beltran underestimated the resolve of the Mexican navy, which continued to track him using multiple, highly reliable informants.

In less than a week, he was traced to another upscale community, where a two-hour gun battle occurred with members of his security detail. The Mexican marines were ready and had over two hundred soldiers, helicopters, and army tanks surrounding the residence. Beltran's bodyguards threw at least twenty fragmentation grenades to keep the marines from advancing. The heavy fire from the marines easily penetrated the walls of the house and ripped the wooden furniture into small splinters. The bullets eventually found their mark and ended the life of Beltran and three gunmen while a fourth bodyguard committed suicide by shooting himself in the head as troops advanced on the house. Inside, the navy found over $40,000 US currency, five assault rifles, pistols, Canadian currency, and numerous religious scapulars and medallions. One of the navy officers killed in the assault was buried a few days later with full military honors. And to further emphasize the savagery of this gang, the following day, unknown gunmen killed members of the dead marine's family, including his mother, in revenge for the death of Beltran.

■ ■ ■ ■

The true Godfather of the Mexican drug trade was Miguel Ángel Félix Gallardo, born near Culiacán, Sinaloa. He came from a poor family and had little education. He took the first job opportunity available to him and joined the ranks of the Sinaloa State Police, one of the most corrupt organizations in the country. The state police in Mexico are very different from the state police in the US who are tasked with primarily patrol and traffic-management responsibilities. In the US, they are uniformed except for their investigative units. Their counterparts in Mexico are plainclothes officers responsible for enforcing state laws dealing with general crime, including homicides, theft, robberies, and drug trafficking. Regrettably, most of the state and municipal police forces in Mexico are riddled with corruption and work closely with drug traffickers and other criminal organizations. The Mexican military and the federal police refuse to work with them and with good reason.

Félix Gallardo caught the attention of Leopoldo Sánchez Celis, the governor of Sinaloa, who made him a bodyguard and trusted confidant. Félix Gallardo saw it as an opportunity to develop other high-level political connections that would serve him well in later years. He became exposed to major drug traffickers operating in Sinaloa and saw an opportunity to go from a salary of approximately $600 US per month to making millions. His big break came when he was introduced to the Honduran trafficker, Juan Ramón Matta-Ballesteros.

Matta grew up on the tough streets of Honduras in abject poverty. His mother cleaned homes in Tegucigalpa and barely made enough money to support her family. He married Nancy Marlene Vasquez from Cali, Colombia, whose family had longstanding ties to the cocaine trade. Through these connections, Matta began his drug career processing coca paste into cocaine and eventually rose to become an international trafficker with extensive ties to Mexico. He became the primary source of supply to Félix Gallardo and the Guadalajara cartel.

Similar to the historical European pattern of marriages for political, economic, or diplomatic reasons, in Latin America, some drug trafficker's married to solidify the drug empires of organizations with shared interests. In this case, Félix Gallardo became the godfather to Ramón Jr., Matta's son. This created greater trust and solidified the nexus between the two major traffickers. Félix Gallardo rose to become the most significant figure in the Mexican drug trade. He shipped tons of cocaine into the US and made millions of dollars for himself and Matta. Félix Gallardo was generous with his bloodstained money and greased the hands of many politicians and other government officials who protected his organization. He advocated violence to retain control over the drug trade and was responsible for the murders of hundreds.

He was also involved in the kidnapping and killing of DEA agent Enrique "Kiki" Camarena. Félix Gallardo was finally arrested several years later and charged with the murder of Agent Camarena as well as racketeering, drug smuggling, and numerous violent crimes. His arrest by Mexican authorities exposed widespread corruption. Until he was transferred to the Altiplano maximum-security prison, he continued to run his organization from behind bars. The MFJP comandante who transported him to the maximum-security prison told me Félix Gallardo cried the entire trip to the prison and lamented it would be the end of him. It was an accurate assumption.

The Federal Social Re-Adaptation Center No. 1, Altiplano, was built between 1988 and 1990 by then President Carlos Salinas de Gortari, and the first inmates were sent there in 1991. The facility is located in the Santa Juana neighborhood of Almoloya de Juarez, in the state of Mexico, approximately twenty-five kilometers from Toluca. When it was constructed, the Mexican government feared the prison could be assaulted from the outside and reinforced the walls to as much as one meter of thickness to discourage ramming. The air space near the prison is restricted, and prison officials also claim cell-phone transmissions are limited within ten kilometers of the facility to impede communications between inmates and their criminal associates outside. Armored personnel carriers are stationed close to protect it against a potential assault. After incarceration there, the reign of Félix Gallardo ended, despite his power and wealth.

All drug traffickers suffer one of two fates that await them: jail or death. Drug trafficking is not an escape from poverty, but nothing more than a temporary escape from reality, with an inescapable, devastating fate that will sooner or later knock on the door of the trafficker. Ironically, most traffickers have the morbid opinion that it is far better to live one good year than ten bad ones. This attitude also makes them formidable and dangerous. To them, enormous wealth and power, albeit for a short time, is preferable to a lifetime of mere existence.

■ ■ ■ ■

While I was still in Hermosillo, two informants came to my office and provided information on a major drug dealer operating in Culiacán, Sinaloa. They reported the dealer was responsible for distributing large quantities of heroin he produced in several clandestine laboratories in the Sierra Madre mountain range near the opium-poppy cultivation areas.

Many dealers established heroin-conversion laboratories close to the opium-poppy fields, because it reduced the risk of transporting the opium great distances and running the gauntlet of police roadblocks. Additionally, by quickly conducting the conversion process from opium to heroin, they reduced the overall bulk significantly making transportation and eventual smuggling into the US much easier. The conversion process is ten to one. It requires ten kilograms of opium to produce one kilogram of heroin.

The informants advised they could arrange an undercover meeting with the heroin dealer, but I would have to travel to Culiacán, the heart of Mexican drug trafficking, alone. I provided the informants with money for travel to arrange the meeting. I gave them instructions on the cover story they would provide to the trafficker, making sure we were all on the same page.

Within a few days, I received a telephone call from them saying *"todo está listo"* (everything is ready). I booked an Aero Mexico flight, and a day later I was in the air on my way to Culiacán. Upon arrival, I took a cab to the MFJP office located on the outskirts of the city. I met with Comandante Jaime Alcalá and his deputy Gerardo Serrano. Comandante Alcalá dressed in expensive tailor-made suits and always wore a large five-carat diamond as a tie tack. His superiors in Mexico City had sent him to Culiacán to bring crime under control where drug traffickers had completely taken over the city and were killing people at random and raping women whenever they felt like it. Culiacán had become a totally lawless city where machinegun fire could be heard throughout the night. The law-abiding citizens were terrified to leave their homes at night for fear of getting caught in crossfire between rival drug gangs.

Alcalá immediately started to purge the criminal element by torturing and killing them. It was known he had created his own unmarked cemeteries in remote areas where he buried hundreds of violent criminals. His right-hand man, Gerardo Serrano carried out Alcalá's orders to the letter. His loyalty was beyond reproach, and he had become a trusted confidant in all matters. Serrano looked like a harmless college student, but in reality, he could kill without hesitating or flinching. Other MFJPs would say, *"El tiene un chingo de cojones"* (he has a lot of balls). Serrano had killed under the direction of Alcalá.

Because of their *extralegal* renditions in disposing of the local criminal element, the violence in Culiacán subsided, but not entirely. By the same token, the absolute powers given to Comandante Alcalá to stem the violence also made him corrupt. He began taking bribes from drug kingpins and made no effort to hide his wealth. Alcalá rapidly became one of the most powerful men within the MFJP. Despite his shortcomings, he worked well with the DEA, as long as our operations did not conflict with the drug organizations paying him for protection, as was the case with many of his peers.

I met with Alcalá and explained the pending operation. As we planned the details, he invited me to a breakfast of *huevos rancheros* and warm tortillas at a little wooden shack very close to his offices. It had been converted into a rustic cafeteria with two cooks who prepared food for MFJP personnel any time of the day or night. Alcalá paid for the food and services for his personnel. In addition to that perk, all MFJP agents stayed at one of the most exclusive hotels in Culiacán, again courtesy of Comandante Alcalá.

The comandante told me he would provide a group of his most trusted and experienced agents, many of whom I knew and had worked with in the past. He said, *"Te mando mas agentes si los necesitas"* (I will send you more agents if you need them).

I took the group of MFJP to the Hotel Ejecutivo, located in the downtown area, and rented the necessary two rooms. As I expected, they were armed to the teeth and brought their weapons through a service elevator in the rear of the hotel in order to not attract attention. I had one last meeting with the informants and instructed them to meet with the dealer to get a sample of the heroin prior to bringing him to the hotel. I had an MFJP agent in the room with me as we waited for the informants to return. He was the one who killed Pedro Avilés Pérez, the legendary drug trafficker. He looked like an NFL linebacker, and apart from his imposing appearance, I liked him, because he had a good disposition and a sense of humor

After what seemed to be an hour, there was a loud knock. Believing it was the informant's, I slowly opened the door and noticed the two of them were now in the company of eight other men dressed in jeans and expensive cowboy boots. All had semiautomatic pistols visibly tucked in their waistbands and made no effort to conceal them. One finally spoke and said, *"Don Miguel, podemos hablar con ustéd?"* (Don Miguel, can we speak with you?) Thinking quickly, I told him only he could enter the room, insisting the others would have to wait out in the hallway. The irony of me giving orders to a group of heavily armed men who could easily overwhelm the MFJP agent and me was plain.

As sometimes happens, the Mexican agents in the surveillance room next door were not paying attention and were oblivious to the ongoing situation. The armed man entered the room and casually ran his right hand through my lower back. He was attempting to determine whether I was armed, which was a good tactic on his part, because he undoubtedly felt the Walther PPK pistol concealed in my waistband. He remained calm and sat on a dresser and began to size me up. The trick was to remain incredibly calm during these dangerous situations. The more intense it became, the calmer I stayed, which undoubtedly saved my life in this and numerous other occasions. The man spoke, rambling on in confusing riddles.

Then it suddenly dawned on me he was there to extort money, fully believing I was a drug trafficker. As it turned out, he and his men were state judicial police officers who had watched the exchange of the heroin sample in a nearby park and had stopped the two informants.

In order to protect themselves, our informants did not mention we were agents, but unfortunately led them to our location. I had worked in Mexico long enough to know this situation could turn volatile very rapidly. I had to act quickly. I drew my weapon and shoved it into the mouth of the state police officer, knocking him down on the floor. I took his weapon and told him if he moved, I'd put a bullet in his head. He nodded in acknowledgment and remained quiet.

I opened the door of the hotel room and charged out with the MFJP agent, weapons in hand, hoping for the best. If the corrupt state police decided to shoot it out, we were so heavily outnumbered that our chances for survival were dismal at best. Luckily, they were so shocked and surprised they raised their hands in total compliance. We disarmed the remaining seven and brought them into the room. By this time, the other MFJP agents waiting in the next room, having heard the loud yelling and chaos, arrived and began to manhandle them. They finally arrested, handcuffed, and spread them out face down on the shag carpet. It was another close call and once again underscored how critical it was to expect the unexpected. What could have become a bloodbath fortunately ended with no casualties.

In later years, Jaime Alcalá left the MFJP and started his own business. He was in his office doing paperwork one afternoon when several men stormed in with AK-47s and riddled his body with bullets. He was found in a large pool of blood by one of his secretaries. Alcalá probably expected his longevity would be significantly shortened when he severed his ties with the MFJP. That's one of the great risks of being in law enforcement in Mexico.

An individual receives some protection while being a member of Mexican law enforcement, but if you're fired or you retire, all protection ceases to exist. In essence, you have a target painted on your chest, fair game for drug traffickers and criminals in general. Most of these gruesome killings go unsolved, which provides incentive to the traffickers bent on revenge. Gerardo Serrano met a more hideous fate. Drug traffickers captured him, tied his arms and legs to two vehicles, and slowly began to stretch him until they literally pulled him apart. It is said that his last words were, *"Que chingen a su madre"* (Go fuck your mother). Knowing Serrano, there is no doubt in my mind those were his last words.

Chapter 7

Corruption, Power, and Greed

Some call him a legend; I call him an American hero. Mike Vigil was without a doubt, the most respected DEA official outside the beltway. He was truly an agent's agent. On a moment's notice, and with only a phone call, he could summon the resources and cooperation of any international law-enforcement official. They only had to hear Mike say, "I need your help, my friend." On numerous occasions, these officials would order their personnel to authorize the landing of a DEA aircraft in a remote location, snatch a DEA fugitive, and have him back in a U S courtroom in less than twenty-four hours. Those were the days …

—Michael P. McManus
DEA Chief of Operations, Mexico
and Central America Section (Ret.)

Mexican law enforcement agencies are divided among federal, state, and municipal agencies. Currently, there are 2 federal agencies, 31 state police organizations, and over 1,700 municipal police departments. This translates to about 500,000 police officers or about 366 police officers per 100,000 people. This compares to 251 full-time sworn personnel per 100,000 people in the United States in 2008. These generous ratios of police officers to citizens, however, have not resulted in a more safe and secure Mexico. Police forces are poorly trained and equipped, and salaries are meager. Corruption is endemic at the state and municipal levels, which tragically undermines Mexico's ability to deal with drug trafficking and other criminal activities.

When I worked in Mexico, the state and municipal police were nothing more than organized criminal organizations that conducted their nefarious activities from behind a police badge. The situation hasn't changed, which creates a recipe for disastrous consequences in which the security of Mexican citizens is severely jeopardized. Furthermore, the Mexican federal police and military continue not to trust each other or share information that would be invaluable in dismantling major drug networks operating in the country.

I believe donor countries, including the US, have no coherent strategies to develop the capabilities of many underdeveloped countries in combating drug trafficking. Each year, as we provide millions of dollars in training, equipment, and technology to foreign countries, most of these resources are wasted and overshadowed by systemic political graft and corruption. Funding and resources should be provided in tandem with the development of civil-service programs, whereby police officers and other security forces are paid decent salaries and benefits, promotions are based on knowledge and ability, and selection of police candidates is focused, ultimately, on developing professional institutions. Better salaries and benefits would help discourage the culture of corruption that currently exists and allow for an effective infusion of resources for a meaningful change.

In Mexico, the government has found it very difficult to provide police agencies with adequate salaries and protection to counter the assault of threats and bribes from the drug traffickers. Mexico has made efforts to reform the federal police by dismissing a tenth of the thirty-six thousand agents in the first eight months of 2010. And in recent times, there has been a move to increase the militarization of policing. Forty-five thousand troops of the Mexican army were mobilized to fight the violent drug cartels, and that number increased in 2010 to over fifty thousand and continues to climb. This strategy has its pros and cons. Without question, the Mexican military is needed to counter the resources and tactics of drug traffickers like Osiel Cardenas Guillen, the former head of the Gulf Cartel who traveled with a heavily armed security escort of seventy to a hundred thugs. It is virtually impossible for police agencies to muster a large enough force to counter an opponent this large. This makes the shootouts in Mexico between the police/military and the traffickers more like a military battle in southern Afghanistan than a law-enforcement action.

The drawback to using the military is they are not trained investigators and therefore don't exploit available evidence crucial for the successful prosecutions of these violent drug traffickers. Recently, I met with one of the Mexican deputy attorney generals, a personal friend of mine. He confessed the rate of successful federal prosecutions is currently less than 3 percent. This is abysmal, and he attributed it to a lack of training and ability to identify and collect evidence by the military. As a result, the federal prosecutors are taken away from their principal duties, sent to crime scenes to collect evidence, and develop criminal cases. Unbelievably, at the state and municipal level, the successful prosecution rates are even lower than at the federal level.

The Secretaria de Seguridad Publica del Districto Federal (Secretariat of Public Security of the Federal District), unlike the federal police and the ministerial federal police, does not have national reach, but does have a force of over ninety thousand police officers in the federal district (DF). This agency is charged with preserving public order and security in Mexico City. The principal police force in Mexico City is the Protection and Transit Directorate also known as the traffic police.

It should be noted that Mexico City has the second-highest crime rate in Latin America. All thirty-one of the Mexican states have a state judicial police force, which report directly to the state's governor. The responsibilities of the state and federal police are not always transparent and often overlap. Most offenses come under the state police, while drug trafficking, crimes against the government, and multijurisdictional offenses are under the auspices of the federal police. State police forces operate from precinct stations called *delegaciones*, with approximately two hundred police officers. Only some of the municipalities of Mexico have their own municipal police forces, which are responsible for minor civil disturbances and traffic violations.

■ ■ ■ ■

The Mexican Attorney General's office (PGR) petitioned the DEA to assist them in developing a criminal case against the *alcalde* (mayor) of Ciudád Madera, Chihuahua, who was trafficking quantities of marijuana by the tons. The assignment was given to me since my office in Hermosillo provided coverage to the state of Chihuahua. The PGR had a potential informant who lived in Ciudád Madera who might be able to provide some valuable information. I contacted him there, but he was apprehensive about talking on the telephone and unwilling to travel to the city of Chihuahua to meet with me. I didn't like the situation, because I didn't know the potential informant, and Ciudád Madera was located in rugged, mountainous terrain in northwestern Chihuahua. If it were a trap—always a possibility—it would be very easy to make me disappear.

I flew to the city of Chihuahua via Mexicana airlines to meet another DEA agent coming from Mexico City, so we could discuss the situation and strategy. The agent from Mexico City was very apprehensive about going to Ciudád Madera, and I realized this was going to be a one-man operation. Sarcastically, the other agent asked, "How long is it going to take you to make the case against the mayor?" Knowing I would push his buttons I replied, "Less than thirty days."

The next morning, I had breakfast at the hotel and took a taxi to the local bus station, purchased a ticket for a few dollars, and boarded a dilapidated bus. The trip was several hours long on a very bumpy and dusty road. I had done some research on Ciudád Madera and knew it was a logging town located in an area where there was little control by the federal or state governments. The town was two hundred seventy-six kilometers from the city of Chihuahua. It was lawless, and Mexican law enforcement had no presence in the area. It is also the place where on September 23, 1965, a guerrilla attack on the military took place. This gave rise to an urban socialist guerrilla group that took its name to commemorate their martyrs. The subversive group was called the Liga 23 de Septiembre (the 23rd of September League). I strongly suspected the Mexican government was more interested in putting the mayor behind bars for his involvement in this guerrilla organization than anything else, but drug-trafficking charges would provide the same outcome.

I was hot and tired when I walked out of the small bus station and immediately caught the attention of several locals loitering outside. They looked suspiciously at me, knowing I wasn't from the area and likely wondering why I was there. Most of the men were dressed in dirty denim jeans, dusty cowboy boots and hats, and some even had pistols tucked in their waistbands. The women only glanced at me, lowered their eyes to the unpaved street, and scurried away. I knew I had to limit my time there and needed to leave before nightfall, when I would be an easy target.

I hired the town's only taxi, an old Ford truck with seats so torn, the padding and springs were bulging out. I got out a few blocks away from the informant's house so I could walk the rest of the distance. The house was very small and badly in need of a coat of paint. There was an old dog sprawled in the front yard, who barked loudly once, and after performing his duty, went back to sleep. I knocked on the door, and seconds later, a middle-aged man wearing the typical dress for the area opened it. He motioned for me to enter, and I followed him to a tiny kitchen with only a table and two folding chairs. The dust from the street was everywhere, covering the furniture and everything on it.

He began his story by saying the mayor was involved in large-scale marijuana trafficking and had large plantations hidden in the mountainous areas several miles from the town, and numerous, heavily armed men guarded the plantations. According to him, the mayor was smuggling marijuana into the United States and using the illicit profits to consolidate his political power throughout the region. Furthermore, he confirmed the mayor was involved in the 23 of September League opposing the dominant PRI political party.

Bingo! Now I knew the real reason they wanted him out of the way, but regardless, he was still a drug trafficker and needed to be in jail. The informant was unwilling to become more personally involved. I couldn't blame him, because he would undoubtedly be killed once they identified him as the source of information. After a few hours of conversation, he drove me back to the bus station in his truck. The engine sounded like an old Maytag washer and probably had a top speed of twenty miles per hour, but it got me there. I purchased a ticket back to the city of Chihuahua, where I spent the night. I was tired and slept most of the way despite the jostling over the poor, potholed roads. The next day, I returned to Hermosillo and began to develop my strategy targeting the mayor. The informant provided by the PGR would definitely not be an effective resource, so I began to task the large pool of informants I already had in Mexico. I told them to find me someone intimately familiar with Ciudad Madera and the surrounding area.

Days later, one of them brought an older man who explained he was very familiar with the area and aware of the mayor's drug-trafficking activities. I debriefed him for several hours, and he provided more information regarding the mayor and other members of his organization. He had a friend who could assist in gathering additional information, and less than twenty-four hours later, he returned to my office with his friend. I documented both as informants, which entailed completing DEA forms, exemplars of their signatures, photographs, and fingerprint cards. They were given a number that would be used in subsequent investigative reports rather than identifying them by name. I provided them with enough money to travel to Ciudad Madera. The idea was to drive there hauling a couple of horses, so they could ride in the rugged mountains where no roads existed to locate the marijuana fields.

I heard nothing for a couple of weeks until they suddenly appeared in the office with a large burlap flour sack containing stalks of marijuana plants. With a map I provided, they were able to pinpoint numerous marijuana plantations belonging to the mayor and his criminal associates. They had waited until the guards had temporarily left the fields and quickly cut some of the plants to be used as evidence. They also were able to identify the storage areas where the processed marijuana was stockpiled before being moved to staging areas on the US border. Later that afternoon, I met with the local MFJP comandante and turned over the marijuana plants and the geo-coordinates of the fields and storage areas. I was also able to give him all available data on the mayor and members of his organization.

We planned and mobilized an operation in Ciudad Madera resulting in the arrest of the mayor, who stood shocked, as the handcuffs were being placed on him. He argued that the arrests were political, but in fact the truth remained: he was a drug trafficker and deserved a long prison sentence. Another seven top leaders in his organization were taken into custody, along with several tons of marijuana, weapons, and vehicles. Also, true to my word, the entire operation had taken twenty-eight days.

I received a telephone call from the PGR in Mexico City congratulating me on the successful operation. In appreciation, they sent me a bottle filled with tequila so strong it could have choked a horse. Tragically, and on a very sad note, several months later, the two informants I used in this investigation were found tortured and killed in Chihuahua. After their murder, they were placed in their truck and pushed off a steep mountain. It took several days to recover their remains, already in an advanced state of decomposition. Later, I learned they had been in Chihuahua telling people they were DEA agents, which eventually led to their demise.

■ ■ ■ ■

On a very hot April 14, my birthday, I had a small party at the DEA office in Hermosillo and invited the MFJP. The comandante came with several of his agents—one nicknamed *the smiling assassin*. The story went that he was involved in a raid on a house where several drug traffickers had barricaded themselves. He apparently had entered with a machinegun and killed all of them, never losing his wide grin. He was a short man with blond hair and had the most unusual green eyes, closely resembling a Hollywood space alien. The smile seemed frozen on his face, and his teeth were capped in gold, creating an eerie glow in the light and completing the picture. The comandante told me they had been in a small town looking for fugitives and had sent the "smiling assassin" to bring potential sources of information to their makeshift office for questioning. He returned herding every man, woman, and child from the village. With a chuckle, he added he'd even brought the town dogs. We all laughed and kidded him, but staying in true character, he just kept smiling and remained silent.

The comandante handed me a brown paper bag as he walked into the office, and I laid it on my desk chair while we ate. It was always a great time, sharing each other's stories. The MFJP were known for their keen sense of humor—especially in describing their interrogation techniques. When they questioned a drug trafficker, they would say they were taking him to the "*casa de la opera donde todos cantan*" (the opera house where everybody sings).

As they expounded on their methods, I recalled an occasion where they arrested several drug traffickers in one of my cases. The next day one of the Mexican agents told me before he could extract information, they uncontrollably began "spilling their guts" to the point that the only way to stop them was by slapping their heads. They used a variety of techniques, one of which involved the *chicharra* (cattle prod), a long tube with two electrodes at the tip. The suspects were given electrical shocks until they confessed and provided information on other traffickers. But their preferred method was mineral water—water boarding. One of the Mexican federal prosecutors told me he had attended a symposium in Phoenix, Arizona, where different companies were displaying the latest law-enforcement equipment and technology. He laughed and said he had the best interrogation device at the convention and showed them a bottle of "Tehuacan" (a Mexican brand of carbonated water). Definitely, an unusual sense of humor.

The stories moved to a much lighter side and continued for several hours. The *smiling assassin* had a great time, and even while he ate, the grin never faded. After they left, I started to clean up the plates and cups scattered on the tables and desks, when I noticed the paper bag with my birthday present from the comandante lying on the chair. I opened it and in total disbelief saw it contained half a kilogram of marijuana! It was a common practice among some of the MFJP to use the marijuana they seized, and he obviously believed the DEA did the same. Forget the leftover cake, I spent the next half hour flushing the marijuana down the toilet and hoping it wouldn't backup. The following year, I made sure to tell them "no *gifts*." They showed up with a bottle of tequila.

As one light-hearted moment passed, ominous dark ones replaced it. An opportunity arose for me to coordinate an investigation involving Rafael Caro Quintero's organization in Caborca, Sonora, with Enrique "Kiki" Camarena who was then assigned to the DEA Guadalajara office. A reliable informant had provided detailed information that Caro Quintero had over twenty tons of marijuana worth hundreds of millions of dollars in an isolated ranch on the outskirts of Caborca. The informant also indicated several men armed with AK-47 assault rifles were providing security. He said they were extremely violent and would probably confront police or military elements. According to the informant, the marijuana was the highly marketable sinsemilla (without seeds) type.

In cultivating sinsemilla marijuana, the sex of the plant is crucial. Plant size is a good indicator of sex. The males are usually removed as soon as they are identified, so the females will not be pollinated, thus producing sinsemilla, buds with a high content of the active ingredient THC.

Based on the accurate information provided by the informant, we began to carefully plan the operation at the ranch. Kiki traveled from

Guadalajara on a commercial flight, and I met him at the Hermosillo International airport. He was tall with a stocky build and was always in good spirits. He'd been in the US Marine Corps and later joined the El Centro Police Department. He soon became a drug agent in the department and a year later, was hired as a special agent with the DEA. His first assignment was Calexico and after three years was transferred to Fresno, California. He served four years there and was then assigned to the DEA office in Guadalajara. We became close friends while I worked in Hermosillo and he was based in Calexico. Who would imagine a few years later, he would be brutally tortured and murdered while working in Guadalajara?

After a long afternoon, we agreed, based on information we were provided by the informant, it would be prudent to use a good-size assault force of both soldiers and MFJP agents. Later, we met with the MFJP comandante and briefed him on the pending operation. He thought it was wise to include the military in the operation and would contact the local military commander for the necessary support. A few hours later, the comandante informed us he had been able to obtain thirty soldiers for the raid on the ranch the next day, but with one small problem in logistics. The Mexican army could not spare a truck, and therefore, we had to provide transportation. Neither the MFJP nor the DEA had a vehicle large enough to move military troops, so we needed to develop a solution fast.

As I have explained before, flexibility and the ability to improvise quickly are crucial character traits for an effective leader. I contacted a local rancher who owned some very large cattle trucks. Luckily, he had one not being used and offered to rent it for seventy-five dollars per day. I provided the fuel, and in return, he promised to clean and wash it. The next morning, we loaded thirty soldiers into the back of the old truck and began our journey to Caborca.

The Mexican soldiers were used to enduring hardships and didn't complain about the rough ride. They sat and stood in their camouflage uniforms and webbed helmets, carrying a vast assortment of assault weapons and a significant amount of ammunition. These sturdy soldiers were very alike in appearance, short and dark-skinned. As with most military forces in Latin America, the Mexican forces were primarily staffed by those of Indian descent, with the exception of the officers. I respected their hardy resilience and their ability to operate in rugged terrain for long periods of time with little food or water.

The drive to Caborca was long and I'm sure it seemed much longer to the poor soldiers being tossed back and forth in the truck as it hit the hundreds of ruts the road. As we continued, the MFJP were in two vehicles; Kiki and I traveled in a separate sedan. This was actually one of the few times where the MFJP and the Mexican Army were working together on a joint drug operation.

When we entered Caborca, I noticed there was little activity on the streets, with the exception of a few milling around looking at our small caravan with suspicion. They were used to confrontations between the police and drug traffickers. Through long association, they were desensitized to the drug-related violence that had become so prevalent in their lives. We finally found the narrow dirt road that would lead us to the ranch being used to store tons of marijuana. Tall weeds and sage with strong, sweet smells permeated the air and lined the road. The area was flat and sparsely populated with a few small ranches sprinkled throughout the countryside. We hadn't passed any vehicles, so it was deadly quiet other than the whine of our engines as they pushed along the makeshift road.

The ranch finally came into view about half a mile away to our left. The informant had done an excellent job in describing it, saving us invaluable time. It had a metal gate, which had been left open. There was a small, wooden house with a large barn located directly behind it less than a hundred yards from the front gate. We stopped twenty yards from the house and began to exit our vehicles, when the roaring thunder of rapid gunfire erupted. A barrage of bullets filled the air like a swarm of angry wasps, and many rounds hit the ground kicking up dust in small clouds. We charged the house, forcing the armed traffickers to run into a small cornfield behind the barn. They continued to fire at us as they made their retreat. As the exchange of gunfire intensified, most of the traffickers tossed their weapons and fled, with the exception of one who decided he would engage us in a gun battle. Astonishingly, his mortality didn't appear to influence his actions. As five soldiers and I came into sight, he lifted his assault rifle and began to aim it. A heavy barrage of gunfire brought him down. He died in a black pool of blood quickly absorbed by the dry sand.

A later search of the barn revealed more than ten tons of sinsemilla marijuana carefully packaged in large boxes used to ship eggs. The next day, I received a telephone call from one of the Mexican federal prosecutors who said, "Mike, I went to the scene of the shooting to conduct an investigation on the death of the drug trafficker, because I have to prepare a formal report." He added, with a chuckle, "It was very interesting, because the trafficker killed in the gun battle had handfuls of raw marijuana stuffed in his pockets." The soldiers wanted to make sure there would be no question the dead man was involved in drug trafficking and had taken marijuana from the barn and shoved it into his clothing. They were masters of the obvious and further proof that efforts against the major drug organizations involved deadly violence and ruthlessness on both sides.

To gain a better understanding of the role of the Mexican military in dealing with drug trafficking and transnational crime, it is important to understand its structure and objectives. The Mexican Armed Forces comprise the army, which includes the air force as a subordinate component, and the navy, which also has the naval infantry and naval aviation. The three primary objectives of the armed forces is the repulsion of foreign aggression, protection of internal security, and to assist the civilian population in the event of a large natural disaster. There are three primary components of the army: a national headquarters, territorial commands, and independent units. The Ministry of Defense controls the army by a very centralized system and a large number of general officers.

The army has a modified continental-staff process in its headquarters. Without question, the army is the largest branch of Mexico's military.

At present, there are twelve military regions, which are further divided into forty-four subordinate military zones. There is no established number of zones within a region; therefore, they can be tailored to meet operational requirements. The army consists of approximately one hundred ninety-two thousand combat-ready ground troops.

The air force national headquarters is located in the army headquarters in Mexico City. It is divided in four regions: northeast, northwest, central, and southern. The air force has a total of eighteen air bases and the capability of quickly creating forward-operating bases, depending on the operational circumstances, for rotary and light, fixed-wing aircraft.

The navy's headquarters is located in Mexico City and is considerably smaller than the army's. The Junta (Council) of Admirals has a significant advisory role within their headquarters, which is an indication of the importance placed on seniority and cliques dating back to the admirals' time as cadets in the naval college. As a result, they are a close and exclusive group who work well with one another. The navy's operational forces are comprised of two separate units: the Pacific and Gulf forces.

The president has a military role based on the Mexican constitution and is considered the Supreme Commander of the Armed Forces. Furthermore, the president is considered the army's only five-star general, according to the Mexican constitution. Of importance is Article 129 of the 1917 Mexican Constitution, which states, "No military authority may, in time of peace, perform any functions other than those that are directly connected with military affairs." The army's involvement in drug investigations and tactical operations are clearly outside their mandate. This has caused great consternation within the Mexican congress and mass media. The military has to play a critical role given the fact many of Mexico's drug lords travel with very large security forces, numbering over a hundred well-armed individuals with assault rifles, state-of-the-art communications, and bullet-resistant vehicles.

Mexico's soldiers earn only two-thirds of their Colombian counterparts, despite the fact that Mexico's gross domestic product (GDP) per capita is 50 percent higher. In 2010, it was estimated Mexico spent slightly less than $4 billion on its military. This amounted to 0.4 percent of their GDP. In comparison, Chile spends eight times more than Mexico and Brazil four times more. Only Guatemala spends equally modest sums on its military, despite being a major transit country for drugs between South America and Mexico. In order to put it further in perspective, the budget for Mexico's oil company PEMEX, with less than half of the personnel of the military, spends well over 40 percent more on salaries for employees. It's not difficult to understand how low wages can contribute to corruption.

Chapter 8

Mexico: Where Good Guys Wear Masks

During Mike's time at DEA, his vision took it from a fledgling agency to the most-renowned narcotics force in the world. Under his remarkable leadership, the DEA Caribbean Division conducted numerous and unprecedented multinational drug-enforcement operations that would forever alter the strategy in which DEA would battle international drug-trafficking organizations. In response to the tragic events of September 11, 2001, as the DEA's chief of international operations, Mike implemented Operation Containment, which united the counternarcotics efforts of the DEA and law-enforcement agencies from twenty-five countries, primarily from Central Asia. Operation Containment successfully diminished the flow of opium from Afghanistan that was used to fund terrorism. When I address Mike, I refer to him as "El Comandante."

—Frank J Mazzilli
Section Chief (Ret.),
DEA International Operations
Europe, Middle East, and Africa

Los Zetas, one of Mexico's fastest growing and most violent drug-trafficking organizations, was founded by soldiers corrupted by the so-called Gulf Cartel under the control of Osiel Cardenas Guillen, now in prison in the United States. Los Zetas not only engage in international drug trafficking, but also participate in assassinations, kidnapping, extortion, and other transnational crime. It was founded by a small group of forty former Mexican Special Forces deserters and includes former federal, state, and local police officers. The organization began as the military wing and private mercenary army of the Gulf Cartel, but after the arrest of Cardenas Guillen, the Zetas began taking a more active role in drug-trafficking activities. In 2010, the Zetas started to operate more independently, which was considered by Gulf Cartel members to be in conflict with their interests. The split of the Zetas and the Gulf Cartel led to violent and bloody turf battles, predominantly in the states of Nuevo León and Tamaulipas.

Zeta violence has not been restricted to rival traffickers. They have also engaged in multiple massacres and vicious attacks on civilians, including a 2011 Monterrey casino attack where fifty-two innocent people were killed. The same year, the Zetas killed one hundred ninety-three people in the state of Tamaulipas and were also responsible for the murder of twenty-seven farmers in Guatemala. It is believed they also massacred two hundred forty-nine in Durango. Their transformation into a major drug-trafficking organization has completely changed the landscape of Mexico's national security. They pose an enormous threat to the government of Mexico by engaging in wholesale slaughters of innocent citizens. Their objective is to intimidate the government and gain control over the country's drug trade. They regularly exploit the brutal aspects of murder using beheadings and dismemberment of their victims. It is my opinion that the Zetas, in the future, will be the most formidable drug-trafficking organization in Mexico and much of Central America. They have already begun to spread their tentacles into Guatemala.

The Mexican government will have to use the services of the military and police agencies more effectively to secure both their northern and southern borders. Their northern border is being used to funnel both drug profits and weapons used to further threaten the national security of Mexico. Recently, I met with Genaro García Luna, the cabinet secretary for Public Security (SSP), who indicated during the course of ten months they had seized over thirty-three thousand weapons and ten thousand fragmentation grenades. He expressed Mexico's frustration with the number of weapons being smuggled from the US into Mexico, which were used to escalate the violence throughout the country.

Mexico, on its southern border, has the same issues facing the US on its southwest border. There are drugs, illegal immigration, and weapons being smuggled into Mexico, primarily through Guatemala. It is disheartening to me how Mexico and its security forces are under continuous siege by an insidious criminal element so powerful it will take extraordinary measures to bring it under control. I traveled, not long ago, to the Mexican state of Tamaulipas to work with the Mexican marines. Many of their vehicles were bullet-riddled from encounters with the Zetas, who operate extensively throughout the state. The marines will no longer travel anywhere without a convoy and use trucks armed with 50-caliber machine guns. The Zetas will confront these military convoys in an unbelievably brazen manner and have killed many soldiers. Their latest tactic is to establish roadblocks on roadways to rob citizens and tourists. If military convoys approach, they will not immediately retreat, but open fire. The soldiers now wear masks to prevent being identified by drug traffickers who will kill them or their families. This has become a complete reversal where the *good guys* are now wearing the masks.

While at the office in Hermosillo, I was contacted by an informant in Agua Prieta, Sonora, who provided information for money. He was familiar with a large drug-trafficking organization involved in the distribution of heroin, cocaine, marijuana, and *methaqualone*. He said the criminal organization was smuggling the illegal drugs across the border primarily in hidden compartments built into a fleet of cars and trucks crossing through the Douglas, Arizona, port of entry. More often than not, women drove the vehicles into the United States for a modest fee.

He indicated the enforcers for the organization had killed several local police officers and members of rival gangs and had become so powerful they intimidated the municipal police and local politicians. First, they offered bribes, and those who didn't take the money were killed. It was the traditional *plata o plomo* culture of drug traffickers, where they would offer silver (plata) or lead (plomo). Most accepted the silver and were "corrupted" through intimidation.

The informant also reported the drug traffickers in Aqua Prieta were currently in possession of several million methaqualone tablets and were asking one US dollar for each tab. They could be sold in the US for three to five US dollars, and so the profit margin was significant. Methaqualone is a sedative-hypnotic drug and a central nervous system depressant. Its use was at an all-time high in the 1960s and 1970s as a hypnotic for the treatment of insomnia and as a sedative. It has also been used as an illegal substance and recreational drug. It is commonly referred to by its street name Quaaludes.

I told the informant to arrange a meeting with the drug traffickers in Agua Prieta to buy a few million methaqualone tablets. He was streetwise, but it is imperative in undercover operations that instructions are specific and the cover story is simple and uncomplicated. In this case, he was to introduce me as a buyer from Phoenix who wanted to buy a large amount of drug. The undercover agent and informant have to work in unison to undergo questioning and scrutiny by the traffickers. It was a very dangerous situation, especially in Mexico, where one could be killed and the remains disposed of, never to be seen again. I had played this game many times and knew the intricacies of these operations and the high stakes.

Agua Prieta was a rough city where drug traffickers had taken over through sheer force. It's a pueblo and municipality in northwestern Sonora on the US–Mexico border, adjacent to the town of Douglas, Arizona. At the time, the population was no more than thirty thousand. It was a key area during the Mexican revolution where Plutarco Elias Calles and Lazaro Cardenas, two future presidents of Mexico, both lived during their early years. Pancho Villa made a daring night assault there, but the forces under the command of Elias Calles repelled it. He would turn over in his grave knowing what he and his entire army were unable to accomplish had been done by a group of thugs dealing drugs. Since there was no way I could trust the local police, my only option was to take MFJP agents from Hermosillo who I knew and trusted with my life. The MFJP comandante made arrangements for ten agents to accompany me on a trip that took several hours on a narrow, winding two-lane road strewn with rocks and the ever-present potholes. It was hot and dusty, made worse by the slow-moving commercial trucks. The entire group was tired and thirsty by the time we arrived on the outskirts of the pueblo.

I met with the informant who had set up a meeting with the traffickers at the Silver Dollar Saloon in the middle of Agua Prieta. I made final plans with the MFJP and arranged a bust signal, the trusty opening of my car's trunk. To err on the side of caution, I also gave them a secondary signal, placing both my hands on my head. The ten MFJP left for the saloon to get into position. It was getting late in the day, and darkness wouldn't be in my favor. Surveillance agents needed the daylight to clearly observe the events unfolding at the saloon. I gave the MFJP half an hour to establish themselves at vantage points. Prior to leaving Hermosillo, I had placed stacks of copier paper in a large bag to give the appearance and weight of money. Not taking money would create a challenging situation. As savvy businessmen, most traffickers wanted to see the cash before making a drug delivery. It would be something I'd have to deal with during the negotiations.

The sun was setting when we arrived at the cantina. I parked my car in front with the rear end sticking out into the street, which would give the MFJP agents a line of sight to clearly see the trunk signal once it was given. The Silver Dollar looked like a prop for a Western movie sitting on a dirty street. Its façade was dark because there were no streetlights. Several trucks were parked in front, and many rough-looking men stood outside. As we stepped out of the vehicle, my informant greeted a group of six men who were huddled together next to the stucco building. All were wearing the usual expensive ostrich-skin cowboy boots and Western clothing.

A dark-complexioned man approached the informant and shook his hand. He introduced me as the buyer, and the Mexican trafficker grinned and briskly shook my hand several times. The other men glared menacingly as they watched my every move. Their shirttails were slightly pulled out of their pants, which meant they were probably armed. The apparent leader wanted to make small talk, but I quickly got to the point, since it was beginning to get dark. He assured me he had several million tablets of methaqualone at a safe location. He'd been drinking, and I could smell hard liquor on his breath. He slurred his words as he asked to see the money. I countered, telling him that I was on their home turf and at a distinct disadvantage. I forcefully demanded to see the drugs before providing them with access to the money.

After half an hour of negotiations, it was agreed they would take my informant to see the methaqualone, and only then would I show them the money. They wanted to see cash before they brought the drugs to the saloon, so I would have to play this one with great cunning or experience an ugly turn for the worse. The leader motioned to his men, sending four of them to a black Chevy Silverado truck and told the informant to accompany him in another vehicle. I stayed there making small talk with the other traffickers who remained behind. They casually mentioned I wouldn't have any problems with the authorities as long as I did business with them. They bragged about having complete control over Agua Prieta in deciding which politicians would hold political office. These traffickers were ruthless men who had killed anyone who opposed their criminal activities. Their prime objective was to enrich themselves, and they did it without concern for the misery that inevitably followed in their wake.

As we stood in front of the saloon, I noticed the telltale bulge at their waistbands, confirming they were armed. The others returned forty minutes later with the informant and pulled next to my car. The informant assured me he had seen the methaqualone. In whispered conversation, I asked only one question, "Can you find your way back to the location?" He nodded. As I went to my car, a wind came down the street throwing thick, opaque clouds of dust into the air. I opened the trunk and hoped the MFJP agents would see the signal. The traffickers were all focused on my movements as I began to very slowly pull the suitcase out of the trunk. Seven MFJP charged down the street, guns drawn.

In the fleeting moment it took them to run from their vantage point, the traffickers drew their weapons and shots were fired with me in the middle of the confrontation. The traffickers began to scatter, but I chased several of them into the building. I had a Walther PPK .380 semiautomatic pistol in my hand and hoped they didn't have AK-47s. I aimed my pistol at five traffickers, who quickly dropped their weapons, and I shouted for them to lie down near the bar. Taking it up a notch, MFJP agents entered yelling obscenities and began to pistol-whip the traffickers already on the floor.

I scanned the room for potential problems and noticed a long, narrow hallway leading to the back. I entered cautiously, again with my weapon drawn. The hallway was almost totally dark and wreaked of urine and cigarette smoke. I walked slowly and quietly with my gun cocked and my finger on the trigger. Halfway down, I saw a sudden movement from a small closet in the passageway and came face to face with a man holding a gun in his hand. I began to squeeze the trigger when he dropped his weapon and yelled, "*No dispare!*" (Don't shoot.) I grabbed his shirt and yanked him out of the closet. In another split-second, one or both of us would have been dead. I marched him back into the bar where the other prisoners were lying on the floor and the MFJP were still yelling and cursing them.

At that point, it was critical to quickly get to the location where the informant had seen the methaqualone. If the traffickers were able to move the drugs, the Mexican government wouldn't have a prosecutable case, and they would be set free. I grabbed three MFJP agents and my informant. Time was of the essence. We sped toward our destination, dodging dogs and pedestrians along the way in the dark. The informant said the traffickers had loaded the methaqualone in the trunk of one of their vehicles, for transport to the Silver Dollar once they had seen the money.

We approached a house surrounded by wire fence, where a large Ford sedan was parked in front. The informant pointed at it and said, *"El carro está enfrente de esa casa"* (the car is in front of that house). I breathed a sigh of relief: no calls had been made and no one had moved the car. The house was empty. No one seemed to be in the immediate area, and we needed to move rapidly before other traffickers were able to mobilize. I took a tire iron, and with the help of the MFJP agents, we were able to pry open the trunk. Inside were several large, green plastic bags filled with methaqualone in pill form. We loaded the bags into our car and left as quickly as we had come. The operation netted over ten arrests and millions of dollars' worth of methaqualone. As important, it decimated the drug-trafficking organization that had established a stranglehold over the citizens of that little village.

The situation in Agua Prieta and all along the US–Mexico border is virtually the same, where drug traffickers rule through intimidation and violence. Although the drug trade is highly complex, the ultimate objective is simple: to get the drugs from the source countries to the consumer markets within the US, the principal consumer in the world. As with any supply chain, the drug shipments that originate in the source countries are extremely large but, as they get closer to the retail level, are broken down to more numerous and smaller loads. A ton of cocaine transported into Mexico from the south will be smuggled across the northern border in parcels that may consist of no more than a small percentage of the entire load. The tactic is to avoid risking a complete loss due to interdiction efforts by law enforcement officers. Once in the US, the drug loads are usually broken down even further as they're sent to different distributors. When drugs are transported from South America into Mexico they can be measured in tons. Once they cross the border into the US, seizures are reported in kilograms, and by the time they are seized on the streets of urban areas, the drugs have been divided into ounces and grams. Mexico uses the metric system, which is very different from the English system and I learned, through time, to make the conversion. For example, in the English system, a ton has 2,000 lbs., but in the metric system it is 1,000 kilograms and an ounce is 28 grams.

This creates a tenuous situation where a multitude of federal, state, and local law-enforcement agencies across the country are generating efforts to seize ounces, pounds, and kilograms on individual and/or collective investigations. This requires an enormous expenditure of funding, resources, and manpower. It has always been my opinion, that by having more resources in key source and transit countries, US federal agencies such as the DEA have a better opportunity to seize drugs at the level of tonnage, before they are divided into smaller parcels, which would also require less funding and fewer resources. It is perplexing why some agencies prefer to have an office in a US city that has no significant drug problem, rather than in a key foreign area where they could definitely get a bigger "bang for the buck" by attacking first- and second-tier drug-trafficking organizations. The answer lies in that the heads of many law enforcement agencies are political appointees who do not have an understanding or the experience to make informed decisions. It takes years to gain the knowledge necessary to develop strategic plans.

While the Mexican drug-trafficking organizations do have members in the US, they also have to rely on other groups to handle the retail aspects of drug distribution. More often than not, this requires that operations be compartmentalized so, in the event a member is arrested, they cannot divulge extensive information. The drug organizations employ criminals with specialized skillsets, such as truck drivers, pilots, and boat handlers, who transport their product from one area to another. They also need money launderers to handle the huge amounts of money derived from drug sales and individuals who can corrupt public officials with bribes, to protect the operations of the organization. They also rely heavily on trained security personnel who provide protection from law enforcement and rival groups.

US gangs play a key role for the Mexican drug organizations in smuggling drugs across the border and providing security. They also act as assassins in Mexico and easily flee across the border where they are relatively safe. Members of the border gangs are usually young and seeking to make large amounts of money through illicit activities. Most of the gang members have family in Mexico and are easily recruited by Mexican drug dealers to do their dirty work. However, the US gangs are not formal extensions of the Mexican networks and have their own traditions, structures, and operating areas. They are also engaged in more than just drug trafficking. They participate in robberies, kidnappings, extortion, and property crime.

The Barrio Azteca gang, operating in the El Paso, Texas, area is violent and responsible for numerous homicides on both sides of the border and is affiliated with the Juarez organization. They made national news when they were connected to the murders of US Consulate employee Lesley Enriquez and her husband, Arthur Redelfs, both U.S. citizens, as they were leaving Juarez, Chihuahua, heading home to El Paso.

Enriquez, who was four months pregnant, and her husband died in a hail of bullets as they left a children's birthday party in their white Toyota SUV. Their seven-month-old baby was found screaming in the back seat. One of the chief enforcers for the Barrio Azteca gang stated the "hit" had been authorized because Enriquez allegedly assisted a rival gang in obtaining visas in Juarez. Later, it was determined that Redelfs, a correctional officer in El Paso, was targeted for allegedly mistreating incarcerated Barrio Azteca members

Another individual, Jorge Alberto Salcido, the husband of a Mexican employee of the Consulate, was also killed after leaving the same birthday party in a separate but similar vehicle, a white Honda SUV. One of the assassins remarked they had shot at both vehicles because they were the same color and they were unsure which held Enriquez—the intended target.

The Juarez drug organization is currently in conflict with the Sinaloa organization, which has led to unprecedented violence in Juarez. Several thousand have been killed in the city of approximately 1.3 million people. The enforcer also confessed to the killing of fifteen teenagers at a party believing it was a gathering of rival drug members. Gang enforcers are not trained in specialized operations and therefore make horrific mistakes by needlessly killing innocent people.

Another border gang with an established culture of dealing drugs and a propensity for violence is the Logan Heights gang based in San Diego, California. It was created during the 1960s when several individual Mexican street gangs from the neighborhoods of Logan Heights unified. Although they are based in San Diego, the influence of the gang has spread to include Los Angeles, Las Vegas, Denver, Minneapolis, and Tijuana, Mexico. It has been allied with the powerful Tijuana drug-trafficking organization headed by the Arellano Félix family for many years becoming an unholy alliance predicated on greed and violence. Their solidarity was firmly established in 1992, when Joaquín Guzmán Loera, a.k.a. El Chapo, and his associate Hector Palma Salazar, a.k.a. El Guero, attempted to kill some of the Arellano Félix brothers who were visiting a popular discotheque in Puerto Vallarta, Jalisco. Although the Arellano Félix brothers were able to escape with the assistance of a Logan Heights gang member, David Barron, eight members of the Tijuana organization were killed by automatic weapons fire.

The Logan Heights gang and, in particular, David Barron gained the respect of the Arellano Félix brothers for returning a barrage of fire that allowed them to escape. As a result, they made him chief enforcer for the cartel. Barron, known by his street name Popeye, committed his first murder when he was only sixteen years old. While in prison, he was recruited by the Mexican Mafia (La EME). As a career criminal, he engaged in drug trafficking and carried out *hits* and kidnappings for the Tijuana Cartel.

Later, Barron and a group of "hit men" were sent to Tijuana to kill journalist Jesús Blancornelas, who had recently published photos of cartel members. While driving to work one morning, he was ambushed with a barrage of lead from all sides. His driver was shot thirty-eight times, and Blancornelas was hit four times but survived. One of the bullets fired by one of Barron's own men ricocheted and hit Barron in the eye, killing him instantly. He fell against a wall propped up by his shotgun, and his blood poured into a gutter. His finger was still on the trigger of his weapon.

Chapter 9

Expect the Unexpected

Mike Vigil is a visionary leader who never forgot his beginnings as an agent. He firmly believes that ... the expansive sharing of information, unbridled cooperative efforts at the national and international levels, and the development and effective execution of global strategies are the only ways to disrupt and eliminate transnational drug trafficking and terrorism. During his career with the DEA, he achieved huge successes and deservedly attained the highest level of the Senior Executive Service. He won numerous protracted and violent struggles against major international drug-trafficking organizations headed by some of the most ruthless and murderous criminals in the world, such as Juan Ramón Matta Ballesteros.

Mike would never ask anyone to do something that he had not already done himself. He had the unparalleled ability to summon the assistance of high-ranking leaders throughout the world in support of ongoing operations. Mike did not view international borders as impediments, but rather embraced them as an opportunity to conduct multinational counterdrug initiatives that were unprecedented in history. Mike always disliked the status quo and aggressively

implemented innovative strategies. I am honored to call him
"Jefe" and privileged to have him as a friend.

—Pedro Peña
Group Supervisor, DEA

I received a telephone call at the office from an old friend of mine, Gary Wheeler, also originally from my home state of New Mexico. Gary had likewise joined the DEA and was serving in La Paz, Bolivia. Although we never met in college, we had both graduated from New Mexico State and became close friends. Gary was a terrific agent who spoke fluent Spanish. He had blond hair, always had a smile on his face, and would give you the shirt off his back. Everyone liked him. He also had a keen ability to work well with foreign counterparts in Latin America. He treated them with respect and didn't have the "Ugly American" attitude so many US government officials display when working in foreign countries. Gary asked if I was interested in working in Bolivia for a few months, since they were shorthanded and had a large workload. I immediately volunteered, knowing it would provide me the opportunity to work in a major source country. Bolivia was a critical area and was second only to Peru in the cultivation of the coca plant and manufacture of coca paste and cocaine base. With great enthusiasm, I jumped at the chance to work there, relishing the idea of working in such an interesting environment. I flew into the La Paz International airport, located high above the city. Gary was waiting on the tarmac with his usual wide grin. We were happy to see each other and pleased to have the opportunity to work together.

Also on temporary assignment in La Paz was Sandalio González, who was assigned to the DEA Los Angeles office. Sandy, as most people called him, was of Cuban descent, and also a very talented agent. He had a contagious laugh, and we would become long-term friends. Sandy would later be responsible for the capture of Rafael Caro Quintero, who was one of the main traffickers who had abducted and murdered DEA Special Agent Kiki Camarena.

The three of us chatted as we drove the road down into the capital city of La Paz. From the car window, I watched the poor Bolivian women washing clothes in the dirty water of a small river running along the highway. They were referred to as *cholitas* and wore hats that looked like derbies, and colorful dresses spread wide with countless petticoats. It was a slang word for indigenous women who wore polleras (bright colored dresses). The word was not one of disrespect and was used by all Bolivians. They had predominant, Incan features, were very short-statured, and probably hadn't evolved much from their ancient ancestors. I knew Bolivia's economy was one of the poorest in the Americas, ranking ahead of only Haiti. The source of the cocaine trade, the coca plant, had become the primary cash crop of the country and provided hundreds of millions of dollars to the local economy, but the peasants received little benefit from it. Each year, hundreds of hectares of valuable forestland were being cut in order to plant more coca plants. Adding to the deforestation, enormous amounts of chemicals were being dumped into the water supply and countryside, damaging the environment.

The cultivation of the coca plant is a tradition in Bolivia that can be traced back to 3,000 BC, having religious, cultural, and medicinal purposes. Natives have chewed it to eliminate fatigue and hunger and alleviate altitude sickness, a daily occurrence for many. During the colonial period, the Quecha and Ayamara Indians chewed the coca leaf as they labored in the silver mines. They called it the *hoja sagrada* (sacred leaf) and used its stimulant properties to endure their hard labor. The 1865 discovery in Europe of how to process it into cocaine transformed it into a highly profitable, but illegal product.

The two principal growing areas in Bolivia are the Yungas and the Chapare. The Chapare, a rural province, and the Yungas, a tropical forest, are both located in central Bolivia. It is rugged terrain and most of the inhabitants engage in the cultivation of the coca plant. Coca is an ideal cash crop for the poor peasant farmers, because it's pest resistant, easy to cultivate, and produces an average of four harvests a year. Its high value-to-weight ratio makes it easy to move from rural areas, where transportation systems are poor or nonexistent.

Coca production in Bolivia increased significantly in the 1980s, a time of political and economic crisis there, when the demand skyrocketed in northern countries, such as the United States. Inflation, severe drought, and the adoption of a program that closed state tin mines in 1985 combined to create a very desperate situation for thousands of Bolivia's poorest. This predicament was even more difficult for the indigenous peasants who comprise the majority in the rural areas.

Two factors coalesced that further stimulated the expansion of coca cultivation in Bolivia. Government policies that opened international borders resulted in prices plummeting for local agricultural products, affecting about 70 percent of the country's food. Second, rural areas were already in distress as populations grew and the average size of landholdings diminished because of the division of land among members of each successive generation. The shrinking plots of land had become inadequate to live on. In desperation, small farmers and displaced miners flocked to the Chapare and the Yungas to grow the coca plant, which had become a financial bonanza. They weren't aware of the damaging effects of cocaine, and in a bid for survival, it probably wouldn't have mattered.

While in La Paz, we made contact with an informant based in Cochabamba, who reported he was in touch with a large cocaine-trafficking organization supplying Colombian drug dealers with hundreds of kilograms of cocaine. The informant said the organization was very dangerous and had been involved in numerous murders. Based on that information, I traveled with Gary on a Lloyd Aereo Boliviano (LAB) flight to Cochabamba, the fourth largest city in central Bolivia, also known as the City of Eternal Spring, because of its yearlong moderate climate.

When we landed, we took a taxicab to a local hotel, where we met with the informant. Although he spoke a little English, we opted to speak Spanish. A few minutes into our discussion, I knew he was probably heavily involved in the drug trade. He was very familiar with many aspects of the business and apparently very friendly with several major traffickers. He explained Cochabamba had become a major hub for cocaine trafficking in Bolivia. We debriefed him thoroughly and asked if he was willing to introduce me as a potential buyer. He agreed but wanted to be paid for his services, which wouldn't be a problem. His motives were twofold: he wanted money and also wanted to eliminate local rivals that were cutting into his profits.

We made arrangements for another meeting to take place the next day with some of the key members of the targeted drug-trafficking organization. This meant preparations had to be initiated to include coordination with the Bolivian National Police. I told the informant to advise the traffickers I was a major Mexican heroin trafficker who wanted to diversify into cocaine, since the demand in the US was at peak level. It took more than an hour for him to finally grasp all of the nuances of the cover story, and I quizzed him one more time just to make sure. We selected another hotel nearby and reserved an undercover room that I would use and a second one that would be used by Gary and the Bolivian National Police, who would conduct surveillance.

Later that afternoon, we met with local commanders of the Bolivian National Police to brief them on the situation and the proposed plan, which they readily accepted. As a precautionary measure, we didn't reveal the names provided by the informant. It was always a good idea not to lay all your cards on the table, because your investigation could easily get compromised because of endemic corruption in the country. The stage was set, and that evening we enjoyed a nice dinner at a local Chinese restaurant and went to bed early. The next day would be a long one, and remaining mentally alert was imperative, because you never knew what might happen—*expecting the unexpected*.

It was unusually hot the next day, but a slight wind made it tolerable. In the morning, we rented the two rooms we needed at one of the better hotels. Eight Bolivian National Police officers in plainclothes quietly filtered in and went to a room directly across from mine. Within an hour, the informant called saying he had met with the traffickers and set the meeting for early afternoon. I made sure he had properly laid the groundwork so we wouldn't get our wires crossed. Once everything was done, I waited in the hotel room and hoped things would unfold according to plan.

Sitting quietly in the corner, I psychologically prepared for the high-stakes negotiations that would decide the outcome of the operation. When there was a knock on the door, I opened it, and the informant, accompanied by another man, entered the room. He was smiling as he introduced me to Fernando.

As we shook hands, Fernando was obviously attempting to determine if I were a legitimate drug dealer. After a short discussion about the weather and my trip, he said he'd been told I was from Mexico and was interested in purchasing large quantities of cocaine. I told him my nationality was Mexican, but during the past few years had several bases of operation in the US to distribute heroin produced in my labs located throughout Mexico. I explained the drug of choice in the US was now cocaine, and I wanted to establish a reputable and trustworthy source of supply in Bolivia.

He wanted to know the amounts of cocaine I was interested in purchasing, and I estimated it would be approximately two tons each month. He immediately showed his enthusiasm by smiling and happily slapping me on the back while dollar signs flashed in his eyes. I expressed my apprehension about bringing millions of dollars into Bolivia, because I was unfamiliar with the area and didn't yet have a network of individuals who could assist me. Fernando said there would be no problems as long as I did business with them. He reached into his pocket and pulled out the credentials and a badge identifying him as a senior-ranking officer in the Bolivian National Police. He laughed and said that *they* would take care of me and ensure I would not be arrested.

I told Fernando before doing transactions for ton quantities, it would be beneficial for me to purchase a sample of fifty kilos to judge their capabilities and the quality of product. It was couched as a best business practice. He had no problem with that and inquired when I wanted them. I told him it would have to be that same day, and the delivery would be made at the hotel. He said it would take him an hour to get the cocaine, and as he started to leave, I told him I would be having lunch in the lobby restaurant and would meet him there in an hour. He grinned and said he was looking forward to doing business with me for many years. I estimated it would be more like hours, and the clock was now ticking.

Once Fernando left the room, I called Gary and briefed him on the situation. We decided to have only two surveillance agents in the lobby restaurant, while everyone else would remain in the room. The chances of Fernando recognizing some of the Bolivian National Police officers, especially those who had been in Cochabamba for a long time, was too much of a risk.

I went to the restaurant and sat at an uneven table that rocked back and forth, sending plates and silverware sliding across the tablecloth. The chicken sandwich was dry, but the potatoes made up for it. The waiters were bored and stood in a semicatatonic state near my table, since business was slow and only a handful of people were in the restaurant. A loud couple entered, which added some life to the deadly dull establishment. It perked up the waiters, who scrambled to their table and offered them mate de coca (tea made from coca leaves). Over an hour passed.

Out of the corner of my eye, I saw Fernando and five uniformed Bolivian soldiers enter the restaurant carrying several large bags. They sauntered over to the table and dropped the bags on the floor next to me. I could see numerous tightly wrapped kilogram packages of cocaine inside them. They hadn't even bothered to conceal them, and the waiters didn't bother to give them a second glance. The soldiers maintained a somber demeanor and allowed Fernando to do all the talking. They were his partners and obviously more were outside the hotel providing security. I told him to accompany me by himself to the room where the money was being safeguarded to make the exchange. I didn't want to take the soldiers and risk a major gun battle as the operation began to unfold. It would be much easier to arrest Fernando first and then, with the element of surprise, take the Bolivian soldiers into custody.

Fernando helped me take the heavy bags of cocaine upstairs while the others waited in the restaurant. He told me they could provide any amount of cocaine and it was the best in all of Bolivia. He reiterated that by doing business with *them*, I would be afforded all the protection necessary from the police and the military forces. We entered the elevator with other guests of the hotel, who were not the least concerned with obvious cocaine packages bulging out of the large bags. From the elevator, we walked to the room where Gary and the National Police officers were waiting. When I opened the door, using the rusty hotel key, several police officers appeared in the doorway. Fernando dropped the bags he was carrying and smiled, extending his hand to the other officers, whom he immediately recognized. It was too late, and he was quickly taken into custody and unceremoniously thrown into the room. I told Gary and the police officers about the Bolivian soldiers in the restaurant and the others outside the hotel. Rapidly mobilizing many of the Bolivian police, we went downstairs with guns drawn to arrest the stunned soldiers in the restaurant and several more in front of the hotel, who offered no resistance. A total of twelve arrests were made without a shot being fired, thanks to good planning and the element of surprise.

While drug-related corruption is not uncommon in most drug source and transit countries, during this operation, I was able to see firsthand the high-level involvement of Bolivia's security forces and government in the cocaine trade. It came as no shock, since Bolivia was at the tail-end of the Luis García Meza regime, which literally transformed the country into a cocaine superpower. Prior to assuming the presidency of Bolivia, García Meza was an army general and a leader of the right-wing faction of the military, which was not pleased with the return of Bolivia to civilian rule. He, like many officers, had been part of the Hugo Banzer regime and disliked the ongoing investigations of political and human-rights abuses by the new Bolivian Congress. García Meza and many of his fellow officers wanted a strong anti-communist dictatorship that they were used to under Banzer. They were willing to take great risks to reestablish the old political system. Unfortunately, García Meza and other officers had close ties to major drug traffickers operating in the country. They used the military to protect the cocaine trade and act as their enforcers, transporters, and protectors in exchange for huge payoffs and bribes. This tainted funding heavily supported the coup that put García Meza into the presidency. It was for this reason it was called the Cocaine Coup. The traffickers, in reality, were purchasing the Bolivian government by assisting García Meza with his political ambitions.

Initially, a military junta forced then President Lydia Gueiler to name García Meza as the Commander of the Army. Several months later, in July 1980, García Meza and the junta of military commanders initiated a violent coup. Many citizens who resisted were killed or imprisoned. Despite the hundreds of coups that have taken place throughout its turbulent history, this was one of the worst. Allegedly, the Argentine intelligence service participated in the coup, because Argentina had political ambitions in Bolivia.

The García Meza coup brought together one of the most unholy alliances to ever exist in the world. García Meza was supported in his rise to power by the Nazi war criminal Klaus Barbie. Barbie fled Germany after the Second World War using one of the so-called ratlines—a system of escape routes for Nazis and other criminal fascists fleeing Europe. The routes led to safe havens located primarily in the South American countries of Argentina, Paraguay, Brazil, Uruguay, and Chile.

The García Meza regime embraced Barbie and used his skills for intelligence collection, torture, and interrogation techniques. Barbie worked closely with Bolivian Colonel Luis Arce Gómez, named the Minister of Interior by García Meza. Arce Gómez referred to Barbie as his "teacher." Adding to this collection of heinous characters, were the cocaine traffickers operating in Bolivia. Many of the most significant ones supported García Meza and now demanded protection for their illicit activities. This was no problem, but they were still required to pay millions of dollars to García Meza and other government officials. Arce

Gómez provided oversight to the massive corruption activities and, with complete arrogance, emptied seized-cocaine storage areas, redistributing the cocaine to select traffickers. The largest share of the proceeds was distributed between García Meza and himself. Arce Gómez was the cousin of Roberto Suarez, the most significant cocaine trafficker in Bolivia at the time, and became known as the minister of cocaine.

Adding to the alliance, Arce Gómez and Barbie recruited several psychopathic neo-fascist terrorists who formed the Novios de la Muerte (Grooms of Death). This paramilitary unit was used by Arce Gómez to drive certain traffickers out of business to consolidate the cocaine trade and their control over it. The group also acted as a death squad to eliminate political opponents. Killings and brutal repression were the hallmark of the García Meza regime. The rival political parties were dissolved, opposition leaders exiled, unions repressed, and the press was silenced. The Bolivian army killed thousands within months and became a well-tuned instrument of terror. Arce Gómez issued an ominous warning to the citizens of Bolivia to "carry their last will and testament under their arm."

Following both external and internal outcries, García Meza resigned as president in August 1981. He left the country and was tried and convicted *in absentia* for the massive human-rights violations that he ordered while president. In 1995, he was extradited to Bolivia from Brazil and sentenced to thirty years in prison. His principal collaborator, Arce Gómez was extradited to the US, where he served a long prison sentence for drug trafficking. Once released from prison in the US, he was promptly deported to Bolivia, and since 2009, he has been in a prison in Bolivia. He returned to his country an old and pathetic man whose power base had completely eroded. No one even recognized him when he arrived at the airport in La Paz. Barbie was later sent out of Bolivia, initially to French Guyana and then to France, where he was convicted of war crimes. He only served four years before dying in the same prison where, decades before, he brutally murdered many innocent victims.

The Bolivian military was unable to sustain itself in power for very long and eventually, literally, retreated to its barracks with their reputation completely tarnished and its leadership in shambles. Bolivian cocaine kingpin Roberto Suarez Gómez was sentenced in 1988 to fifteen years in prison but was released in 1996, only to die four years later of a heart attack. His son Roberto Suarez Jr. was killed in a shootout with Bolivian authorities. The Novios de la Muerte were disbanded and faded into obscurity.

Chapter 10

The Deal in Brazil

I worked for Mike Vigil as the Country Attaché for the countries of Poland, Germany, and the Czech Republic. Mike always displayed boundless leadership, vision, and was a master strategist in crafting global initiatives such as multinational operations and the international sharing of information on transnational crime and terrorism. During Operation Containment, Mike delivered stellar and unprecedented results. He was able bring together the expertise and intelligence systems of countries worldwide in a joint effort to stop the flow of opium and heroin from Afghanistan. The coalition also included the Russians and the Chinese, who for the first time in history participated in an operation such as Containment. He actually convinced the Iranians to attend the planning session, until the political statement was made that they were part of the "axis of evil"[and] derailed it. The operation resulted in record seizures and arrests.

Mike demonstrated exceptional initiative and the ability to exceed at all levels. Mike is a true warrior whom the law enforcement community worldwide has placed their extraordinary trust and confidence in his friendship and leadership capabilities.

—Bob Mangiamele
DEA Country Attaché for Poland,
Germany, and the Czech Republic

During my temporary assignment in Bolivia, I had occasion to work with a female informant who had extensive knowledge and ties to major drug traffickers in Bolivia and other countries. She was an older woman and was tougher than most people who controlled large organizations. She dressed in expensive, designer clothes and had a weakness for Gucci handbags. She could be deadly and did not attempt to conceal this fact. She was also a mercenary and wanted to work for the DEA to earn money by providing information on traffickers she didn't care for or had distasteful experiences with in the past. I called her Juicy Lucy, because she had the mouth of a sailor.

During several meetings, she reported that the son of the minister of justice under the García Meza regime was a significant trafficker who operated primarily in Bolivia but also in Brazil, where he currently resided with his family. According to Juicy Lucy, the trafficker, Ruben, had been a Bolivian consul in Corumba, Brazil, representing the Bolivian government. She also reported that Ruben had married a Brazilian woman and was currently living in São Paulo.

Based on that information, I contacted the DEA office in Brasilia, Brazil, and made arrangements to meet with one of their agents in São Paolo in order to initiate and coordinate the investigation. It was our policy to coordinate with the local DEA office if we were going into their area of responsibility and also a good idea—primarily for safety issues, in the event they had to assist an agent in danger. I packed my suitcases and traveled to São Paolo, accompanied by Lucy.

We arrived at the international airport on a dreary day and were met by the agent who had arrived the day before from Brasilia. After exchanging greetings and small talk, we made our way to a downtown hotel. During the drive, I was able to get a perspective of the city, which reminded me of New York City with its subway systems and cramped buildings. São Paulo is the tenth-richest city in the world and the largest financial center in Brazil. At the time, the population was approximately fifteen million. It ranks as one of the most expensive cities in the world ahead of London, Paris, Milan, and New York City and is also one of the most ethnically diverse cities in Brazil.

That evening, the agent from Brasilia and I met with Juicy Lucy to discuss the cover story she would use when meeting with Ruben. The other agent would also accompany me in an undercover capacity. The informant was instructed to tell Ruben I was a major drug trafficker, based out of Mexico, who was seeking to develop a new cocaine supplier, because my current source had been arrested during the past month.

The agent from Brasilia spoke some Portuguese, but the negotiations would be in Spanish, which was great for me, since I wouldn't need a translator. It was important that nothing was lost in translation and would allow me to develop the interaction so critical during undercover operations.

We went over the cover story to ensure everyone had it straight, in order to minimize risk. The next morning, we met with members of the Brazilian federal police, who were highly professional and adept at conducting counterdrug operations. We discussed the pending operation and were provided several who would work with us.

Officially, known as the Departamento de Policia Federal (DPF) and headquartered in Brasilia, the Brazilian federal police are tasked with investigating criminal activities of an interstate or international nature. They are the first line in preventing and suppressing the illicit traffic in drugs and perform the functions of coast guard (enforcement only), air police, and border patrol. DPF units are present throughout the states and territories and are highly skilled in tactical operations working closely with Interpol, the famed international police organization.

After our meeting, we went to a typical Brazilian restaurant where servers brought food to the table on large skewers, shaving the meats and sausages onto plates until our digestive tract went into overdrive. I was in awe of the police accompanying us, who were able to consume as much food as they did and probably could have eaten more had we stayed longer. I could barely stand up from the table and was uncomfortable as we relocated to the lobby of our hotel to continue planning the operation. Our discussions were long and tiring but worth every minute in order to ensure in-depth coordination. It gave me the opportunity to get a feel for the counterparts who would be working the investigation with us. I was pleased they acted confident and obviously were used to working with foreign law-enforcement agencies. We established that the undercover introductions to Ruben would be initiated the following day at his residence. The informant would make the arrangements later that evening.

The next morning at breakfast, Juicy Lucy said she had contacted Ruben and he was expecting us at his home in the early afternoon. I went upstairs, changed into an expensive suit, and put on a few gold chains, topping off the look with several large diamond rings—all attire and accessories befitting a wealthy drug kingpin from Mexico. The other agent and I drove with the informant to an affluent residential area in downtown São Paulo.

We arrived at a secure condominium complex and were allowed entry by a security guard who obviously knew we were coming, since he rapidly facilitated our entry. We took a spacious elevator to the third floor, which opened to two large doors with metal bars for added security. Lucy rang the doorbell, and seconds later, a man opened the door. He smiled at her, introduced himself, and shook our hands.

Ruben was of medium height and build and had a crooked smile that looked more like a smirk. His light-brown hair went wild in ten different directions. He graciously escorted us to a sofa in the middle of the living room with obviously expensive furnishings. As we all sat down, a very thin, attractive woman entered the room, accompanied by a small boy who was about three years old. Ruben introduced his wife and young son. She was very personable and offered us something to drink.

I had brought a large basket of wine, fruit, and cheese wrapped in cellophane and tied with a bright red bow. The wife expressed her gratitude and watched their son begin to remove the bow and tear the cellophane. I wondered why Ruben was jeopardizing his freedom and, more so, the well-being of his family to engage in cocaine distribution. There was only one answer and that was greed. The wife excused herself and carried her son into another room.

Ruben began to ask me questions with the obvious intent of corroborating Lucy's story. We had done our homework well, and he seemed to relax as the conversation continued. After a twenty-minute feeling-out period, we began serious negotiations. I explained my lucrative heroin business and my plan to develop a reliable source for pure cocaine in order to replace the one I had lost as a result of law-enforcement actions. Ruben said he was part of a group based in Bolivia that could supply tons of cocaine and had a fleet of aircraft that could transport it anywhere within the region. My preference would be to have it delivered to Brazil, since I had contacts that would provide support and security. Ruben inquired about the quantity I was interested in purchasing, and I explained my intent was to initially purchase five hundred kilograms, and if everything went as planned, larger quantities would follow. He smiled and said this could easily be arranged. We negotiated the price and agreed on $5,000 (US) per kilogram, with a total purchase price of $2.5 million. As we sat there bargaining, in the back of my mind, I was thinking, *How in the world am I going to pull this off, especially considering I have no money to show him?* I'd have to cross that bridge when the time came. Ruben said he would contact his associates in Bolivia and I should call him in three days. He wrote his telephone numbers on a small piece of paper and handed it to me as we left.

After the initial undercover negotiations, I removed Juicy Lucy from any further activity in the investigation. She had done her job as my informant, and in the interest of safety, I made arrangements for her to return to La Paz the following morning. During the next couple of days, we coordinated and continued planning with the federal police. We took the opportunity to spend time together having lunch and dinner forming close personal relationships. Prior to meeting with them we made sure we were not being watched by the traffickers by conducting counter surveillance. As the Brazilian police followed us they could determine if we were being followed by others before we met. Additionally, when working in a large metropolitan city it is easy to escape scrutiny. They were a likable bunch and had a great sense of humor. It was dry, but humor nonetheless. I made them aware that Ruben and his associates would, in all probability, transport the load of cocaine from Bolivia into Brazil by aircraft, and they should begin looking for a suitable area that could serve as a clandestine airstrip.

I called Ruben a few days later to check on the status of our pending deal. He answered the phone and cryptically explained his associates had expressed interest in consummating the deal and were even more interested in establishing a long-term relationship. He said they needed a few weeks to prepare the logistics and security for the pending operation. In the meantime, I wanted to return to La Paz, so the federal police took me to the airport and dropped me off in front of the main terminal. As they drove away, I suddenly realized I had a Smith and Wesson .38-caliber revolver in my small portfolio, along with several documents. I was working undercover, so I didn't have my DEA credentials and found myself in a real predicament. I opted to take my chances and walked up to the security area and handed my bag, with the weapon in it, to the airport security official. He rummaged through it in a cursory manner but never saw the handgun. Next, I walked with the bag through the magnetometer, which didn't activate. Great security. Lucky for them, I was a DEA agent.

I returned to São Paulo a few weeks later. The flight was quick, and I met with the agent from Brasilia, who was waiting at the airport. That afternoon, we rendezvoused with the federal police agents who advised us they had found a suitable location for an airstrip at a ranch located in a rural town called Avaré. The ranch belonged to one of their friends who had graciously allowed them to use it during the operation. According to federal police, the town was three and half-hours from São Paulo. I called Ruben the following day and, to set the stage even further, asked him if he was interested in seeing the airstrip we would be using. He was eager to ensure it was in an isolated area and not under surveillance by local police.

On a rainy morning, we drove to Ruben's home and found him waiting as we pulled in front. Our driver was an undercover federal police agent who knew how to get to the ranch in Avaré. As we drove, our conversation was about taking precautions and the importance of security on both sides when doing the large drug deal. He indicated his organization was fully protected by the highest levels of the Bolivian government and had political contacts in Brazil. He asked me how I planned on transporting the cocaine to Mexico. I told him during the past five years I had acquired a Beechcraft King Air and an Aero Commander. I also said one of these airplanes would be used in the operation and that my cousin was a pilot and would fly the cocaine to one of my ranches in southern Mexico. Ruben said his father was a high-ranking official in Bolivia.

We eventually came to the outskirts of Avaré, an agricultural and cattle-raising town of forty thousand. The federal police driver began to take a series of roads that were unpaved, and dust began to kick up in large, brown clouds. The vehicle didn't have air-conditioning, but the alternative of opening the windows and choking on the dry dust was far worse. We arrived at a small, rustic ranch house surrounded by trees, with an open pasture where I could see several head of cattle grazing on the thick, green grass. The house was nondescript and, behind it, jutting up from the flat ground, was a very tall water tower. We showed Ruben the pasture, which was fenced on both sides, but sufficiently wide to accommodate a twin-engine aircraft. He carefully inspected the area to be used as the landing strip and walked the length of it. He liked the fact it was very isolated and no other ranches were in the immediate area.

We had lunch at the ranch house and enjoyed some sandwiches, potato chips, and soft drinks. Not the best meal, but we were all famished and that made it more palatable. The return trip to São Paulo was uneventful, and Ruben dozed off for most of the time. We were all tired when we finally left him at his home in the early evening and watched him walk slowly to his front door and wave good-bye.

I called him the next day to discuss what I hoped to be the final details of the drug deal. His associates were about to throw a monkey wrench into the plan, which I had anticipated from the very beginning. He said his partners wanted him to see the money before moving any further with the transaction. For several weeks the negotiations were intense. I argued this was the first time I had done business with them and had not seen any cocaine. I was in their territory and would not bring millions of dollars in cash all the way from Mexico until I was sure everything was ready on their end. The traffickers stood their ground, not knowing my cash on hand was the $300 in my wallet. It would be impossible with all the bureaucratic red tape to obtain the large flash roll required for this operation in such a short time frame. The agent from Brasilia was getting frustrated and called the case a "hummer," saying it wasn't going anywhere. I ignored his opinion and persisted with the negotiations, which went on for a few more weeks. In my conversations with Ruben, I kept dangling the money carrot. They would be making huge profits by establishing a pipeline for cocaine through my organization into Mexico and then funneling it to the United States.

We had reached an impasse. I finally played my last card, telling him that I no longer had time to waste and would go to someone else to purchase the cocaine. It was a last-ditch effort to focus on every drug trafficker's personality trait: greed.

Another week went by before I spoke with Ruben, who by this time was enthusiastic that everything was ready to proceed. To break the stalemate between both parties, he had advised his associates in Bolivia he had seen the money. His lie set the wheels in motion for a disastrous end to their criminal organization. He was convinced I was a legitimate drug trafficker and wanted to circumvent the suspicions of his partners. Ruben informed me two of their best pilots would be traveling to São

Paulo and would need to see the airstrip in Avaré in order to get their bearings and ensure the aircraft could safely land. The pilots would arrive the following week, so with a lull in the operation, I decided to take a flight to Rio de Janeiro, since I'd never been there and wanted to take the unique opportunity to visit this spectacular city. I packed a few clothes and took a quick flight, landing at the Galean International Airport.

Rio is a beautiful city and the twenty-sixth largest in the world. It was the capital of Brazil from 1763 to 1815, which was later changed to Brasilia. My first stop was the giant statue of *Christ the Redeemer* located on the top of Corcovado Mountain, which overlooks the entire city. Next on my list was to visit some of the eighty kilometers of beautiful coastlines of the Copacabana and Ipanema beaches, and like any tourist, I took the cable car to the top of Sugarloaf Mountain. The restaurants were saturated with ambience and served everything from exotic dishes to street food. Rio is truly one of the great cities of the world, and its people are some of the most gracious I have met in my world travels. Even though my stay was too brief, I was still able to see most of the city and sights.

Working undercover exacts a mental and physical toll. It is unbelievably intense and requires a type of focus unattainable by most. It is crucial to allow the mind and body to relax and balance the stress and tension. One misspoken word or move due to exhaustion can undo months of planning or, worse, get you killed. These small diversions kept my head clear and were as critical as good planning.

Returning to São Paulo a little more relaxed, I touched base with the federal police. We reached a consensus that two of their agents would take the Bolivian pilots to Avaré when they arrived. It didn't make sense for a drug kingpin, the role I was playing, to be taking the pilots of another organization to see an airstrip. Ruben mentioned that because he had already seen the clandestine field, only the pilots would be making the journey.

We had the federal police meet them at their hotel and drive them to Avaré. The following day, Ruben reported the pilots were satisfied and wouldn't have problems landing their airplane at the designated location. He also indicated they were in final preparations, but several more days were required to put everything in order. I fabricated a story that I would be returning to Mexico to prepare my logistics for the transportation of the bulk currency to Avaré, where it would be exchanged for the half ton of cocaine. I advised Ruben I would return on the aircraft with the money in about a week and would contact him at that time. But of course, I remained in São Paulo and continued planning with the federal police.

The cat-and-mouse undercover operations are as psychologically tiring as a world-championship chess match where a mistake caused you to not only lose, but get killed. I had to be on top of my game and anticipate the moves of my opponent. My role portraying a drug kingpin had to be nothing short of an *Oscar*-winning performance. It had to be flawless, and many times I had to improvise and react to nonscripted situations.

The investigation involving the Bolivian traffickers was predictably difficult, because like most, they operate in a subculture of violence and distrust. The saying "there is no honor among thieves" is undeniably accurate. Money is their only friend and objective in life. They are willing to jeopardize their lives and the lives of others for the power that comes with it and conduct their illicit business with an unjustified sense of invulnerability and the feeling they can overcome any obstacle in their path. They lose all sense of morality and humanity. Their natural ability to judge right from wrong is perverted into a foul narcissistic philosophy of "what benefits me and what does not." Some may enjoy lavish lifestyles, but often this is short-lived when they become wards of the state in small, sterile prison cells or, worse, inhabit a *dirt dormitory* when their lives are cut short by violence.

I let six days pass before calling Ruben and telling him I had returned with the money. He said he would contact his people in Bolivia and I should contact him later that evening and I would be very pleased with the quality of the cocaine. In a later conversation, he assured me everything was set and the cocaine would be delivered in a few days. We could pick him up in two days, and he would ride with us to the Avaré airstrip.

It was the news I wanted to hear, and now we began to finalize our plans with the federal police. They would arrive in the area a day before to establish a large force around the ranch to conduct close surveillance and arrest the traffickers when the cocaine was delivered. The police would wear camouflage uniforms to prevent detection from the air. The plan was solid, and we left no loose threads hanging to entangle us later.

We drove to Ruben's home, and as usual, he was waiting outside— this time with a small bag in his hand. I immediately thought he might be carrying a weapon and would have to be neutralized quickly during the arrests. He greeted us and slid into the rear seat. He was in a jovial mood, and his unruly hair seemed more ruffled than usual. We joked on the way and drank bottles of juice that had a chalky taste but were at least cold. Ruben began asking questions about my trip and whether I had encountered problems. I told him everything went well and uneventful. He asked if my airplane was at the airstrip in Avaré. I explained we had initially landed there but moved it to another area. The cocaine and money would not be at the same location at the same time until the deal was going to be consummated in order to avoid potential problems. Once the cocaine arrived, we would retrieve the money only a short distance from the airstrip. Ruben appeared to have no issue with my explanation and dozed off. I was relieved that he had fallen asleep, because that meant I could also relax and not have to be on my guard for the entire three-and-a-half-hour trip.

We arrived at the airstrip three hours later and carried the bags of food we had brought into the small ranch house. As with most drug deals, the traffickers are seldom on time, and we could at least have something to eat in the event they were delayed. While this may seem inconsequential, it is another small detail very important to the logistics of a drug operation. Having food and something to drink can keep tension under control.

Ruben immediately walked to the airstrip and began to examine it. It was clear he was checking for the skid marks that should have been left by my aircraft when it landed. As he walked back and forth several times, he came within twenty feet of at least two federal police in camouflage uniforms lying prone on the side of the makeshift landing strip. It had rained the previous day, and in reality, the water would have erased the skid marks. I could explain the lack of skid marks. That would have been easy. I would not have been able, however, to explain the presence of Brazilian federal police.

Hours came and went, making it feel as if we'd been waiting an eternity. I prodded Ruben for an estimated time of arrival, but he didn't know. His nonchalant attitude was "they would get there when they got there." I was concerned he would want to go *sightseeing* again and come across the camouflaged police who were thick as locusts in the area. In order to avoid a last minute disaster and compromise of the operation, I kept Ruben engaged in conversation for several hours. Each time he stood up to move around, I was ready to pull him into another conversation. In essence, I was handcuffing him with words. It was critical that every movement be limited, to minimize his chances of seeing some of the federal police hiding close to the ranch house.

At five in the afternoon, I heard the distant hum of aircraft engines. The sound was so faint, that for a second, I believed it was nothing more than my imagination. It became louder and louder, and I knew we were minutes from a critical stage where if anything went wrong, a lot of blood could be spilled. My adrenaline was pumping with excitement, but I kept it contained and remained calm. Ruben reached into the bag he had brought with him and pulled out a red shirt. He removed the denim shirt he was wearing and replaced it with the red one. He walked to the middle of the field and lit a cigarette. Both were obviously signals to the pilots that everything was fine and it was safe to land. The aircraft dropped to a few hundred feet and made two circling passes around the makeshift airfield. They observed the *all-clear* signal from Ruben and began to make their approach. The twin-engine aircraft landed gently on the field and taxied to the end where we were all standing. The pilots turned the engines off, and within a minute, four men exited the brand new airplane.

We exchanged greetings with Ruben, making the introductions. The pilots were aloof, but the other two were much friendlier. Inside the plane were numerous duffle bags containing kilogram bricks of cocaine wrapped in the standard packaging of thick brown tape. We walked to the ranch house and offered them something to eat and drink. They said their trip was long and tiring. After minutes of small talk, I told Ruben we were leaving for a few minutes to get the money from my cousin who was safeguarding it nearby. The agent from Brasilia and I got into our vehicle and began driving away from the location. A half a mile from the ranch house, a federal police officer stood guard by a gate and saluted as we drove past him, which had the eerie feeling of something directly out of *Mission Impossible*.

A half hour later, it was all over. The Brazilian federal police had moved in quickly after we left, to make the arrests, and seized the five hundred kilograms of cocaine and the aircraft. During the arrest, one of the men pulled out a fragmentation grenade, displaying his finger on the pin. He was surrounded by machinegun-wielding federal police and decided to release it, letting it drop harmlessly to the ground. This man, who was about fifty years old, turned out to be the head of security for the Bolivian minister of justice, Ruben's father.

The seizure of cocaine was the largest in the history of Brazil at the time, and the federal police were elated. All the major Brazilian newspapers and television stations covered the story. We met with the director general of the Brazilian federal police, whose congratulations gave everyone a great sense of accomplishment, having immobilized a major international cocaine-trafficking network.

Two decades later, at an International Drug Enforcement Conference (IDEC), I met a high-ranking Brazilian federal police official, and in conversation, I mentioned the case to him. He looked at me wild-eyed and, by incredible coincidence, said he had been in Avaré during the operation. Not only was he there but had been in the rickety water tower behind the ranch house for almost six hours with water up to his chin. We hugged each other and became friends for life. What a small world we live in.

1974 Graduation from DEA Special Agent training, Washington, D.C.

Working undercover in Brazil

Operation in the Colombian jungles

Boat marijuana seizure in Cartagena, Colombia

Cocaine seizure taken from the Albatross in Florida.
Tom Scarantino, John Fernandes, Bob Martin, Mike Shamus, me

Cocaine seizure in Miami. John Fernandes, me,
Tom Scarantino

Afghan Deputy Minister of Interior, General Muhammed Salangi presenting me with a king's robe

In Afghanistan along the Pakistani border with Mujahadeen fighters

Seizure of clandestine cocaine laboratory in
Colombia

An operation with Colombian National Police in the Sierra
Nevada mountains

With the Mexican Marines in Michoacan, Mexico

Receiving Top Cop award from Mariska Hargitay and
Chris Meloni

Using trash bags as rain protection in Mexican jungle
while destroying marijuana seizure

In the jungle on a search and destroy operation
with Mexican Army

With Mujadidi, former Afghan President in Kabul, Afghanistan

With Khyber Rifles in Pakistan

Cocaine seizure on Colombian north coast

Marijuana seizure in Colombian jungle

Chapter 11

The Lure of White-Powder Wealth

Mike Vigil is definitely one the most knowledgeable counterdrug and terrorism experts on Afghanistan. He has worked closely with the highest leadership of the Afghan government in developing large-scale operations and intelligence programs. He is highly respected in our country and was made an honorary general by the Ministry of Interior. This is an honor which has never been bestowed to anyone else

—General Mohammad Tahir Ebad
Afghan National Police

Back in Hermosillo, I received an unexpected call from Juicy Lucy in Bolivia, who had assisted with the significant case in Brazil. She was in a good mood and wanted to know if I were interested in a group of Bolivian cocaine traffickers operating out of Santa Cruz de la Sierra. According to her, one of the principals was the wife of a Bolivian ambassador. Lucy said Patricia was enamored with the finer things in life and the salary of a Bolivian ambassador was, unfortunately, rather meager. Patricia was also connected to several of the largest cocaine traffickers in the country, most of them living in Santa Cruz de la Sierra.

One of my first questions to Lucy was whether or not she thought Patricia would be willing to deliver a quantity of cocaine to Mexico. By luring her out of Bolivia, I could ensure she would not be released, which would in all likelihood occur if the operation were conducted in her country. Undoubtedly, her husband had powerful political connections and would make the case quickly disappear. Juicy Lucy said she would speak with her and let me know within the next few days. I told her to tell Patricia I was willing to pay more for the cocaine if the delivery were made in Mexico. When working undercover, I always relied on the greed factor, which usually clouded their judgment and caused them to make critical mistakes.

Having spoken with Patricia, Juicy Lucy said she was willing to deliver the cocaine to Mexico City for $2,000 more per kilogram. I wanted to purchase twenty kilograms. The total price per kilogram would be $8,000. My order could have been much larger, but I knew Patricia would personally transport the cocaine because of her diplomatic status and it would be difficult to carry more than that amount.

Lucy agreed to accompany Patricia and probably one other person to Mexico City. She let me know the cocaine would be smuggled in hidden compartments of several suitcases. Patricia had skilled people who modified them, and these cases were difficult to detect. Lucy said it would take a few days to prepare for the delivery but she'd let me know once everything was ready to proceed.

The following week, she called to say the cocaine had been hidden in several suitcases and airline tickets had been purchased. They planned to arrive in the capital three days later, not giving me much time to prepare. I contacted our office in Mexico City briefing them on the pending operation and made reservations to travel there myself. The next morning, I took an Aero Mexico flight into Mexico City and was met at the airport by two agents who were assigned there. We immediately went to the MFJP offices to confer with the comandante in charge of operations. We would coordinate with Mexican Customs officials at the airport to allow Juicy Lucy, Patricia, and the third person to pass without a search. I would take all three to a local hotel a few miles from the US Embassy, on Avenida Reforma. The MFJP would provide a large van and an agent to act as the driver. They would also have agents follow us from the airport to the hotel. The DEA would rent two rooms at the hotel with an adjoining door to facilitate the arrests of the traffickers at the time I gave the arrest signal.

The only aspect troubling me was the surveillance from the airport to the hotel. I was fully aware the MFJP were not very adept at conducting a moving surveillance, but for whatever reason, the comandante insisted on doing this. It was his country we were operating in, so ultimately, I'd have to deal with it and not argue.

That evening, I called Lucy in Bolivia and confirmed their travel. She provided the flight information and said Patricia was bringing a male associate named Antonio. She described him as being about forty years old, dark complexion, black hair and eyes. He also had a scar from an old knife wound on the right side of his face.

I asked her to call me on the morning of their departure, because I wanted a description of the clothing Patricia and Antonio were wearing. We didn't want any mistakes in identifying them. This was important in the event they became separated before going through customs inspection because the Mexico City airport was always very chaotic.

On a Wednesday morning filled with heavy smog, Lucy called me to say she was at the La Paz airport with Patricia and Antonio. She described Patricia as wearing a tight, short, black skirt with a red blouse and carrying a large, red purse. Antonio was wearing black dress pants, white shirt, and several gold chains around his neck. She also said they had a total of eight large suitcases with false bottoms containing the cocaine. I passed the descriptions to the MFJP who immediately sent three agents to the airport to coordinate with customs and wait for the flight.

A few hours later, I left for the airport accompanied by an MFJP agent in a large white van that would accommodate the traffickers and all of the suitcases. Traffic was heavy, and it took an extra half hour to get there, but we still arrived with an hour to spare. I went with the

Mexican federale to the terminal handling international flights to meet with customs managers and several other MFJP. They would identify Patricia and Antonio shortly after they disembarked from the aircraft and point them out, so other personnel would ensure they passed freely through the customs area. I would wait with my Mex-Fed driver in the terminal and connect with the Bolivians once they cleared Customs.

We didn't have long to wait before the flight arrived. I watched the Customs search area from where I stood. They had an interesting system to determine whether someone was searched or not. Arriving international passengers were told to press the button on an electronic system. If the light turned green, there would be no search, but if it turned red, you were asked to proceed to an area where your suitcases were inspected and x-rayed. I had undergone the same process many times traveling in and out of Mexico and found it humorous, because there was a small hidden button that Customs personnel pressed to ensure the light turned whichever color they wanted. They were obviously selective as to who passed without a search. Eventually, I saw Lucy, Patricia, and Antonio approach the search area. Patricia was a tall, beautiful woman in her early forties. She had jet-black hair and green eyes; her skirt was high above her knees, and as one would expect, every man stared at her.

They approached the electronic system; one of the MFJP agents nodded to the customs agent who reached for the button to ensure a green light for all three. They pushed the carts containing their suitcases through the customs area and into the main terminal. Lucy quickly saw me and walked in my direction. She gave me a hug and then introduced Patricia and Antonio. They were visibly relieved they were not searched and thought they were home free. Patricia had a very sexy voice and was obviously adept at using her beauty and sex appeal to get her way. She said the trip from La Paz was long but worthwhile, since it would be profitable for everyone. She also said the cocaine was pure and would be very marketable. On a future transaction, she wanted me to travel to Bolivia and spend some time in Santa Cruz de la Sierra with her. We walked to the van in the parking lot and loaded the suitcases in the back.

Traffic was still heavy leaving the airport, but we were able to weave our way onto the main highway. Antonio was quiet and visibly nervous. He kept looking out the back window to determine if we were being followed. Once we entered the always-congested downtown area of Mexico City, I realized the MFJP surveillance vehicle was following too closely behind us. Their surveillance was anything but discreet.

Antonio also saw the car that was literally stuck to our rear bumper and yelled, *"Nos están siguendo"* (We are being followed)! The expression on Patricia's face immediately changed to concern. I told the driver to lose the vehicle, but he was unable to accelerate or make abrupt movements due to heavy traffic. I finally told him to pull over to the curb, and sure enough, the MFJP also stopped abruptly behind us. I jumped out hoping to defuse the situation!

Hurriedly, I walked away from the van over to the MFJP vehicle and told them they were following too closely and strongly suggested they go straight to the hotel or risk putting the operation in jeopardy. I reached in my pocket and pretended to hand them something, while Patricia and Antonio fearfully watched the entire animated discussion. The MFJP hastily left and I returned to the van. I told Patricia and Antonio the men were local police officers who had seen them at the airport and decided to follow them, probably to extort money. I told them not to worry because the cops had accepted a bribe and would stay away. At least part of my story was true.

They understood bribery. It was also a way of life in their country, and they breathed a sigh of relief. We arrived at the hotel, where a bellboy brought a large cart to assist us with the mountain of suitcases. As we entered the lobby, I spotted a few MFJP agents loitering about. We piled into the large elevator and went to my room, located on one of the upper floors. It was poorly lit and smelled like stale cigarette smoke, which had permeated the curtains and rugs.

Antonio didn't waste time, placing the suitcases one by one on the large bed; he began removing bundles of clothes that he threw on a chair. He pulled out the suitcase lining exposing the false bottoms, which were neatly segregated into numerous small squares, each containing a plastic bag of cocaine about an inch thick. The compartments were virtually undetectable, and undoubtedly they had used this technique in the past to smuggle cocaine from Bolivia. Antonio began piling the bags of cocaine on the bed and explained they would be smuggling the payment money back to Bolivia in the same false-bottomed luggage. I grabbed one of the bags and pretended to examine it and said loudly enough to be heard in the next room, *"Parece que la coca es pura"* (It appears the cocaine is pure). This was the arrest signal. The door to the adjoining room burst open as the Mex-Feds charged into the room brandishing AK-47s and yelling, *"No se muevan!"* (Don't move.)

In the chaos, one of the MFJP agents, who obviously didn't know who I was, mistook me for one of the traffickers and struck me on my neck with the butt of an AK-47. Stars exploded in my head, and the blow almost knocked me out. This unplanned attack made my arrest appear even more genuine than I anticipated. Fortunately, another agent pulled him aside and whispered in his ear. The MFJP pretended to arrest Juicy Lucy and me in an effort to take suspicion away from her. They handcuffed everyone and took us downstairs where they loaded Patricia and Antonio in a separate car. After they drove away, the MFJP removed our handcuffs and drove us to the DEA office at the US Embassy.

Later that day, they called to thank me for the operation and seizure of twenty kilos. They were happy to inform me that Patricia and Antonio had confessed and signed statements regarding their criminal activities. At the time, I wondered if the MFJP had used the *chicharra* or the Teohuacan to motivate and persuade.

The following morning, I drove Juicy Lucy to the airport for her return to Bolivia. She waved as I left her at the terminal, but I had not seen the last of her.

Weeks passed, and back in my office in Hermosillo, I was attempting to make some headway on the backlogged investigative reports and other documentation, when the telephone rang and it was Gary Wheeler. He was barely audible because of the poor telephone communications in

Bolivia and Mexico. Communications in and out of underdeveloped countries were extremely poor and frustrating, especially when involved in matters of critical importance. I was able to understand that Juicy Lucy was in contact with a significant African American drug-trafficking group based in Chicago. This group had been engaged in trafficking large amounts of brown heroin throughout the Chicago area for many years. Their suppliers for the heroin were members of the infamous Herrera organization based in Durango, Mexico.

The head of the Chicago organization was Robert "Blood" Lewis. He had been a strike-force target for fifteen years but had eluded law enforcement because he allowed his underlings to take the risks handling and distributing the heroin. Juicy Lucy told Gary the organization was attempting to develop a source for cocaine and apparently had been in contact with her.

We decided to pursue the investigation, given the stature of this criminal organization. Arrangements were made to travel to the *Windy City* where Gary would bring Lucy. I contacted the DEA office in Chicago and asked that agents be assigned to support the operation. My suitcases were packed again, and I flew there three days later. I took a taxicab to the hotel where Gary and Juicy Lucy had already arrived, and checked in. We met at the hotel restaurant to discuss the pending operation.

Because the drug-trafficking organization headed by Lewis wanted to purchase cocaine for distribution in the Chicago area, we agreed to conduct a *reverse*. This is an operation where the undercover agent poses as the *seller* of drugs rather than the buyer. It is a sensitive activity and requires extensive coordination with other law-enforcement agencies in the area to *deconflict* any possibility that another agency was inadvertently posing as the buyers. There is always the likelihood two agencies believe they are dealing with drug traffickers when they are not. The inherent confusion in these situations could have lethal consequences with a worst-case scenario being agents shooting at each other.

We met with one of the Chicago enforcement groups and briefed them on our strategy in dismantling the Lewis organization. They were very familiar with Lewis and indicated he'd become wealthy selling heroin. Members of the Herrera family, a Durango, Mexico–based organization who dominated the heroin trade in Chicago, provided Lewis large amounts of brown heroin on consignment but, frequently, were arrested and went to prison for a number of years. This worked out well for Lewis. Imprisoned men could not collect the money he owed them.

The next twenty-four hours were spent planning. The Chicago office agreed to be responsible for coordinating with other agencies in the area to ensure other operations weren't in conflict with ours. They also advised they would obtain additional support from one of the Chicago Police Department's drug units. We had our informant contact Queen Esther Freeman, a member of Lewis's organization, to establish a meeting for the next day. Lucy made arrangements to meet at a hotel in the downtown area, where we would conduct an initial undercover introduction. I would play the role of a major source of supply for cocaine, based in Bolivia, and speak poor English with a thick Hispanic accent to enhance my undercover role. It gave me more credibility, since many South American traffickers speak broken English or none at all.

Queen was an older woman who obviously took pride in the way she dressed. Lucy introduced me, and when she extended her hand, it felt like hard, sun-dried leather. She had black eyes, but her disheveled hair didn't fit with her expensive ensemble. Her vocabulary was made up of street slang, and her grasp of the English language was exceptionally impoverished. She butchered more words than I did in my undercover persona. There were times when *she* actually needed a translator.

I told her the purpose of my trip to Chicago was to meet with Lewis and discuss the possibility of a cocaine transaction. She strongly assured me Lewis and his wife, Ruth, were major traffickers in Chicago. She also added Lewis had heroin distributors on every street corner "doin' bidness fo' 'im." According to Queen, Lewis and his wife wanted to get involved in cocaine, because the demand was now higher than for heroin. She said that later in the evening she would return and take us to the Lewis home.

After Queen's departure, we met with DEA and Chicago PD agents to discuss the surveillance that would occur later in the day. They were familiar with the Lewis residence and would establish themselves there prior to our arrival. Other units would follow us to and from the location.

Queen returned as promised, and we accompanied her to the central part of Chicago. The house was actually a mansion, but it appeared out of place in such a poor area, surrounded by old, dilapidated buildings. Glass from broken bottles and trash littered the streets, and few of the streetlights were lit. Queen sauntered up to the porch and rang the doorbell. A white maid opened the door and invited us into a large dining area containing an enormous wooden table surrounded by other expensive furniture.

As we sat on a sofa near the table, I looked around the spacious room with an oversized fireplace and high ceilings. There were Persian carpets, pieces of Waterford crystal, porcelain figures, and other expensive objects with price tags still attached. Obviously, the Lewis's wanted visitors to know how much they had paid for each article. It reminded me of Minnie Pearl, who left price tags dangling from the hats she wore on stage. Minutes later, Ruth Lewis entered the room and introduced herself. She welcomed me to Chicago and apologized that her husband was out on business, but definitely wanted to meet with me the next day.

Ruth was a short, heavyset woman and wore clothes that were not off the rack. She had expensive jewelry studded with large diamonds that were definitely meant to impress. She told me she and her husband were very much interested in purchasing cocaine. She explained further they had a large organization but at the present time were only involved in the trafficking of heroin. She asked about the amount of cocaine I could deliver. In "broken English," I told Ruth there would be no problem in furnishing any amount they wanted to purchase. I explained most of my business was primarily with Miami-based traffickers who purchased tons of cocaine on a regular basis. She was visibly impressed, but the doorbell interrupted our discussion.

A young, African American man entered the dining room. He had short-cropped hair and wore a thick leather jacket and blue jeans. He stood at the dining room table, and as Ruth approached him, he pulled out a brown paper bag from the inside of his jacket. He dumped large stacks of money onto the table, which scattered, covering a large portion of the surface. Ruth stared at him and asked "if it was all there." He told her it was and would return in the morning. He turned and left the house as abruptly as he had entered. He was a drug dealer obviously working for Lewis and had just turned in proceeds from the day's drug sales.

Ruth didn't bother to count the money and left it lying on the table for all of us to see. Being a perfect hostess, she gave us a tour of her home. Each room was filled with decorative items, all bearing price tags. The home had a temperature-controlled room loaded with fur coats and also a sauna that, with the press of a button, produced a warm tropical rainfall—all paid for by their enormous drug profits.

After telling her how impressive her home was, arrangements were made to meet with her husband the following day. The evening, however, was not yet over, because Queen wanted to have pancakes. I was starved, and it sounded good to me, so at midnight, we all sat at a diner on the south side of Chicago having a stack of blueberry pancakes. Queen wasn't entirely loyal to Lewis, and it sounded like she had an ax to grind. Ironically, she thought they had accumulated wealth on "the backs of others." Regardless, she was engaged in drug-trafficking activities with them and was part of the conspiracy. I was full and, finally, went to bed at about three in the morning.

I received a phone call in the early afternoon from Robert Lewis asking if he could come to the hotel to meet. I told him that we could meet in a few hours because I had some pressing issues in Bolivia that needed to be addressed immediately. I stalled as much as I could, because we wanted to put a listening device in the room, so surveillance agents could listen and record. Like clockwork, Lewis arrived, knocking loudly on the door. Juicy Lucy allowed him to enter, and he hugged her and then introduced himself to me. He was a tall, heavyset man who wore expensive dress slacks and a white linen shirt. We made small talk, feeling each other out, much like boxers during the early rounds. He asked questions regarding Bolivia, which I easily answered, before we began to discuss the issue of cocaine. Lewis was cautious but said he was interested in purchasing large quantities. I assured him it wouldn't be a problem to furnish whatever amount he wanted. I also warned him that logistics would be slightly more complicated if he wanted the cocaine delivered to Chicago.

Lewis wanted to know how I smuggled the cocaine into the US, and my response was purposely vague. I told him that I brought it into a clandestine airstrip in southern Florida. Understandably, most traffickers will not divulge much information about their operations or *modus operandi* (MO). They survive by being paranoid and suspicious, even of other drug traffickers. As with most large drug deals, several meetings to negotiate price and quantities are normal, and this one followed the same pattern. Lewis said he would be in contact to discuss quantity. Apparently he wanted to check his finances and liquid solvency, because most drug deals are *cash-and-carry* transactions. He excused himself and left. He was much more confident and relaxed by the end of the meeting, which was a good sign that he believed I was a legitimate cocaine trafficker. His overconfidence and greed would lead to his demise beginning with the proverbial dollar signs.

During breaks in the undercover negotiations, Gary and I had time to spend with the DEA agents from Chicago, John Bott and Joe Peckos. Both had a well-developed sense of humor with compatible personalities. They had been assigned to Chicago for a number of years and were very familiar with the city. They had great working relationships with local law-enforcement agencies, especially the Chicago PD. The agents showed us around and took us to some great ethnic restaurants. It was always good to have some free time to relax and mentally plan your next moves and countermoves. I liked working with Gary because he would always *watch my back*. I trusted him with my life, and this is something I do not say lightly. While working undercover, it was imperative that someone was there to support me in the event of sudden violence, which, in this business, could erupt at any moment. This kind of work required putting my life on the line, and when hot lead started to fly, I needed courageous colleagues who would also risk their lives by stepping into the den of death with me.

Less than forty-eight hours later, Lewis initiated contact. He came to the hotel and asked how long it would take me to move a quantity of cocaine into Chicago. I told him it would take at least a week and involved my return to Bolivia to make the arrangements. He was initially interested in fifty kilograms. I said each kilo would cost $21,000 since he wanted it delivered to Chicago. The fifty kilos would come to a total of $1,050,000. He didn't blink, but wanted to negotiate an initial payment and then pay the balance. Lewis said he would pay $100,000 when the cocaine was delivered and the rest in increments. I agreed to the terms, since the ultimate objective was to put this significant trafficker in prison and stop him from spreading poison.

Before ending the meeting, I told Lewis I would return to Bolivia the following day to make all necessary arrangements and would contact him once the cocaine had arrived in Florida. He must have been mentally figuring his take, since his mood changed from somber to jovial, and he began to make small jokes. As he left, he shook my hand like I was his long-lost brother. Obviously, I wasn't going to Bolivia, but would remain in Chicago to plan the final stages of the operation. We opted to use one of the DEA's twin-engine aircraft that had been flown into the Midway airport and placed in one of the hangars for safekeeping. The plan was to call Lewis in a week and tell him I was in Florida with the cocaine and have him meet me at Midway, where the cocaine and the initial payment would be exchanged. Gary would pose as one of the pilots, and the Chicago agents would provide surveillance and make the arrests. The operational plan was polished during the following days, and the trap was set.

After a week had passed, I called the Lewis residence and spoke to Ruth. I told her I had arrived in Florida and that everything had gone according to plan. She wanted to make small talk, and to cut it short,

I quickly interjected, telling her I would be at the airport the next day between noon and one in the afternoon. I further explained the cocaine would be transported in one of my aircraft—there would be no customs search, since the flight originated in Miami. Customs was only involved if the plane came from a foreign country. She seemed excited and assured me her husband would be there on time. I reminded her that he should bring the initial down payment.

Gary and two other agents posing as my pilots/bodyguards accompanied me to the Midway airport with fifty kilograms of fake cocaine packaged in kilo bricks. In order to be able to charge Lewis and other members of his organization with possession, we placed a small amount of actual cocaine in two of the packages. We loaded the suitcases into the plane and waited at the other end of the airport, out of sight from the private-air-service area, where we were to meet Lewis. Surveillance agents would alert us when he arrived. I also agreed to wear a wire, which I disliked, but it was important for surveillance units to monitor the conversation with Lewis and keep abreast of the operation as it unfolded.

Forty-five minutes later, we were advised Lewis had pulled into the airport. The pilots switched on the engines of the aircraft, and we began to slowly taxi to the area where they were waiting. The plan was to give the illusion we had just landed, and no doubt, Lewis would be suitably impressed when he saw the shiny, sleek airplane.

Once at the private air service, I opened the door of the aircraft and stepped onto the tarmac. Almost immediately, I saw Lewis standing by another man, who was later identified as James Perry. I approached them and asked Lewis if he had brought the money for the cocaine. He explained he had half of the $100,000, which consisted of $8,000 in cash and a certificate of deposit in the amount of $41,000. He added he would have the rest of the down payment the next day. I smiled, and laughingly said, "Okay. I know where you live, anyway."

During the conversation with Lewis, Perry stood listening a few feet away. Shortly afterward, Lewis told him to get their vehicle, which was parked very close to where we were standing. Perry was obviously one of

Lewis's underlings and bodyguards, because he jumped as Lewis gave the order. When Perry drove up in a station wagon, both Lewis and I got in. I sat in the front seat alongside Perry and Lewis sat in the back seat. Lewis handed me a large envelope with the cash and check. As I examined the contents of the envelope, Lewis kept surveying the area and watching the (DEA) pilots, who had by now also walked outside of the aircraft.

Abruptly, Lewis got out of the car and said he would let Perry load the cocaine. Perry drove the station wagon a few hundred feet to the airplane and parked near the wing closest to the door. At that point, I got out of the vehicle and walked over to where Gary and the other DEA agents handed me the suitcases of fake cocaine.

Meanwhile, Perry stepped to the rear of the station wagon, opened the tailgate, took the suitcases and began to hastily load them. I spoke briefly with Perry, who quickly tied himself to the criminal conspiracy by asking if the cocaine was all there. I gave the arrest signal and could hear the immediate screeching of tires as agents moved in to make the arrests. Lewis attempted to flee on foot, and as he ran his pants fell down to his ankles. He was quickly apprehended. It was one of those rare, humorous moments, where I watched Lewis being marched across the tarmac at gunpoint in his underwear. Robert and Ruth Lewis, James Perry, and Queen Freeman were all convicted in federal court on charges of conspiracy, possession, and intent to distribute. As usually happens with drug traffickers, the bill finally came due for the many years they engaged in selling drugs. Lewis's organization ceased to exist without him to supply his army of dealers with drugs.

I returned home to Hermosillo and was notified I had been selected to take charge of the office in Medellin, Colombia. I began looking forward to the new assignment, which I instinctively knew would offer many new challenges.

Chapter 12

A Culture of Violence and Death

Mike Vigil is an international expert in the complex subculture of illicit drugs and terrorism. He is a hero to many countries in the region, because of the major counterdrug operations that he developed throughout the world. Operation Containment, for example, had a profound impact in the Middle East, Central Asia, and Europe. The success was due in large part to Mike's incredible ability for strategic planning and execution of multinational operations.

—Boyko Borisov
Prime Minister, Bulgaria

I had applied for and was selected for the position of Resident Agent in Charge of the office in Medellin, Colombia. Normally, the DEA did not allow agents to be in foreign assignments for more than six and a half consecutive years. I strongly suspect the agency didn't have a lot of applicants for the position, since Medellin, at the time, was known as *the most violent and dangerous city in the world.* They undoubtedly made an exception to the policy because of this reason.

It was a well-deserved reputation, as I would later personally experience. Medellin is the second largest city in Colombia and located in the Aburrá Valley, with an elevation of almost five thousand feet. I distinctly remember being on an Avianca flight that flew over the valley, then made a sharp turn in the opposite direction. The plane went into a steep dive and barely cleared some of the buildings. The airport was right in the middle of the city, making takeoffs and landings dangerous and heart-pounding experiences.

DEA Agent Joe Almanza met me at the airport. He was originally from southern Texas and had previously worked in Mexico City. I'd known him for a number of years. We drove to the Intercontinental Hotel, located on a large mountain in a suburb called El Poblado, one of the best residential areas in the city. Joe lived there and said it had some excellent restaurants and entertainment. I stayed at the hotel until suitable housing could be located—security would be very important.

The next day, Joe took me to the office, located in the downtown area. It was in an old building that also contained several stores and businesses and was definitely not secure. It sent up red flags. The elevators allowed anyone to access our office. DEA occupied half of the fourth floor, along with a small engineering firm. The entire building had one guard, posted on the ground floor, who carried an old rusted handgun that he probably had never fired. It is unlikely that it *could* fire.

We had a difficult time ahead of us, given the entrenched and growing power of the Colombian drug cartels. They had accumulated enormous wealth and power by not only corrupting, but also intimidating politicians, security forces, and a vast majority of the judiciary. The great marijuana bonanza had laid the foundation for the power of these drug organizations that cultivated large fields of marijuana along the Venezuela border and the northern part of Colombia. Individuals who previously could not afford a pair of socks were suddenly driving Chevy Silverado trucks and wearing pretentious jewelry. On the north coast, many people were killed just for the sin of honking their horn at the new drug lords. This new breed would step out of their bright new trucks and pump bullets into their unsuspecting neighbors if they dared offend their machismo. It is easy and cowardly to act macho when you're armed to the teeth and the other person is not.

These new drug barons got their starts purchasing cocaine paste and base from sources in Bolivia and Peru to meet the new consumer market in the US. Though morally bankrupt, Colombian drug traffickers are savvy businessmen, and they began to cultivate coca in Colombia to eliminate middlemen and increase their profit margins. The cocaine empire paved the way for drug traffickers to solidify a massive power base and become a national-security threat to their country. Violence became their calling card, and they took the concept of *silver or lead* to an entirely new level. To further secure their power, they financed the campaigns of the politicians who protected their organizations. Government officials who opposed them, on the other hand, would be given plenty of lead and quickly eliminated, thus serving as a very visible example to others. More often than not, their families would also be killed, because compassion and mercy are definitely not in the vocabulary of the Colombian traffickers.

The propensity for violence in Colombia began with the period known as *La Violencia* (The Violence), beginning with the April 1948 murder of Jorge Eliécer Gaitan, a popular left-wing Liberal Party leader in Bogotá. This, combined with civil unrest and dissatisfaction with the Conservative Party–led government, sparked a murderous conflict between the Liberal and Conservative political parties. During a period of sixteen years, over two hundred thousand citizens were killed, in a country less populous than the state of New York. To put it in perspective, this was more than six times the total casualties suffered by all US forces in the Korean War. The label *La Violencia* was not coined because of the prolific number of killings, but rather from the way the atrocities were committed. Many were beheaded and dismembered.

The Colombian *corbata* (necktie) originated from this genocidal period of civil war, where the throat was slit and the tongue pulled out through the gaping hole, giving the appearance of a necktie. During the peak years of La Violencia, it is estimated between twenty to thirty thousand armed rebels operated in the country. They organized themselves into guerilla units that attempted to create small, independent republics in the southern regions of Colombia.

A few weeks after my arrival, I became fully aware of the social impact caused by the long-term violence inflicted on the population. I frequently saw dead bodies strewn along the roadsides and watched passersby step over them as if they were just the natural hindrance of a tree branch or rock. There was no revulsion or expressions of horror displayed on their faces. Regrettably, they had become desensitized to violence and death and accepted it as normal. It had become part of everyday life, and their culture became steeped in death. The homicides were so numerous on some days that the Colombian authorities were unable to recover and transport all the cadavers to the morgue in a timely manner. On my return trip home from the office late in the day, I saw the same dead bodies still lying there covered in blood and flies and bloating in the tropical sun. Drug trafficking and crime in general were rampant there, and life had little value.

Medellin happened to be the operating base for the most significant cartel in the country, certainly the most violent. It was a loosely knit group of separate organizations, with Pablo Escobar Gavíria being the most powerful. The other members were José Gonzalo Rodríguez Gacha, also known as *El Mexicano*; Carlos Lehder Rivas; and the Ochoa brothers, Jorge, Juan David, and Fabio. Rodríguez Gacha came from another violent mafia in Colombia that has dominated the emerald business for decades. He kept a low profile but was just as deadly as the rest of the Medellin Cartel. The Ochoa brothers were from a fairly wealthy family who owned expensive horses and Las Margaritas restaurant. Lehder was a short, flamboyant man with the personality of a typical con artist. He had served time in the US for auto theft, and while in prison, made several contacts that later assisted him in the transportation and distribution of cocaine.

Interestingly, the Medellin Cartel came together first as a means of self-protection against kidnappers who targeted their families for

...om. The Ochoas' sister, Marta Nieves, was kidnapped. This event led to a meeting between Escobar, Rodríguez Gacha, Lehder, and the Ochoas, who formed an organization named Muerte a Sequestradores (Death to Kidnappers). Marta Nieves was eventually rescued, and later, Escobar's father was also taken but rescued after a few days. The kidnappings and the traffickers resolve to protect their families created a closer working relationship between the separate organizations and led them to share drug-trafficking routes, sources of supply, conversion laboratories, and transportation systems. Universally, there is nothing as effective as a common enemy to bring people together.

Pablo Escobar Gavíria, the third of seven children, came from humble origins. His father, Abel Escobar, was a peasant farmer and his mother, Hermilda Gavíria, was an elementary-school teacher. Money was tight for him and his closest friend and cousin, Gustavo Gavíria. Both of them began to engage in petty crime. They stole gravestones and sandblasted off names and dates before selling them. Eventually, they became exposed to the more-profitable business of cocaine. Early in their drug-trafficking careers, Pablo and Gustavo were arrested for possession of approximately sixteen kilos of cocaine. Bribes were quickly paid, and they were released without serving time in prison. As a compelling message, several weeks later, all of the arresting officers were hunted down and killed.

The Medellin Cartel began to establish significant sources of supply for coca paste in Bolivia and Peru. The raw material was transported to clandestine labs hidden in the Colombian jungles where it was converted into cocaine hydrochloride. Within a few years, the cartel was making hundreds of millions of dollars. In his book, *The Accountant's Story*, Roberto Escobar (Pablo's brother) wrote that they were spending $2,500 a month on rubber bands just to hold the stacks of money together. They hid the staggering amounts of drug money in warehouses and had an acceptable annual loss of 10 percent of their profits, because rats ate the paper currency.

The DEA office worked very closely with the Colombian National Police (CNP), who lived under the constant threat of death. Escobar had placed a $600 bounty on their heads that essentially painted a bull's-eye on them. The CNP were one of the most professional national police forces in all of Latin America. Their wire-intercept operations center, however, was rustic and could only intercept a few lines at a time. Knowing the importance of intelligence, I used some of my operational funding to develop a much larger wire-intercept center, including the purchase of several Marantz 220 tape recorders. The actuators, which turned on the recorders when a call was made or received by the target phone, were built from nuts and bolts for $1.50 each. We built a cabinet where the recorders were placed and separated to determine the lines being monitored and recorded. I also obtained pen registers to record the telephone numbers of incoming and outgoing calls. It took me a little more than a week to construct an effective wire-intercept center. We provided the CNP with constant suspect telephone numbers, and they selected the ones they wanted to focus on, but more often than not, intercepted most of them.

The Colombian legal process for intercepting telephones is very different and not as complicated as ours in the United States. We are required to develop an extensive affidavit, listing investigative efforts and probable cause, which is reviewed by the US Attorneys' Office and forwarded to main Justice for further review. It normally takes at least thirty days. In Colombia, the request to intercept a telephone is a one-page document, signed by a judge and forwarded to the telephone company, which will make the necessary arrangements. It was, however, fraught with problems, because the telephone-service providers or employees of the judiciary tended to sell the information regarding the telephones being intercepted. On one occasion, a call was intercepted as one trafficker told another he had just received the latest list of telephones being targeted and boasted that none belonging to them was listed. Perhaps, feeling a twinge of guilt, whoever sold them the information, had obviously not given them a complete list.

One of those telephone numbers being intercepted belonged to Harold Rosenthal, a fugitive from the US. He was a former bail bondsman ad become involved in the drug trade as a result of his exposure to various drug traffickers. He realized money from drug trafficking was much more profitable than posting bond for criminals. Rosenthal was eventually arrested and given a lengthy prison sentence. He was a skilled con artist who came across as a *good ol' boy* and convinced someone to give him a prison guard's uniform, which he used to literally walk out of the federal prison in Memphis, Tennessee. The escape was well planned, and through the help of his criminal associates, Rosenthal was able to travel into southern Florida. From there, he was transported by boat to Colombia and settled into a nice colonial house in the El Poblado area of Medellin. The house was located along a narrow road, which led to a major avenue close to the downtown area.

Shortly after his arrival in Medellin, Rosenthal brought his girlfriend, Veronica Wahl, to move in with him. Wahl was an attractive blonde from West Germany who thought drug trafficking was the ultimate adventure. She was just as volatile as he was and talked on the phone incessantly with a thick German accent. She linked Rosenthal, during the intercepted calls, to the Ochoa clan, who had become his primary sources of supply for cocaine. She also revealed that Roberto Suarez, Jr. (Robby), the son of Roberto Suarez, the most significant cocaine trafficker in Bolivia, had met with Rosenthal and other traffickers in Colombia to discuss potential cocaine transactions. Wahl would disparage Harold constantly on the telephone, and after a particularly violent argument, he took several of her expensive diamond rings and threw them out the front door across the road. Those involved with Rosenthal clearly showed drug trafficking was an equal-opportunity-employment enterprise. This major Colombian cartel was working, through Rosenthal with good ol' boys from Tennessee and Georgia, as well as with members of the Gambino organized crime family. Greed and money overcomes cultural and ethnic differences like nothing else.

We delayed arresting Rosenthal, because several DEA divisions in the US were still conducting investigations that formed a broad criminal conspiracy code named "Southern Comfort." Undercover agents had penetrated drug traffickers who were tied to Rosenthal and were collecting valuable evidence that would lead to successful prosecutions. He and his associates had been responsible for sending tons of cocaine into the US and used skilled pilots with twin-engine aircraft. He was under the impression he was safe operating in Colombia, especially under the protection of the Ochoa brothers. I followed him on occasions into a grocery store close to his house and noted he was always in the company of a Colombian man, whom we learned was from Barranquilla, located on the Colombian north coast. This man acted as his assistant and translator, since Rosenthal didn't speak Spanish. Rosenthal always dressed casually and usually wore an old, beige baseball cap. He had dark hair, was of medium build, and didn't stand out in a crowd. Rosenthal didn't know it, but his inconspicuous days as a fugitive were rapidly coming to an end.

During one of the intercepted phone calls, he made a death threat against the Colombian minister of justice. The Colombian government didn't take the threat lightly, given Rosenthal's connections with the murderous Medellin Cartel. Our written request for the expulsion of Rosenthal was rapidly approved, and planning to arrest him was coordinated with the CNP. Three DEA agents and a US Marshal from Georgia arrived in Medellin to assist with his removal to the US. Pete Charette, a close friend of mine, led the team from Atlanta. Pete was another good agent who had domestic and foreign experience and could be trusted in tight situations.

A few days after their arrival, we met with a young CNP lieutenant, Gonzalo Betancur, at our office to discuss the operation to capture Rosenthal. We reviewed maps of the area and photos of his home. We decided several CNP officers would conduct surveillance of the residence from the wooded area across the street, and a team consisting of CNP, DEA, and the US Marshal would be further down the road near a major avenue. Radio communication would allow the surveillance agents to notify the arrest team when Rosenthal was heading in our direction. We put the plan into effect early in the morning two days later. Several hours passed, so we did what is usually done on surveillance, we made small talk about women, music, and our war stories, waiting for Rosenthal to leave.

In the early afternoon, the CNP radios crackled as we were notified that Rosenthal and his assistant from Barranquilla had left the residence and were in a white sedan. We saw the vehicle coming down the hill heading in our direction. I yelled, "Prepárense!" (get ready), alerting everyone to prepare their weapons for the trap that was about to ensnare a major drug trafficker and fugitive. The sedan approached the intersection heavily congested with traffic and came to a stop. It was immediately surrounded by gun-wielding agents running in from all directions, weapons drawn and shouting.

Several people in nearby cars, petrified with fear, jumped out into the street and began running from the area, believing it was another typical assassination attempt by drug traffickers. Rosenthal and his assistant, judging by the expressions on their faces of surprise and fear, thought the same thing. For a few seconds, they believed they were going to die. Ironically, he breathed a sigh of relief when he learned he was only being arrested and not the target of a rival drug organization. Several CNP agents took him and his associate into custody and left the area.

We accompanied the remaining CNP to Rosenthal's house to conduct a search for evidence of his drug-trafficking activities. The house was surrounded, with entry made from the front and rear, but it was vacant. Wahl was not at home. We found several kilograms of cocaine in a large, clear plastic bag in a trunk containing numerous porn magazines and sexual devices. After finishing the search, as we left, I watched many of the CNP agents carry out some of the sex toys dangling from their back pockets. The following day, Rosenthal was on his way to the US where he would be facing significant federal charges. The LODI News-Sentinel reported the following:

Lodi News-Sentinel: Huge Drug Ring Uncovered

Federal grand jury indictments were unsealed Monday charging 53 people with smuggling 3.8

billion worth of cocaine into the United States in what authorities said was the largest cocaine ring uncovered in the nation's history. Harold Rosenthal of Atlanta, alleged ringleader of the gang, was accused of trying to arrange the murder of drug agents to avenge his arrest and protect other members of the ring. An intensive undercover investigation by federal, state, local authorities led to the indictments, which charge some 5 tons of cocaine were brought from Colombia into Georgia, Florida, Tennessee, and Pennsylvania in 14 shipments. The indictments in the investigation called "Operation Southern Comfort" were unsealed in Atlanta, Miami, Los Angeles and Little Rock, Arkansas.

U.S. Associate Attorney General D. Lowell Jensen said the probe, in which 2,700 pounds of cocaine was confiscated, uncovered the largest cocaine ring ever. "The federal government has uncovered the largest cocaine-trafficking ring in the nation's history," Jensen said. He estimated the amount of cocaine brought into the country annually at 30 to 60 tons and said, "The ability to identify and charge major rings is a major step in the right direction."

Jensen praised the Colombian government for its help in the investigation. "The Minister of Justice and the Attorney General of Colombia both deserve great credit for their assistance," he said. "We believe it marks the beginning of a new era of cooperation between Colombia and the United States in drug enforcement." The indictment alleged members of the smuggling ring were supported by Bahamian officials who permitted the cocaine to land at the West End airport in the Bahamas.

Rosenthal was serving a 31-year sentence when he escaped from a federal facility in Memphis three years

ago. He allegedly fled to Colombia, where he contacted
drug suppliers and financiers and began assembling
shipments of drugs destined for the U.S. Agents arrested
Rosenthal, last fall, while he was stuck in traffic in
Medellin, Colombia. The indictment accuses Rosenthal
of directing that Colombian and U.S. law enforcement
agents be murdered in retaliation for his arrest and to
prevent other ring members from being arrested.

A few months later, I began preparations for travel to Atlanta for
the criminal trial of Rosenthal and his associates. Two CNP agents
who worked in the wire-intercept center would accompany me. The
damning evidence from the wire on Rosenthal's telephone would be
admitted as evidence at the trial. If a competent authority in a foreign
country authorizes a wire intercept, it can be introduced as evidence in
US courts. The trial finally got underway and was chaotic. There were
over fifty defendants, all represented by separate counsel, in a very large
courtroom filled with tables, each covered with legal files and documents.
Interestingly, Rosenthal and some of his codefendants had crafted a
legal defense claiming they were collecting information on Colombian
subversive organizations for the CIA. They also alleged the agency had
therefore sanctioned their drug-trafficking activities. It was laughable
but their only defense, since it would be impossible to deny involvement
in the cocaine trade. The trial went on for weeks while defense attorneys
subjected us to intense cross-examination, but in the end, everyone,
with the exception of one low-level defendant was convicted. Rosenthal
received a life sentence, and all his other criminal associates were given
long-term prison sentences.

While in Medellin, I became great friends with Colonel Jaime
Ramirez, who headed the counterdrug component for the CNP. He
was a small man, but had a great heart and an enormous sense of
humor. I supported him in developing wire-intercept centers in other
key cities located in northern Colombia. They became highly valuable

assets because they collected significant information about many drug-trafficking organizations, which led to numerous arrests and seizures. Colonel Ramirez knew he was the target of many drug traffickers who had been imprisoned or had their drug loads seized. The assassination attempts intensified after the seizure of the infamous Tranquilandia cocaine processing laboratories in the jungles of Caquetá located about 400 miles southeast of Bogotá.

The huge laboratory complex had been built by the Medellin Cartel, but its primary architect was Rodríguez Gacha. Tranquilandia was comprised of nineteen laboratories with dormitories for lab workers, complete with an electrical system and water supply from the Yari River. The cocaine paste and precursor chemicals were flown in, and the processed cocaine was flown out, using approximately ten airstrips carved out of the jungle specifically for that purpose. The DEA was able to locate the complex by placing tracking devices into a shipment of ether, an essential precursor in the manufacture of cocaine hydrochloride, purchased by a Medellin Cartel associate from a company in New Jersey. It was initially tracked to northern Colombia and then to its final destination in Caquetá.

A joint assault by the CNP and the DEA resulted in the total destruction of the complex and approximately 13.8 metric tons of cocaine, valued at over a billion dollars. As the assault on Tranquilandia was underway, the Medellin Cartel sent emissaries to offer a multimillion-dollar bribe to Colonel Ramirez. He ignored it and followed through with the elimination of the jungle cocaine-processing labs. His fate was sealed with a contract placed on his life and many skilled assassins willing to carry out the assignment.

Despite being marked for death, Ramirez treasured the few moments he could spend with his family, and less than two years after Tranquilandia, as often happens, he became careless with his security. He was traveling on a highway near Medellin with his wife and two young sons, when a red Renault intercepted his white minivan. An assassin in the front passenger seat fired a burst from a machinegun striking Ramirez and injuring his

Ramirez was mortally wounded, causing his van to run off the road. One of the assassins calmly approached the van as Ramirez's wife ran up to him pleading for their lives. The gunman pushed her aside as he fired another burst into the lifeless body of Ramirez. The wife and sons, although wounded, were allowed to live. It was obvious the assassin had been paid or instructed to only kill Ramirez.

The violence in Colombia during my tenure in Medellin was extraordinary. The traffickers inflicted heavy casualties against the CNP, who displayed great courage in carrying out their counterdrug efforts throughout the country. Not only did they have to contend with the powerful drug organizations, but also the subversive organizations operating in the urban and rural areas of the country.

On one occasion, the main column of the left-wing guerrilla organization known as the M-19, headed by its overall leader, Carlos Pizarro, were in need of supplies and medicine. They attacked a small town in southern Colombia being aware they would have to first neutralize a small garrison of CNP. It began in the early evening as the M-19 fired rocket-propelled grenades and automatic weapons at the small building housing the CNP. The battle continued through the night, and in the morning, the structure only had three walls remaining. One wall and the roof were completely obliterated. The walls that remained standing had bullet and shrapnel impacts on every square inch.

When the CNP, all young officers, ran out of ammunition, they removed their uniforms and shredded them, using knives, and then destroyed their weapons so the subversives wouldn't use them. When they surrendered, the M-19 lined them up in their underwear. Pizarro approached them and congratulated them for their courage and valor during the battle. He was impressed and offered them the opportunity to join their ranks. The young lieutenant in charge declined, saying they all came from poor families, but they would not abandon the CNP. Pizarro called for his aide to bring him a piece of paper and a pen. He wrote a receipt for the weapons and uniforms the CNP had destroyed, so they could give it to their superiors. Pizarro walked down the line of CNP officers and shook the hand of each one and left the town untouched. It was a testament to the courage of the CNP, who have fought thousands of battles and given their lives to make Colombia a safer place for all its citizens.

The M-19 later collaborated with drug traffickers waging war against the Colombian government over the extradition treaty with the US, which became effective in 1982. The treaty allowed for the extradition of individuals involved in drug trafficking and money laundering. The traffickers greatly feared removal from their power base. They also knew being convicted in the US meant long prison sentences. As a result, they created a group and called themselves Los Extraditables, headed by Pablo Escobar. They used the media and other tactics, including extortion, bribery, and murder, to threaten politicians and judges to eliminate this legislation. Many went into hiding and ordered their assassins to eliminate anyone who supported the treaty. Killings were wholesale, and people were murdered by merely voicing support of the treaty to the wrong person. The Extraditables began to issue death threats to Colombian Supreme Court judges, demanding they repeal and denounce the extradition treaty. The group publicly stated, *"Preferimos una tumba en Colombia a una carcel en los Estados Unidos"* (We prefer a tomb in Colombia to a jail in the United States).

About three years later, the M-19, at the behest of Escobar and his associates, attacked the Palace of Justice. Between thirty-five and forty guerillas laid siege to the large building housing Colombia's Supreme Court justices. As they entered, the M-19 killed the security guards and building administrator, who was in his office. Immediately, the rebels took three hundred hostages including twenty-four Supreme Court justices and twenty other judges. Once inside, they began inquiring about the Supreme Court justice who was to render the opinion of the court in regard to the constitutionality of the extradition treaty between the United States and Colombia.

After gaining control of the building, they forwarded a recorded communiqué to a local radio station, demanding that Colombian president, Belisario Betancur, come to the building to stand trial by an M-19 tribunal. That was never going to happen, and the M-19 was aware of this, however, their actual intent was to buy time to destroy any documents dealing with extradition. Escobar and other cartel members from Medellin were completely obsessed with the issue, and while they didn't fear their own government, were apprehensive of facing the US judicial system.

Just hours after the M-19 took over the justice building, the Colombian army launched its own assault with armored cars and heavily armed soldiers. There would be no negotiations, so they executed their attack. I was in Bogotá at the time, which quickly became a war zone with no quarter asked for and no quarter given. I heard the pounding of simultaneous explosions, and the rapid chatter of bullets filled the air. Automatic weapons fire and rockets created terror within the local population, and people fled from the area in panic. The army was able to rescue the two hundred hostages being held in the lower three floors of the building, but the M-19 held many others in the upper two, refusing to surrender. The final military assault on the top floors resulted in the deaths of the hostages, and the building caught fire, with clouds of dark smoke escaping through open windows.

In the end, over one hundred were killed, including soldiers, hostages, and the guerillas. It took two days to extinguish the inferno, and over six thousand legal documents were destroyed. The famous Colombian television personality and actress, Virginia Vallejo, said Escobar had admitted to her he had paid the M-19 $2 million to attack the Supreme Court. Vallejo was Escobar's paramour for many years and confided in her. He also told her it was not his intent for the hostages to be killed and blamed those killings on the military.

The Supreme Court raid was one of the bloodiest conflicts between the Colombian government and its long struggle with leftist guerillas. After that raid, the M-19 was crippled with the loss of five important commanders who died in the siege. A total of eleven magistrates died in the assault, which began the violent efforts of the Medellin Cartel in opposing the extradition treaty with the United States. In 1991, the Colombian government banned the extradition of its citizens to the US, because of intimidation tactics by Escobar and his associates, but later reinstated it in 1997. Thousands died over the issue, and the ruthlessness of the Medellin Cartel was never more evident.

Escobar had great financial power but wanted political power as well. He had aspirations of becoming the president of Colombia but didn't understand that, by becoming a politician, he would come under heavy scrutiny. He ran for alternate representative to the Chamber of Representatives of the Colombian Congress for the municipality of Envigado. Escobar conducted an intensive campaign. His slogan was, "Pablo Escobar, a man of the people, a man of action, a man of his word." His hired assassins walked through the crowds carrying large suitcases filled with money to be passed out to every person. Escobar enjoyed playing the role of a Robin Hood.

There was a huge mountain of garbage on the outskirts of Medellin, where hundreds of the city's poorest lived in little huts made from cardboard. They acted as human scavengers for bottles, metal cans, and anything they could sell for pennies. Escobar started an organization called Medellin sin Tigurios (Medellin without Slums). He built hundreds of small homes for these poor souls, and the residential area was named after him.

He also created his own newspaper called *Medellin Civico*, in which he published his acts of charity. He never mentioned the thousands of police officers, judges, politicians, and innocent people he had killed. He was eventually elected with tainted drug money as an alternate representative. Soon he would experience a major conflict with a rising politician named Rodrigo Lara Bonilla, named minister of justice by then President Belisario Betancur.

Lara Bonilla was an outspoken critic of drug traffickers and violence crippling Colombia. He publicly denounced Escobar for who he really was, forcing him to abandon his political position. Escobar was very unforgiving and extremely vindictive. He ordered the killing of Lara la, and the plan to move assassins and weapons from Medellin to Bogotá was set in motion.

These killers studied Lara Bonilla's daily routine and chose to strike when he was most vulnerable. He knew he had been marked for death and traveled with a large security detail. As he left the office one evening, he had a vehicle in front and one behind, acting as shields. All three cars were full of security personnel. As they weaved their way through the winding streets, a motorcycle with two men began to follow the caravan. Suddenly, it accelerated and passed the follow car. It quickly swerved to the left side of the vehicle where Lara Bonilla sat and fired a burst from an Israeli Uzi. Several bullets pierced the thick glass window and struck him in the head and neck. He died instantly and slumped against one of his bodyguards, with blood spilling into the seat and onto the floor. The motorcycle rapidly passed the caravan in anticipation of a pursuit. An attempt to negotiate a sharp turn caused it to overturn, and sparks flew as metal and asphalt made contact. The shooter stood and began to fire at Lara Bonilla's security detail and was killed within seconds. He was seventeen years old, and the driver of the motorcycle was nineteen.

The murder of Lara Bonilla brought about public outrage, and President Betancur declared he was going to begin extraditing drug traffickers to the US in retaliation for the brutal and senseless killing. Carlos Lehder would be the first one on the list. Jorge Ochoa was arrested in Spain as he was attempting to purchase a multimillion-dollar ranch to breed and raise fighting bulls. The United States Government immediately filed an extradition request with the Spanish authorities on drug-trafficking charges. Colombia also filed a request, based on a minor charge of illegal importation of animals into the country. Ochoa was sent to Colombia, where he was soon released.

While in a Spanish jail, Ochoa met a member of the paramilitary terrorist organization known as the ETA (Basque Homeland and Freedom) whose goal is to gain independence for the greater Basque region from Spain. The ETA has terrorized Spain for many years using a common tactic of the indiscriminate use of explosives. Ochoa i[?] him to Colombia when the ETA terrorist was released from prison. He introduced him to Escobar, who realized the Basque terrorist could be an invaluable tool to intimidate the government in a further attempt to get rid of extradition. He could also be used as a weapon against Ochoa's mortal enemies.

Escobar's principal assassin and right-hand man, Jhon Jairo Velásquez, nicknamed Popeye, stated in an interview that his boss was elated the ETA terrorist was an explosives expert. According to Velásquez, in the past they had used less-sophisticated explosives consisting of black powder and dynamite with simple detonation devices. With the assistance of the ETA terrorist, they were able to use remote-controlled bombs secreted in suitcases and vehicles. Velásquez said Ochoa "provided the fuel, but backed away when it would be ignited." In other words, Ochoa didn't have the stomach when it came to wholesale slaughter. He also said Escobar was a master criminal and was pleased with the ETA involvement, which could assist him in expanding his acts of intimidation. The term *narcoterrorist* evolved from Escobar's senseless and massive terrorist attacks against the government, the population, and criminal rivals.

To continue his control, Escobar planned to kill Cesar Gavíria Trujillo who was campaigning for the presidency. He bribed an airlines employee to place a suitcase with a bomb on board Avianca Airlines flight 203, believing that Gavíria would be onboard. The aircraft departed the international airport in Bogotá heading to Cali, when the bomb detonated approximately five minutes into the flight. The explosion cut the aircraft in half and killed all 107 passengers, with two Americans among the dead. Three more people were also killed on the ground by debris falling out of the sky. Dandeny Muñoz Mosquera, another Escobar assassin, was apprehended in Medellin, extradited to the United States to stand trial for the bombing, and received ten consecutive life sentences. Gavíria was a very lucky man, and later became president of Colombia.

Escobar also had an immense hatred for Miguel Maza, the director of Colombia's Administrative Department of Security (DAS), because of his efforts against drug trafficking and support of extradition. A month after the terrorist act involving the bombing of the Avianca aircraft, Escobar began planning the murder of Maza. His assassins parked a truck laden with over a thousand pounds of explosives in front of the DAS headquarters in Bogotá and detonated it remotely, the blast killing fifty-two and wounding another thousand innocents. It leveled several city blocks and completely destroyed over three hundred commercial properties. Maza escaped unharmed; it was the second attempt on his life involving the use of explosives.

Working in Colombia, where the homicide rate and violence in Medellin were astronomical, was extremely dangerous. The assassins hired by the drug traffickers used motorcycles to pursue their victims in heavy traffic, where they pulled alongside their target firing weapons at point-blank range. Motorcycles were favored because they provided maneuverability in areas a car did not have, in the event of being chased. The route I traveled from home to the office was narrow and serpentine. Because it was always late in the evening and very dark when I left the office, I never turned my radio on and kept my windows down in order to hear the sound of an approaching motorcycle. It was a security measure. One night while driving home, I heard a motorcycle quickly approaching from behind. The sound became louder and louder, but I couldn't see it. It did not have its lights on. I began to swerve my car from side to side, making it impossible for whoever was following to pull alongside. As I reached my apartment in a gated area, I swerved into the driveway and began to reach for my pistol when two individuals sped by, ominously looking back at me. The passenger was bent over and appeared to be cradling a weapon on his lap. As a visible DEA agent, I was a target and always at risk.

A friend and lieutenant in the CNP invited me to join him at one of the restaurants in the downtown area of Envigado on a Saturday night. The suburb was where Escobar had spent many of his early years, and the people there were very loyal to him. The town square was full of restaurants, and in the evenings the beat of loud music rolled through the night air. It was an extremely lively area packed with people out for a night of fun and relaxation. We took a table at an outdoor restaurant and ordered a bottle of excellent local rum called Ron Medellin. An hour later, three girls asked if they could join us, because all the tables were taken. They were very attractive and personable, so we bought them dinner and drinks.

In the course of light conversation, I asked one where she worked. The young girl nonchalantly said she was a secretary for a group of assassins who did contract killings. Ironically, she made the comment as though it was a normal and common profession and, here in Medellin, considered a regular and profitable job. As the conversation continued, I probed for more details and specifically about the rates. She explained the assassins charged fifty dollars for a regular person, but the price increased if it were a high-ranking government official. This was the type of depravity that permeated everyday life in Medellin completely driven by the drug trade.

As a result of the violence and crime in Colombia, the CNP, although not officially sanctioned to do so, formed *death squads* to kill drug traffickers and habitual criminals. I knew its members who operated in Medellin, led by Captain Laureano Gómez. One night, the squad captured someone known to have killed seven police officers for money. They determined he needed *special treatment* and wanted to send a strong message to other killers, illustrating their fate if they murdered CNP brethren. The man was bound and gagged and, at three in the morning, taken to a residential area, where he was tied to a large tree. Five sticks of dynamite were tied to his waist. The fuse was lit, and the assassin began to squirm, violently attempting to free himself and to shake the dynamite loose. He looked into the sky for one brief moment as though he knew he was going to meet his maker. The dynamite exploded with such force that his torso was blown onto the roof of a nearby house. His legs shook violently for several seconds and then became still. Windows in many homes were shattered and several cars nearby were damaged by the enormous blast.

Three members of the death squad, including Laureano, were identified and placed under house arrest until they could be tried. The CNP headquarters in Medellin was very large with administrative offices, officer's dormitories, cafeterias, and a bar where officers could congregate. Laureano and the other two members were restricted and could not leave the building, but they were permitted full access to the different areas of their headquarters. Once a week, I would go visit them and have a few drinks at the officers' lounge. We always had a good time and enjoyed each other's company. Working with foreign counterparts was intriguing and provided a different perspective. I did not condone their actions, but understood the motive. It was my choice to work with them.

One evening, the three of them got drunk and went to their dormitories to play Russian roulette. They placed one bullet into Laureano's service revolver and took turns spinning the cylinder containing the hollow point. One by one, they put the barrel to their heads and pulled the trigger. On Laureano's second attempt, the gun exploded violently as the firing pin struck the primer of the bullet, sending the lead projectile through his brain. He died instantly, and sadly, I had lost another good friend.

The CNP death squads continued to operate throughout Colombia. The colonels and generals responsible for the various departments chose whether or not to implement them. It was a risk and understood if you were discovered, your career was finished. On the other hand, they pursued the use of extralegal means to eliminate those who were killing their comrades and innocent citizens. It was a double-edged sword, but many decided it was the means to an end. They also realized the need to closely monitor the activities of these groups, because the killing became easier and could spiral out of control. On one occasion, a member of the death squad had a girlfriend who began dating someone else and enlisted other members of the squad to kill the new boyfriend.

Another member came to my office and brought a copy of that day's local newspaper. On the front page was an article regarding five traffickers who had been executed the previous day. They were found lying on their stomachs alongside each other with a single gunshot wound to the head. On the same page was another article reporting that a CNP lieutenant had been treated at a local hospital for a gunshot wound on his lower back but refused to make any comment on the matter. He told me they had captured the drug traffickers and taken them to a remote area to execute them when one of the traffickers started to run. The lieutenant gave chase but was accidentally shot by one of his own men, who fired at the fleeing criminal. It underscored to me, once again, this was a highly volatile and violent time.

■ ■ ■ ■

The DEA used wire intercepts and informants to collect intelligence to monitor activities of the Medellin traffickers. One of our informants reported he was in contact with a distributor who worked for the Medellin Cartel and indicated he could arrange an introduction. Two days later, I was introduced to Jaime at a downtown restaurant. He was a short, stocky man who walked with a slight limp, which he explained was the result of a gun battle where he had been shot twice in the leg. Going back to a familiar cover story, I told him I was from Mexico and interested in purchasing a twenty-kilogram sample of cocaine, which would be a prelude to larger quantities. I could have asked for a much larger amount, but experience told me that would have required me to have an aircraft or a boat and travel to a trafficker-controlled area where I wouldn't have operational control. Plus, on a large deal, they wanted to see the money and probably demand half in advance. Jaime said he could provide the sample, so we arranged to meet at the parking lot in a local mall for the exchange of money and drugs.

I arranged for a group of CNP to deploy to the mall parking lot in advance, where they would conduct surveillance. The arrest signal would be the removal of my sunglasses, and if they didn't see that, I would hold both hands to my head as a backup. Once surveillance was in place, I drove to the parking lot to wait for Jaime. Half an hour later, he showed up in an expensive gray sedan with three other men. They got out and stood nearby surveying the area as he approached me with a nervous smile. He asked if I had the money and indicated the cocaine was in the trunk of the car. When I asked to see it, Jaime opened the trunk to display a couple of shopping bags filled with kilogram packages of cocaine heavily wrapped in tape. As we began returning to my car, I took off my sunglasses. The CNP moved in quickly to make the arrests. Jaime appeared to be in complete disbelief that he had fallen into an undercover sting. A few weeks after the arrests and seizure, my informant had stopped by a small convenience store when a man entered with a machinegun and fired two bursts. The bullets ripped through his chest, and he was dead before he hit the ground. I suspect the traffickers were able to determine he was an informant and put a contract on his life.

The traffickers had a large and effective intelligence network throughout the country. Their sources included corrupt police, politicians, media representatives, military, judiciary, and ordinary citizens. The situation was so bad, if anyone was foolish enough to ask questions about a drug trafficker, it became a death sentence. One of my informants was able to collect valuable information on family members, criminal associates, and assets acquired by Escobar. He was found on the side of a road near Envigado. He had been brutally beaten, stabbed with knives; needles were driven under his fingernails, and then he'd been shot several times in the head. His face was almost obliterated; he was only identified by the documents found in his pockets. He had a torn piece of cardboard on his chest with a message that said, *"Por ser sapo de la DEA"* (For being a toad of the DEA).

Another informant, who had recently retired from the CNP, left his home early one morning, and as he walked down the street, an armed man approached him from behind. The gunman shot him several times in the back of the head and left him to die in a spreading pool of blood. The killer had an accomplice waiting on a motorcycle nearby enabling him to jump behind the driver and speed away from the area.

■ ■ ■ ■

As is the case in all Latin American countries, soccer—*fútbol*—is the most popular sport. The people are fanatical and completely fill the stadiums to support their favorite team. I often went to games in Medellin and occasionally sat several seats away from Escobar and a group of his closest criminal associates and assassins. They did not know my true identity, because I maintained a low profile, and this allowed me to operate more effectively. Despite his enormous wealth, he was always dressed in blue jeans and an inexpensive shirt that could have been purchased on sale at a bodega. He usually wore a pair of immaculate, white tennis shoes, but never any jewelry. Escobar was not by nature an ostentatious man. The criminals with him were dressed poorly as well and resembled a typical street gang found in one of the poor barrios in the US. Their understated appearance gave no impression they controlled the most powerful cocaine-trafficking organization in the world. While Escobar didn't seem concerned about his dress, he did lavish money on other things.

I visited the huge estate he used as an occasional retreat and had named Hacienda Nápoles (Naples). He had built a large zoo there, opened to the public. Families could drive through any day of the week to observe the exotic animals worth millions of dollars that had been imported from countries around the world. The estate entrance had a small, single-engine aircraft sitting on top of the large archway. It was the first aircraft Escobar had used in smuggling cocaine from Bolivia and Peru. Also on the ranch was a long, paved runway, which could accommodate jet aircraft. The hacienda was huge, with a red tile roof and large columns throughout the exterior. Several man-made lakes surrounded the house, along with a massive swimming pool. Life-sized sculptures of animals and prehistoric dinosaurs also covered the grounds. There was a large bullring that could seat thousands of people, which was a source of diversion and amusement for Escobar. Of the hundreds of ranches and properties he owned, Hacienda Nápoles was the one he treasured the most.

An informant with ties to Escobar provided information on a large cocaine-conversion laboratory located in a warehouse close to the industrial section of Medellin. It was an ideal area for a lab, because it was isolated and little traffic used the single, small dirt road. A day later, after coordinating with the CNP, we raided the warehouse and discovered an enormous lab with a huge supply of precursor chemicals, primarily ether. We also found almost six hundred kilograms of processed cocaine. There were large metal trays under hundreds of heat lamps where cocaine was dried prior to being packaged for shipment. Several plastic bins were in one of the corners and used to mix the coca paste with essential chemicals for conversion into cocaine hydrochloride. A thorough search revealed a hidden escape route through a narrow hole on the side of the building. We surmised that several chemists had squeezed through the hole as we entered the front and rear entrances. These types of labs existed throughout many parts of the country and were capable of producing hundreds of kilograms of cocaine each week.

A little over a year after my arrival in Medellin, two independent sources belonging to the CIA and CNP alerted the US Embassy in Bogota that traffickers had hired a Marxist guerrilla group known as the Ejército de Liberación Nacional (National Liberation Army/ELN) to kidnap me. The independent sources revealed the subversive group had been tracking my movements and even knew my favorite restaurants. There was no question, based on the information from the highly reliable sources, that the ELN was conducting surveillance, particularly on weekends.

They had been operating in Colombia since 1964 and were considered an official Foreign Terrorist Organization by the US State Department, because of their kidnapping activities. The ELN coordinated some of its activities with the larger guerrilla organization, Armed Revolutionary Forces of Colombia, better known by its acronym FARC. Both subversive networks targeted civilians and worked with the most powerful drug organizations in Colombia. These two organizations have carried out numerous violent attacks, kidnappings, and massacres against the general population. Their motto was "the end justifies the means." Eventually, the European Union also designated the ELN as a terrorist organization for its transgressions of humanitarian law. It had no respect for human life and wanted to overthrow the Colombian government. Fabio Vásquez, a Colombian rebel trained by Fidel Castro in the early 1960s, had formed the ELN. Che Guevara, the famed revolutionary who was born and raised in Argentina and later joined Fidel Castro in his overthrow of Fulgencio Batista in Cuba, had inspired it.

The US Ambassador to Colombia, Lewis Tambs, weighed the disturbing intelligence and closed the DEA office in Medellin. The bombing of the Marine barracks in Beirut had recently taken place, and the State Department was now very sensitive to threats on US personnel. It was not about to take any chances that I might be kidnapped and killed, creating another international incident. I was ordered to evacuate Medellin immediately and take over the DEA office in Barranquilla, located on the Colombian north coast.

Prior to leaving, the CNP gave me a charcoal drawing of Icarus from Greek mythology done by one of my close friends. The inscription read, "En la vida se presentan dos o tres ocasiones de ser héroe, pero casi todos los días se presenta la ocasión de no ser cobarde" (In our lives we have two or three occasions to be a hero, but almost every day we have the opportunity not to be a coward). I was truly honored by this kind gesture.

Chapter 13

A Two-Million-Dollar Suitcase

Mike Vigil is a tremendous warrior and a true hero of the United States in the universal war against drugs.
—General Leonardo Gallego Castrillon
Former Director of Colombian
National Police Anti-Drug Forces

I left all of my belongings, including my personal car, in Medellin, taking only two suitcases of clothes to catch a flight to Barranquilla. At the time, I didn't know I would be there for two years. I lived in small hotel rooms, alternating among several, since local drug traffickers owned most of them. My office became my only closet and the closest thing to a stable home.

Barranquilla is the largest industrial city and port in the Colombian Caribbean region. It lies next to the Magdalena River, which is the principal river of Colombia and flows north for about 1,528 kilometers and traverses most of the country. The river is a strategic waterway for drug traffickers smuggling marijuana and cocaine. They also use it to move precursor chemicals, such as ether, into the country for the manufacture of cocaine. The traffickers bribed local officials and the indigenous population along the river to assist them with the transportation of cocaine to staging areas on the Caribbean coast. These *helpers* also acted as security, warning traffickers about police or military forces in the area.

Barranquilla later served as a safe haven for European immigrants, especially during and subsequent to World Wars I and II. Waves of settlers from the Middle East and Asia were well versed and skilled in the smuggling of contraband and quickly shifted to a more lucrative product—illegal drugs—providing their skills and services to both the Medellin and Cali organizations. The north coast of Colombia, principally the northeast, stretching from the Guajira to the Department of Cesar and along the Magdalena River, had experienced significant wealth through what was known as the *marijuana bonanza. Department in Colombia is used to signify a state whereas in the U.S. it indicates a division of an organization.*

Most of the coca paste and base originated in Peru and Bolivia; however, marijuana was a product of Colombia. Unlike the cocaine trade, which was controlled in the hands of only a few, a vast number of north-coast inhabitants reaped the financial benefits of the marijuana trade. The Colombian traffickers, many of Lebanese descent, were responsible for the bonanza. They had been engaged in the smuggling of cigarettes, liquor, and household electrical appliances for many generations. Colombia temporarily became the principal supplier to the US for marijuana, which was appropriately known as Colombian Gold. It was actually *more* valuable than gold and led to the creation of an artificial inflation. Traffickers were paying outrageous sums of money for real estate, driving the property prices out of reach for ordinary citizens. The marijuana boom was driven, in part, as a result of the eradication efforts in Mexico and the Jamaican government destroying a high percentage of its marijuana crops.

The Colombian north coast is strategic for drug traffickers because of its access to both the Caribbean Sea and the Pacific Ocean. It is dotted with clandestine airstrips, international airports, major seaports, rivers, tributaries, and isolated areas along the coast, which are used to facilitate drug smuggling. Traditionally, the cocaine-conversion labs were located to the south, and the processed cocaine transported to northern staging areas by land vehicles, aircraft, and boats. Once there, the drug organizations used associates with boats and airplanes with crews available to move the cocaine farther north, with the principal destination being the US. The Colombian traffickers also contracted pilots from the US and other countries to fly large loads of cocaine through the Caribbean and sometimes used transit countries to refuel prior to arrival in the US, The most commonly used routes were through the Windward Passage between Cuba and Haiti, through the Yucatan Channel between Mexico and Cuba, and through the Mona Passage between the Dominican Republic and Puerto Rico.

While assigned to Barranquilla, I calculated a high percentage of cocaine and marijuana were being smuggled by coastal freighters, go-fast boats, fishing boats, or anything that could float and make its way north. The traffickers, like any commercial enterprise, had to quickly and efficiently move their product into the consumer market, since profit was the ultimate goal. The cocaine was usually hidden in secret compartments or mixed in with legitimate cargo. Because of its bulk, marijuana was placed in the holds of large ships and then offloaded to smaller boats near US waters. Colombian drug traffickers also used an extensive network of aircraft and pilots to transport drugs to the US. These pilots were (and are) highly skilled and acted as true mercenaries. Many had been in the military or worked as commercial pilots. The mobility, speed, and the ability of some aircraft to allow for airdrops made air transport a preferred method and also reliable.

Drug traffickers used airstrips they built in isolated areas, pastures, or roads, as well as international airports to stage their air-smuggling activities. On the Colombian north coast, there were over three hundred clandestine airstrips and at least three commercial airports. Many entrepreneurs built airstrips on their ranches and rented them to drug traffickers. The aircraft of choice had two criteria: cargo and distance capability. They wanted to reach the US or transshipment areas such as Mexico, Jamaica, or the Bahamas. At the same time, they wanted to maximize the amount of drugs on each smuggling operation. Many times, greed overcame logic and common sense, leading to disastrous results. They sometimes overloaded the aircraft with drugs despite the advice of their pilots, resulting in crashes before they even left Colombian airspace. While flying missions in northern Colombia, I saw many trafficker aircraft that had crashed in remote areas. On one trip, I saw three twin-engine planes floating aimlessly in one of the many lakes littering the countryside.

Many drug pilots used devices to increase the distance capability of their aircraft. An apparatus used frequently was a rubber fuel bladder, which was understandably prohibited by federal law. They are extremely dangerous and highly combustible. Traffickers also often placed large fuel cans in the interior of the aircraft and ran rubber hoses into the fuel lines. These tactics made the plane a virtual flying bomb where a mere spark could ignite the extra fuel. Pilots were willing to take the chance, because their pay compensated for the great risks. Furthermore, traffickers paid as high as $50,000 to air-traffic controllers to allow their aircraft coming from the US and other countries to penetrate Colombian airspace without being reported to military or police forces. The money was nothing more than an informal insurance policy. The pilots were the best in the business and used very innovative tactics to avoid getting caught.

They frequently used the US Gulf coast to cross the border, because there was heavy helicopter traffic between the Gulf coast states and hundreds of oil rigs located offshore. When flying drug loads to the US, once they reached the middle of the Gulf, they decreased speed to 120 knots, appearing on radar as a helicopter. About fifty miles from the US coastline, the planes dropped to an altitude of five hundred to a thousand feet in order to blend in with the heavy helicopter traffic and not arouse the suspicions of radar monitors.

Once in US airspace, the pilots traveled inland for a short distance and then landed at clandestine airstrips or conducted an airdrop. Waiting individuals loaded their vehicles and scattered in different directions within minutes. The pilots were usually paid $4,000–$6,000 per kilogram, with the average load being three hundred to four hundred kilograms. On a single smuggling operation, a pilot could make over a million dollars. The risks were high, but the money made it worthwhile. With some, it was not only the money but also the adventure and the thrill of the adrenaline rush. Pilots are often risk-takers by nature, and this cat-and-mouse game was simply one more entertaining risk.

I coordinated numerous investigations with the DEA Miami Field Division involving the use of informant pilots being contracted by Colombian traffickers to fly loads of cocaine into the United States. The informants owned or leased the aircraft used in these activities. They were paid large cash advances, which we called "trafficker-furnished funds." The DEA used the money to pay the informants, and the rest was retained as evidence. The traffickers used the pilots and their planes to transport large amounts of cocaine, usually to the south Florida area, where they had a significant distribution infrastructure.

On many occasions, the informant pilots had difficulty finding the clandestine airstrip at night and would make an emergency landing at the Ernesto Cortissoz International Airport in Barranquilla. They had little choice because they were low on fuel by the time they entered Colombian air space and had only a short window of time to locate the strip. Unfortunately for them, they were promptly taken into custody for not having filed a flight plan and charged with violation of Colombian air space. They were thrown in some of the worst prisons in the world, full of dangerous and homicidal criminals, and constantly endured threats and worse.

It was not unusual for me to receive telephone calls from one of the agents in Miami telling me their informants had been arrested and asking me to get them out of prison. This was a tricky situation, because the governors of each respective department had legal jurisdiction on these types of cases. To complicate things, the local media was quick to report on the incidents and track the cases to determine the outcome. This made the governors wary, because they would indisputably be accused of taking a bribe if the cases against the pilots were summarily dismissed.

Two informant pilots in one situation flew to Colombia, spending considerable time searching for the designated airstrip but couldn't find it. For whatever reason, the traffickers had failed to illuminate their gas-powered lamps for a night landing. The aircraft was running on fumes, and the pilots made an emergency landing at the Barranquilla airport at three in the morning. The CNP arrested them and put them in a local prison that was only slightly better than Devil's Island. Mike Powers, from the DEA office in Tampa, Florida, notified me of the situation less than an hour later. Mike was a good friend of mine, and I knew him to be a great "street agent." The next day, I went to the prison to see the pilots. The other prisoners, who fortunately weren't aware they were informants, targeted them because they were American.

By the time I arrived, they had endured many threats and were already in a state of depression and extremely scared. I explained the situation saying that would require convincing the governor to release them and suppress the story with the press. As expected, the governor was very reluctant, being fully aware he would be accused of corruption and having a nexus to drug trafficking. The scrutiny could cost him his political career. We discussed the situation for hours and settled on something that would work for both of us. I would pay a fine, approximately $6,000, which would allow him to say he had levied a fine for violation of Colombia's sovereignty. Within a few days, the informants were let go, and I escorted them to the airport to get their impounded aircraft. This scenario became repetitive. I forget exactly how many informant pilots were arrested, but I got all of them released.

Because of the high incidence of maritime smuggling, I began a joint operation with the US Coast Guard. My office developed a large informant network whose sole purpose was to collect information on ships, primarily coastal freighters, anchored in the Magdalena River. Drug smuggling on this important waterway had become pervasive, and the DEA knew most ships arrived there to get loaded with drugs, especially marijuana, and once refueled, would travel north to southern Florida or other US destinations.

We used a network of informants who collected daily information on the arrival and departure of ships in the area. They also provided a physical description of the ships, including radar systems, color scheme, name, and number of antennas. We also provided them with cameras to take color photographs. This information and the date of departure was provided to US Coast Guard ships operating in the Caribbean Sea. The photos and descriptions were critical, since the traffickers changed the name of the ship once it was in the open sea. It didn't matter though, because we knew the color scheme and all the other details. As a result of this focused operation, we were averaging about nine seizures every month of hundreds of tons of marijuana, worth billions of dollars. The operation had tremendous impact on the smuggling of drugs from the Magdalena River.

One afternoon while at the office in Barranquilla (located at the US Consulate), the receptionist announced that a man wanted to speak to the agent in charge. The name didn't sound familiar, but I asked her to escort him to my office. He said he had been contracted to participate in a smuggling venture out of the Magdalena River but apparently had gotten into a fight with the captain and been thrown off the ship before it departed. He was very angry, because he needed the money. My first thought was, *What a stupid move on the part of the captain. Why would he kick someone off the ship who might seek revenge by informing on the entire drug activity?* It turned out to be his bad luck and our good fortune. The captain's misjudgment was a fatal mistake.

The accidental informant told us the ship was carrying a hundred tons of marijuana that had been cultivated in the Sierra Nevada mountain range in northern Colombia. He also knew the ship was on its way to Cartagena to load a few commercial items before heading north to the US. He provided the name and a full description of the ship. He also said that Julio Cesar Nasser David ("The Turk") was the trafficker responsible for the smuggling operation.

Nasser David was well-known to the DEA and the CNP as head of a large poly-drug-trafficking organization based on the Colombian north coast. The organization used freighters to smuggle tons of cocaine and marijuana to the US, Freighters offloaded the drug shipments to smaller boats positioned close to the US coast. The Turk's wife, Sheila was also actively involved in the organization's trafficking and money-laundering activities.

After thoroughly debriefing the informant, I contacted CNP lieutenant Jesús Antonio Gómez Méndez and made plans to intercept the ship in Cartagena. Jesús Antonio was an aggressive officer who had exceptional skills in operational tactics. Our friendship became very close and was based on mutual trust and respect. We knew Nasser David was a micromanager when it came to his drug operations and began to check the local hotels in Cartagena, finding him at the Cartagena Hilton.

We needed to focus on locating the ship, so I took a small group of the CNP to Cartagena, which was a little over an hour from Barranquilla by car. On arrival, the CNP used one of their small boats to begin patrolling the bay. They located the ship anchored about half a mile from the coast. They boarded rapidly with no incident, because the crew didn't resist. The holds were full of processed marijuana packaged in thousands of burlap bags. It was a virtual mountain worth hundreds of millions of dollars.

We hadn't forgotten about Nasser David and arrested him in his hotel. The room was filled with equipment he used to communicate with his freighter as it traveled towards the US. He was of Lebanese descent and had begun his criminal career by growing marijuana in the Sierra Madre mountain range. During much of the cultivation season, he lived in a tent next to his fields to supervise the cultivation, harvesting, and processing. He also managed every detail of the mule caravans that transported the marijuana from the cultivation sites to the staging areas along the coast where it would be loaded onto large ships. Nasser David also moved drugs for other organizations if the price was right. He had idly become one of the wealthiest traffickers in Colombia. When we arrested him, he was dressed in upscale clothes that did nothing to hide the fact he was a short, heavy set man with a large nose overshadowing his face. We transported him to the local CNP office to begin an intense interrogation, pressing him on his drug dealing. As we anticipated, he had expected this type of questioning and denied any knowledge of the freighter and marijuana. He explained he was in Cartagena on vacation and wasn't involved in any drug trade. We eventually placed him under the authority of the Colombia judiciary and learned a few days later he had been released.

Years later, Nasser David was again arrested by the CNP a few hundred meters from their installation in the northern section of Barranquilla. At the time of his arrest, he was carrying a Colombian *cédula* (identification card) in the name of Jaime Pérez Pena. By this time, Nasser David and his wife, Sheila, had been indicted in Miami on federal drug charges. She was arrested in Switzerland and eventually extradited to the US. In a plea bargain, she surrendered the family fortune in Europe, amounting to $180 million and was sentenced to twelve years in prison.

Two of Nasser David's drug-trafficking associates were also arrested in the US and forfeited properties and money in various bank accounts. That total amount came to $276 million. In Colombia, the Attorney General's Office seized 270 properties, including the luxurious hotel El Prado, located in Barranquilla.

After serving several years in a Colombian prison, Nasser David died before being extradited to the US, while unknown gunmen assassinated one of his sons, Tito, as he walked from a local gym. Incredibly, Nasser David was responsible for smuggling more than fifty-five thousand pounds of cocaine and three million pounds of marijuana into the US. He died a miserable man and left behind a family who also paid a heavy price for their drug-trafficking activities.

Jesús Antonio later became a general and held several important commands in which he performed exceptionally well. After returning to the US, I found out he had named his son after me. I was truly honored by this gesture.

The work in Barranquilla was very intense and constant, fueled by the information we were receiving from numerous informants. One in particular had an uncanny ability to locate drug stashes from the air, despite the heavy canopy of thick trees in the area. He was a virtual human global-positioning system. He went into very isolated areas, observed the drugs as a potential buyer, and mentally noted the location. The terrain was extremely rugged and difficult to travel. There were no roads and it could only be accessed on foot or by mule.

In one operation, we took several CNP helicopters to the Serranía de Perijá, an area near the Venezuelan border. The range is 58 percent in Venezuela, 42 percent in Colombia, and covered by humid, tropical forests. It has also been an area of conflict between the subversive organization known as Colombia's Armed Revolutionary Forces (FARC) and the Colombian government, specifically because of its strategic location. It provides an easy escape from the reach of Colombian security forces and rapid access to Venezuela.

As we flew near the Venezuelan border, the tree cover was so thick we couldn't see the ground. The informant pointed to a small valley and yelled over the noise of the helicopter engines, *"Está por allá!"* (It's over there!) The fleet of helicopters circled, and all but one descended and landed on top of a nearby mountain. The helicopter that remained in the air would provide force protection in the event we came under attack. It was equipped with .50-caliber machineguns on each side of the aircraft, which was small comfort, because once we landed we also ran the risk of coming into contact with one of the FARC columns operating in the area.

Once on the ground, fifteen of us, weapons drawn, charged down the mountain into a ravine we needed to cross quickly using the element of surprise. As I plunged through the heavy brush, I slammed into a barbed wire fence hidden underneath. Two wire prongs penetrated deep into my right forearm, shooting severe pain through my entire arm. I warned the approaching CNP about the tangle of barbed wire, which we knocked down, and then ran up the next mountain. As we neared the top, we discovered a small trail and followed it. At the end, we found a *mountain* of processed marijuana packaged in large bags, each weighing about forty pounds. It was neatly stacked and placed on a platform of branches to prevent it from being damaged by water. The cache was over six tons of high-grade cannabis. Two CNP agents returned to the helicopter to retrieve a container of fuel to burn the marijuana on site.

As we waited for the agents to return, a few of us continued to follow a trail full of mule dung, where we found four other caches that were even larger. The marijuana was ready for shipment and had we delayed the assault by a few days, it would have been on the high seas headed to the US consumer market. We poured fuel on each of the marijuana stockpiles and watched as it started to burn with flames and gray smoke rising high into the air. As the fire became hotter, several large rats living underneath came out of the burning marijuana in a crazed drug-induced state, ran in erratic circles, and then underneath again. The smoke drove them wild. The CNP were amused and reflected that people acted even worse when they smoked it. Hours later after the fire died down, we returned to our helicopters having destroyed approximately twenty-eight tons.

It was late at night when we arrived back in Barranquilla. The barbed-wire punctures on my arm were throbbing, and I had to get to a pharmacy quickly. Some were open twenty-four hours, and luckily for me, I was able to find one. I told the older man behind the counter I needed a tetanus shot. He took me to a back room and gave me an injection. I paid him six dollars plus a ten-dollar tip and went on my way. In Latin America, many of the people working at pharmacies have a wide knowledge of medicine and treatment and have become informal doctors. I was exhausted, hot, and dirty when I returned to my hotel room. As I began to take a much-needed shower, I noticed hundreds of small black dots covering my chest. They were ticks. The marijuana we had just destroyed apparently was full of them, and I spent over an hour pulling them off and throwing them in the toilet. By the time I finished, the water was black.

On a separate occasion, we conducted an operation in the Sierra Nevada de Santa Marta mountain range. Reaching an altitude of 5,700 meters above sea level, the mountains are just forty-two kilometers from the Caribbean coast. The highest point makes it the world's most prominent coastal summit. There were six helicopters deployed on this mission. As we approached one of the highest peaks, we flew over a large caravan of mules loaded with large bales of drugs, one bale on each side. There were at least thirty mules being led by ten heavily armed men. They began to fire and then scatter as the helicopters got closer. The mules also began to run in different directions as we landed nearby. We jumped out and secured the area. The CNP were able to round up most of the mules and confirm the bales being transported were marijuana. I took one of the mules, a white one, and used it to climb the steep area in search of other marijuana stockpiles. We found several others hidden by branches we estimated as forty tons.

By the time we torched the marijuana and waited until most of it was burned, a heavy, dense blanket of clouds had begun to cover the area. We had two options: remain overnight in the area and risk a confrontation with a large force of traffickers who knew the terrain, or leave with little to no visibility and take the chance of crashing into one of the surrounding mountains. We opted to leave, even though by now the clouds were so thick, seeing more than five feet in any direction was nearly impossible. Making matters worse, our helicopters did not have radar systems, so we'd be flying blind. As the pilot next to me started the engine, the rotary blades began to hum loudly. He made the sign of the cross, which was normal, but when he did it five times, I knew the situation wasn't good.

We rose slowly and moved forward, the skids brushing lightly against the treetops. The clouds were extremely dense, and I fully expected to die if the helicopter failed to navigate the narrow pass and crash against one of the tall mountains, as some have in the past. Apparently, the pilot was thinking the same thing, as perspiration poured in large trickles down his face. Flying blind took a great deal of skill and a lot of luck. We flew in tight circles, also risking crashing into one of the other helicopters. Unless we found a way out, it was only a matter of minutes before we crashed into one of the mountain peaks or each other. None of us spoke. All eyes darted in every direction looking for a break in the clouds. The radio crackled loudly, and one of the other helicopter pilots yelled with great excitement that he found a small opening. We looked to our right and there it was, a hole where we could see daylight. With the added light, everyone was startled to see we had been flying only a few hundred feet from the side of a mountain. It was a near-death experience that still haunts me to this day. The image flashes in my mind of what appeared to be nothing short of divine intervention. Unquestionably, everyone was ecstatic we had survived. After it was over, we all went to a bar and had some *aguardiente* in celebration of life and out of respect for the great equalizer ... death.

■ ■ ■ ■

Thomas Telles, a close friend of mine, who at the time was the DEA Country Attaché in Panama, called me and confided he had a high-powered informant who was in contact with a major cocaine trafficker based out of Bolivia. He wanted to know if I was willing to do the undercover operation. I was motivated to work the investigation since it would provide me with an opportunity to visit and learn more about Panama.

A week later, I took a short flight from Barranquilla and landed at the Tocumen International Airport in Panama City, the biggest and busiest airport in Central America. Panama City is the capital and largest city in Panama. It has always been the political and administrative center for the country and the hub for international banking and commerce.

The first evening there, and always appreciating good food, I had some of the best ceviche in the world. This traditional dish is raw fish marinated in the juice of fresh limes, essentially cooking it. The other ingredients are cilantro and onion. In Panama, they use *corvina*, a white, sea bass indigenous to most Central American countries. It has a firm texture and tastes like something between a snapper and salmon. I ate very little else during my stay and considered it a true delicacy.

The next day, Tom and I met with the informant in the lobby of the Marriott Hotel, where I was staying, and conducted a thorough debriefing. He had been in communication with a Colombian cocaine trafficker named Julio who acted as an intermediary for a Bolivian who owned and operated several cocaine laboratories in northern Bolivia. He said the Bolivian worked with several of his brothers in the illicit drug business and had become extremely rich. He also advised us the Bolivian was the main supplier for many of the most significant traffickers in the Cali area. The Bolivian transported the cocaine by aircraft, and they returned with bulk cash. Our plan was to have the informant contact Julio and persuade him to travel to Panama for initial negotiations.

A couple of days later, Julio arrived in Panama City. We met with him in a local hotel room we rented for the undercover meeting. I played the role of a Mexican trafficker, and Tom acted as my bodyguard. Julio was obviously skilled in the distribution of drugs and negotiating with other traffickers. He quickly got down to business and asked about the quantity of cocaine I was interested in purchasing. I told him four hundred kilograms, initially, with larger quantities to follow once a certain level of trust was established. He said each kilogram would cost $12,000, but after some haggling, the price dropped to $9,000. *Never accept the initial price, ever.* He indicated he was an intermediary for a powerful Bolivian trafficker named Pili who could provide ton quantities of high-grade cocaine. Pili allegedly purchased coca leaves from numerous farmers, processed them into coca paste, and then eventually into cocaine hydrochloride at several labs he operated in different locations in Bolivia.

As the discussions continued, I eventually convinced him to speak with Pili and encourage him to come to Panama so we could meet and establish an agreement for the continual supply of cocaine. Julio was excited I wanted to purchase large quantities on a regular basis. He, like ny others, was starting to get blinded by his greed. He agreed to contact the partner later that night and ask him to come to Panama.

After ending the undercover negotiations, the informant left with Julio and Tom, and I met with members of the Panamanian Defense Force (PDF) who were working the investigation with us. The primary liaison from the PDF for all DEA activities and operations in Panama was Luis Quiel, who had been placed in that position by Panamanian strongman Manuel Noriega. He was always helpful and provided some of the best members of the PDF to work the ongoing international investigation. Quiel said Noriega had ordered him to work closely with us and provide all necessary support.

Noriega, who controlled the country with an iron fist, was running Panama at the time of the investigation. He was a career soldier who had gained most of his education at a military school in Lima, Peru. He also received intensive training in intelligence and counterintelligence at the US Army base in the Panama Canal Zone, Fort Gulick, and was trained in psychological operations at Fort Bragg, North Carolina. When Omar Torrijos became the *de facto* leader of Panama, he promoted Noriega to lieutenant colonel and appointed him as Chief of Military Intelligence.

In 1983, Noriega solidified his position as the de facto ruler of Panama after Torrijos was killed in a plane crash by promoting himself to full general. He continued to work closely with and was paid by the CIA for information he provided on political issues in the region. His relationship with the CIA was longstanding, and he was a valuable source and ally. He was actually invited to visit CIA headquarters in Langley, Virginia.

I recall the killing of Hugo Spadafora, who publically criticized Noriega and accused him of drug trafficking. Spadafora declared he was returning to Panama in order to oppose Noriega but was captured by a death squad at the border with Costa Rica and decapitated. His head was found in Costa Rica, and the rest of his body in Panama wrapped in a US Postal Service bag. Noriega was in Paris during the murder, but a telephone intercept recorded a conversation between him and his Chiriquí Province commander, Luis Córdoba. Córdoba stated, "We have the rabid dog." Noriega replied, "And what does one do with a dog that has rabies?" Time and circumstances were steadily developing against Noriega and his regime.

The investigation took a dramatic turn when Pili arrived in Panama. Julio called my undercover number telling me his business associate was in town and was eager to meet with us. We arranged a meeting for later that evening in the same hotel room. We had also made arrangements to borrow several millions of dollars from the CIA. They have large amounts of money on hand and can move it quickly around the world as needed. The CIA station chief allowed us to use it to facilitate our investigation. We bought a large beige-colored Samsonite suitcase and stuffed it with the money. The cash was all in hundred-dollar bills stacked neatly together with bank wrappers. It took two of us to lift it bulging with the weight of money.

We drove to the hotel early and borrowed a luggage cart from the doorman. We took the elevator to the third floor and placed the suitcase in the surveillance room where the PDF agents were to take their positions. I locked the suitcase and kept the key. Several hours later, we met with both Julio and Pili in the undercover room. The informant was also there with us, and I could see from the corner of my eye he was nervous, as beads of sweat began to form on his forehead. Julio introduced Pili with great deference. Pili was tall, with a head of thick, wavy hair. He resembled a Latin soap opera star and had several diamond rings on his hands. He was wearing white shoes, black pants, and black shirt. A wide white belt, also in remarkably poor taste, complemented the shoes. You could see him coming from a mile away and only proved to me, yet again, that wealth didn't necessarily correlate with good taste in fashion.

Pili obviously wielded extreme power, as Julio deferred to him and would remain quiet with a mere glance. He boasted about being able to supply ton quantities of cocaine each month and having very large conversion laboratories hidden in different areas in Bolivia and clandestine airstrips constructed near the laboratories to facilitate the movement of cocaine to Colombia. He eventually asked if we had the money to buy the four hundred kilograms. I told him we had several accounts in Panamanian banks with millions of dollars that could quickly be withdrawn. As we continued to talk, Tom left the room and returned pushing the luggage cart and suitcase full of money. Pili was impressed it weighed so much that it had to be moved on a cart. I opened the bag and let Pili look at the millions of dollars. Tom quickly removed the suitcase from the room to avoid a potential rip-off. It had the effect we wanted, because after Pili saw the huge amount of money he was ready to do the deal. Again, greed seems to anesthetize brain cells.

Once he returned to Bolivia, he would send one of his most-trusted financial experts who would be responsible for taking control of the money once the cocaine had been delivered. He explained to us that this person knew what to do with it. In final negotiations, Pili said Julio would continue acting as the intermediary. He would return to Bolivia the next day to prepare the quantity of cocaine that he agreed to deliver to Panama. I told him one of my workers would go to Bolivia in the next few days to coordinate matters. Pili smiled and said that it wasn't a problem and offered to pick him up at the airport and let him stay at one of his ranches. We shook hands, and he and Julio, accompanied by the informant, left the room and were seen leaving the area of the hotel.

The first order of business was to return the money to the CIA and begin to plan an operation that would undoubtedly get much more complicated. In the interim, Tom was able to identify another reliable informant we could send to Bolivia to be with Pili during the critical stages of the operation. He looked like a member of the Beach Boys, with long, wispy hair. We briefed him on his role, warning him to communicate with us on a daily basis once he arrived in Bolivia. He was enthusiastic about traveling there, and three days later, we drove him to the airport, gave him a ticket to La Paz and $3,000 for expenses. We also provided him a reliable cell phone. He didn't have any luggage, and only carried a small bag with a couple of shirts and pants. Two days later, we received his call saying he was safe and had been met at the airport, as promised, by Pili and several of his underlings. He added Pili and his people were busy preparing the four hundred kilograms for transport and promised to call the next day, assuring us he was being treated very well.

We began to coordinate with Quiel and the PDF to find a suitable and remote airstrip to use in the operation. We found an area about a two-hour drive from Panama City. It was remote and surrounded by heavy vegetation and could accommodate most twin-engine aircraft. It wasn't an airstrip as most people would envision, but a flat, dirt field without many potholes. It was a completely believable choice, because the traffickers' pilots were used to landing in these types of fields.

A day later, Pili's financial expert, Roberto, arrived. We picked him up at the airport, took him to the Marriott Hotel, and got him checked into a large suite. He was an older man, but distinguished-looking in his expensive suit. Roberto told us he was from the banking community and would be responsible for laundering the millions of dollars we would provide for the cocaine. He had decided to bring his family to Panama and introduced us to his wife. She was pleasant and gave no indication she was involved in the drug trade.

Problem number one began when the informant, who had made the initial introductions, called and said there was an issue with Roberto. Apparently, he had not only brought his wife, but also his paramour. The wife had caught him going to his girlfriend's room, in the same hotel. Our informant complained that the wife was furious and threatening to call the authorities to tell them about the drug operation. She obviously knew more than I had previously thought, and now it seemed I had to play marriage counselor or referee. I told the informant to bring both Roberto and his wife to my room.

I sat them down for a long conversation. I explained this was not the time to be engaging in marital spats and demanded that Roberto get rid of his mistress or the whole deal was off. Roberto was clearly scared and he stood silent as I continued to lecture him. His wife had a broad smile on her face and was clearly enjoying her husband being shamed. Roberto said he would comply and his wife was satisfied with the outcome. She thanked me profusely and promised not to compromise the deal. Understandably, she was still angry with her husband and asked me to kill him if he continued to see his mistress. They left the room with a truce of some sort, realizing there was more at stake than their marriage. This typifies one of the many sharp turns a situation can take and how undercover agents must be able think incredibly fast and resolve issues on the fly, but still remain *in character*.

Most drug deals don't go smoothly, and this one was no exception. Problem number two came when I got a call from Julio explaining things were delayed because of inclement weather in Bolivia. There were also ongoing police operations in the area where Pili had the cocaine, and they were being very careful. He would call us back in the next two days. The informant with Pili in Bolivia called that evening and confirmed Julio's information.

As promised, Julio called again and told me everything was ready, but that Pili had decided it was too risky to have one of his aircraft transport the cocaine all the way into Panama. He apparently wanted to fly the cocaine into Colombia, where we could retrieve it and move it to Panama ourselves. Problem number three. I had a very heated discussion with Julio, but knew he was not calling the shots and was just passing on the message from Pili. This change would require a complete deviation in plans and strategy.

A few hours later, I spoke with my informant in Bolivia and instructed him to accompany the cocaine when it was transported to Colombia. I also told him it was important for him to obtain the exact geo-coordinates of the location where the cocaine would be temporarily stored. This wasn't an unusual request, since Pili would be expecting us to send one of our planes. We received word from Julio that the cocaine was now in his country in an area south of Bogotá. Within twenty-four hours, the informant we had sent to Bolivia arrived in Panama and informed us the cocaine was being stored in a small, isolated farmhouse.

He also handed me the geo-coordinates written down on a scrap of paper.

With the changing scenario, we were forced to incorporate a third informant into the operation. Problem number four. We selected an individual who was a skilled pilot and owned a twin-engine aircraft but was not a brave soul. Our strategy was to bring the cocaine to Panama and reward the PDF for all their hard work with the seizure and arrests.

We had to regroup to deconflict the operation and ensure another Panamanian agency didn't stumble onto our investigation, causing disastrous consequences. Tom and I met with Nivaldo Madrinan, the head of the Panama secret police known as the National Investigations Department and one of Noriega's most trusted advisors. Madrinan radiated a persona of absolute power. He was friendly and accommodating in support of whatever actions we wanted to undertake. Later, in 1989, when Noriega was indicted in the US by the DEA on drug charges and Operation Just Cause was launched, he and Madrinan sought refuge at the Apostolic Nuncio, the Vatican's de facto embassy in Panama City. Noriega was convicted in the US on drug charges and sentenced to forty years, later reduced to thirty years. Madrinan was tried in Panama and received fifteen years, but has since died as a result of poor health.

Subsequent to making arrangements with the Colombian, we prepared the informant pilot and the other informant ("Beach Boy") who knew where the cocaine was in southern Colombia. Their plane was completely fueled—augmented by a fifty-five gallon drum also filled to reach the amount of fuel required to make the trip to Colombia and back. There would be no fuel available at the location where the cocaine was being stored. We waited with PDF personnel on the side of the runway as the plane started down the airstrip. We watched Beach Boy with the wispy hair seated in the back of the plane, wild eyed, hugging the fuel drum as they accelerated by us. As we stood there, the PDF were all taking bets whether they would clear the trees at the end of the runway. The plane did clear the trees, but by only a few feet. Unfortunately, it then developed mechanical problems and returned less than an hour after it departed. Number five.

We scrapped the idea of bringing the cocaine to Panama. I contacted the CNP in Bogotá and told them I would be sending an informant who could lead them to four hundred kilograms of cocaine. We purchased a ticket for Beach Boy to travel there. Less than a day later, the CNP seized the cocaine left in the old farmhouse occupied by a young woman and her small child. Several men at the farmhouse heard the helicopters and ran from the area. No one was arrested at the site, but the four hundred kilos of cocaine were seized. We let Roberto return to Bolivia where he was arrested with Pili and several others as a result of coordination by the CNP with Bolivian authorities. The CNP arrested Julio and put him in prison for several years.

I was still assigned to Barranquilla, when one of the most tragic incidents in DEA history occurred in Mexico. In 1985, DEA Special Agent Enrique "Kiki" Camarena was kidnapped and then murdered in Guadalajara. The traffickers had tortured Kiki prior to killing him and made tape recordings of the interrogation. The tapes vividly depicted the inhumane torture he endured. A massive global manhunt was initiated to capture his killers that included Miguel Félix Gallardo, Ernesto Fonseca Carrillo, Rafael Caro Quintero, and their Honduran source of supply, Juan Ramón Matta-Ballesteros. The DEA will leave no stone unturned when it comes to one of its own. We began to conduct telephone intercepts around the world in order to locate the traffickers responsible for killing Kiki and one of his informants. We also activated a global network of informants throughout Latin America, the Caribbean, and Europe, who began to provide significant information. As a result, we identified Jaime García, who lived in Cartagena, Colombia, and was a known associate of Matta.

Matta first came to the attention of the DEA in 1970 when he was arrested in possession of fifty-four kilograms of cocaine at the Dulles International Airport, near Washington, DC. He later escaped from the federal prison camp at Eglin Air Force Base in Florida, where he had been serving a three-year sentence for illegal entry into the U[nited] States. He was born to a very poor family in Honduras and became involved in the drug trade when he married Nancy Vásquez from Cali, Colombia. Her family was heavily engaged in the cocaine trade and formed part of the Cali Cartel. Matta became educated in the drug trade by beginning to work as a cocaine chemist and later learned the fundamentals of transportation, distribution, and money laundering. He quickly developed a connection to Mexican traffickers, principally the Guadalajara Cartel led by Miguel Ángel Félix Gallardo, the Mexican Godfather of drug trafficking. It is alleged, although never proven, that Matta had become a friend and business partner of General Policarpo Paz García and had financed the Honduran coup that brought Paz into power. It is also believed he was involved in the Honduran airline SETCO that was used to supply the Contras in Nicaragua with military supplies from 1983 through 1985.

We rented a house across the street from García's residence that was close to the downtown area in Cartagena, where both DEA and CNP agents could conduct surveillance and monitor the movement at the house. Our plan was not to raid the premises until we were absolutely certain Matta was inside. We had a limited view of the home, with an obstructed view of the front door because of the carport. Obviously, we couldn't have anyone standing in front, so one of the agents occasionally walked by on the street to determine whether Matta was there. The vehicles parked at the house had heavily tinted windows, also making it difficult to see the passengers. The occupants never parked on the street and hurriedly left the house to enter their vehicles. Despite our efforts, we still couldn't determine with any certainty if he was actually there.

We initiated a wire on the telephone registered to García's house and intercepted an interesting conversation that provided our first solid clue. García called the housemaid and told her to get everything ready because "el Señor" was coming and everything had to be done. A few days later, we saw a gray SUV leave the house. It traveled to a local hotel, where two heavyset, Hispanic males got in the back seat. We followed the

SUV on CNP motorcycles to a restaurant located a few miles away. The two passengers from the hotel were left at the restaurant and the SUV quickly returned to García's house. Less than a minute later, the SUV left again after someone from the house jumped into the passenger's side. We were still unable to determine if it was Matta because it happened so fast. The vehicle returned to the restaurant and retrieved the same two people who were left there a few minutes earlier. We eventually lost the SUV as it traveled into a densely populated residential area but surmised from surveillance that it was highly likely that Matta was staying at the García residence. It was obvious the person staying at García's didn't want anyone to know. We watched the SUV return to the house, but again, we couldn't determine if one of the passengers was Matta. Being a calculating risk-taker, and based on the suspicious activity, I determined it had to be him.

I spoke with the CNP colonel in Cartagena and requested a force of fifteen officers to conduct an assault. He agreed and piled the officers into two Ford trucks. The colonel almost committed a serious blunder when he parked the vehicles with the uniformed CNP directly in front of the house. If anyone had been looking out to the street, they had ample time to escape. I ran up to the trucks ordering the CNP personnel to cover the back and sides of the house, and like a traffic cop, moved the trucks away from the immediate area. The colonel and I went to the house and banged on the front door. A maid appeared and opened a small window next to the door. I told her we were CNP and had a warrant to search the residence for weapons. She was visibly shaken and began to tremble. I asked her to open the door, but she refused and kept looking to the back of the house. Surprisingly, Matta appeared at the window and asked who we were and what we wanted. I repeated what I had told the maid, and he also refused to open the door, moving away from the window.

I told the colonel we needed to kick down the door, but he wanted to wait. Knowing that waiting would risk the chance Matta would escape, I kicked the door with all my weight close to the doorknob, which is the weakest point. It flew open and knocked the maid, screeching in pain, across the room. I saw Matta fleeing across an open courtyard with a .9

mm pistol in his right hand. As he ran, the weapon was held high and at the ready. He leaped on top of a wall at the rear of the residence and fell between it and another wall, each about five feet high. We determined later he had recently had back surgery, which answered my question at that moment of why he hadn't tried jumping the second wall. He landed on his back, and a quick peek over the side revealed that he was pointing the weapon up, ready to kill whoever came over the wall. I pointed my pistol at him and was seconds away from emptying all the bullets into his miserable body, when he yelled out, *"No dispares!"* (Don't shoot!) He dropped his weapon to the ground, and we pulled him out. He commented he could get out of any prison but not out of a tomb.

Though arrogant, Matta knew he was in a serious situation and was pensive. I knew he was mulling over ideas of somehow gaining his freedom. He sat with me in the same room as many of the CNP brought me documents and other items they thought would be useful as evidence. Matta said, *"Don Miguel, se que ustéd es de la DEA"* (Don Miguel, I know you are from the DEA). He told me neither he nor his *"compadre,"* referring to Miguel Félix Gallardo, had anything to do with the killing of Agent Camarena. He said the marijuana dealer, referring to Caro Quintero, was the one responsible for killing him.

Matta, with great feigned deference, insisted he would not kill a DEA agent, because he knew we would hunt him through the fires of hell. Searching further, we found considerable evidence in his briefcases, including telephone numbers of associates, but failed to locate García, who apparently had left before we arrived. We didn't have anything to charge García with, as it turned out, but it would have been interesting to question him. Matta was quiet for several minutes and then brazenly offered us a $3 million bribe to release him, saying he could have it delivered within twenty minutes. I told him to shove it.

After the search was completed, we took him to the local CNP headquarters to arrange putting him aboard an Avianca flight to Bogotá later that evening. We had a very large convoy to transport Matta to the local airport, which had been completely secured. CNP personnel with long weapons covered all entrances of the facility, and Matta was guarded by at least twenty agents. We positioned him on the aircraft so I could sit directly across the aisle. During the flight, he magnanimously extended his hand and congratulated me for capturing him and reaffirmed that no one else had been able to apprehend him in twenty years. At that specific moment, I felt an enormous sense of accomplishment having apprehended one of the world's most-notorious drug traffickers, who had inflicted incalculable misery and death to others. My thoughts went to Kiki and his family.

We landed in Bogotá, where twenty CNP agents were waiting on the tarmac, armed and on high-alert, ready to transport him to La Picota Prison, which houses the most violent drug traffickers in the country. Several months later, Matta's declaration that he could get out of prison turned out to be accurate. An amazing lesson to be learned is what one can accomplish with enough money. From his cell deep within the walls of the prison, he directed members of his organization to bribe the prison guards with over $4 million. In the dark of night, he literally sauntered out and entered a Mercedes-Benz waiting for him at the front gate. He was driven to the El Dorado Airport to board one of his twin-engine aircraft and left for Honduras. Matta was fully aware that Honduras did not have an extradition treaty with the US. What he did have was an outstanding arrest warrant in Honduras for killing Mario and Maria Ferrari, whose bodies were discovered in a hole on a mountain near Tegucigalpa. Matta quickly paid bribes and the charges were dropped.

While jailed in Honduras, waiting for the double-homicide charges to be dismissed, Matta was asked how he had escaped from the prison in Colombia that was considered the most secure in Latin America. He replied, "Well, the doors were opening as I was passing." A later investigation by Colombian authorities on Matta's escape resulted in the arrests of the guards on duty the night he escaped. A search of their homes revealed bales of money they had received as bribes. It is also interesting to note that Matta once made an offer to then Honduran

President José Azcona del Hoyo to pay the Honduras foreign debt, which was obviously rejected.

After fleeing to his native country, Matta felt he was safe, but the long arm of justice was slowly reaching out to put him on her scales. Negotiations were underway with the Honduran Chief of the Army and high-ranking police officials to allow the US to arrest him. The authorization was finally given, and Matta was arrested as he was returning home from an early-morning workout. He resisted, and seeing his freedom evaporate yet again, was subdued by a stun gun. He was put on a plane and initially taken to the Dominican Republic, then on to New York. The image of Matta leaving the plane with an apple in his hand and a clouded, perplexed expression on his face is still a vivid memory. Within twenty-four hours, he was in the maximum-security prison in Marion, Illinois, which had replaced Alcatraz when it was closed.

The removal of Matta from Honduras provoked major riots, during which at least six people were killed and the US Embassy annex in Tegucigalpa was burned down. As with most significant traffickers, Matta played the role of a Robin Hood, but with the sole purpose of hiding his criminal activities and gaining political favors and protection.

I testified at his lengthy trial in Los Angeles. During the proceedings, considerable evidence was presented including hair samples found in the Guadalajara residence where Camarena was tortured and killed after his abduction outside the US Consulate there. These hair samples matched those of Matta. After both the prosecution and defense rested, a statement from Matta was read to the court that said, "What an irony this is, you are going to sentence a man today for kidnapping as if he were a victimizer, and that man himself [Matta] has been the victim of the most horrendous and illegal kidnapping. I am not asking for mercy from you, but you should be certain that you are going to sentence an innocent man, and that it will be God and your conscience who will have to pay for this."

The federal judge replied, "Amen, thank you," and proceeded to sentence him to three consecutive life sentences.

■ ■ ■ ■

During my visits to Cartagena, I took time to relax and unwind by going to La Boquilla, a poor fishing village located seven kilometers from Cartagena. The village was filled by descendants of African slaves brought there by the Spanish to build fortifications to mine silver and gold. There were no roads leading to the village, and I drove along the seashore with the waves hitting against the side of my vehicle. La Boquilla had thatched-roof structures held up by long wooden poles, and naked children ran along the beach with mangy looking dogs and rather large pigs.

The makeshift structures served as very rustic restaurants where you could enjoy some freshly caught lobster. I felt sorry for the kids and would always give them money, which led the villagers to believe I was a major drug trafficker. Who else gave away money to someone they didn't know? It got to the point where the whole village would come running out when they saw my car approaching. Eventually, they had me baptize many of the infants in the village and I became godfather to over a hundred children in La Boquilla. I came to love the villagers, who treated me like royalty. There is something to be said about humble and sincere people, especially after dealing with violent killers and narcoterrorists.

Chapter 14

Paradise *Cracked*

I worked for and eventually with Mike Vigil for two decades. He never suffered fools gladly and disdained bureaucrats who disguised their risk-aversion behind process. He deftly gamed the system to avoid having to ask permission and never accepted a no from someone who didn't have the authority to say yes. The quintessential maverick who briskly walked a tightrope without a net. A raging bull of a personality and innate leader ... He gathered loyal, drug-warrior followers wherever he served and eventually had amassed a global entourage of would-be conspirators at his service, as this book attests. Count me in that club.

—John Fernandes
DEA Special Agent in Charge
San Diego Division, Senior Executive Service
(Ret.)

After serving in Colombia for three and a half years, I was promoted to Group Supervisor in Miami, Florida, the largest division within the DEA. I was looking forward to returning to the US after serving almost ten consecutive years in Mexico and Colombia. In the 1980s, Miami was one of the most dangerous cities in the world. It was one of the principal gateways for marijuana and cocaine coming from the production areas in merica. Colombia was the primary source country, with direct access to the Caribbean, and Florida acted as a main hub for distribution to other parts of the United States. Miami, in the 1960s and early 1970s, was a sleepy retirement city. With the movement of marijuana and later the tonnage of cocaine into the area, things began to change. Billions of dollars pumped into the economy, built skyscrapers and high-rise commercial and residential buildings, transforming the city. High-end stores and nightclubs changed the face of areas such as Miami Beach, Coconut Grove, Key Biscayne, as construction reached a frenzied level. Drug trafficking played a key role in the development. At one point, it was determined the vast majority of paper currency circulating in the area contained cocaine residue.

In 1979, the Federal Reserve Bank in south Florida reported a cash surplus of $3.2 billion, which at the time represented almost 80 percent of the Federal Reserve System's national cash surplus. The profits initially derived from the marijuana bonanza and later replaced by the cocaine trade were mind-boggling. Individuals were literally walking into Miami banks with boxes and shopping bags full of money. The Medellin Cartel contracted help to launder the millions of dollars that they were generating. The launderers established apartments throughout the city, where they received the large amounts of cash. They had employees counting money all day, every day, stacking it, and preparing deposit slips for different banks. Many banks initially refused to take the money, but others were more than willing to accommodate the drug-trafficking community. In order to compete, many of the holdout banks acquiesced and began to also accept the money that was wire-transferred to Colombia and other destinations.

The traffickers, for the most part, controlled the economy of Miami. Prices of real estate began to skyrocket and exotic-car dealerships began to dot the city. Traffickers called their dealerships of choice asking for luxury cars in a specific color to be delivered to their houses. When they arrived, they paid with shoeboxes full of cash. A multitude of businesses were purchased to assist with the laundering of money. It was almost laughable. In one case, a small clothing store was established that had no parking area for customers, yet recorded millions of dollars in profits each month.

With the prosperity of the cocaine trade also came the typical violence stemming from drug traffickers competing for a larger share of the market. Given the massive profits, the distributors were willing to kill anyone who threatened their empires. Traffickers, informants, law-enforcement personnel, and even ordinary citizens were eliminated if they happened to get in the way. It was a volatile melting pot for different ethnic groups, including Cubans, Colombians, Jamaicans, Dominicans, Haitians, and Canadians. Many within these groups were seeking the American dream, and the quickest way to get there was by engaging in the murky drug world. They were willing to take whatever risks necessary, because the enormous wealth possible through illegal drugs made it worthwhile.

One of the events that triggered a surge of violence in the Miami area was the boatlift from the Cuban port of Mariel, which began in 1977 when relationships between Cuba and the US started to improve. President Carter created what was called an Interest Section in Havana, and Fidel Castro did the same in Washington, DC. Castro agreed to begin releasing political prisoners and allowing Cuban Americans to return to Cuba to visit relatives. But the Carter administration was ridiculously naïve about the intentions of Castro when they created an open policy to all Cuban immigrants.

Immigrants from Cuba were immediately granted refugee status and the rights that went with it. Initially, most people reacted favorably to the refugees, but quickly changed when it was discovered many were criminals and mental patients. Castro had duped the Carter administration by arranging for the inclusion of criminals and the mentally ill among the political and economic refugees in order to rid Cuba of its *undesirables* and to damage the image of all Cuban exiles. Castro publicly announced he "had flushed the toilets of Cuba directly into the United States." Many inhabitants of Miami described the as an invading army, despite the fact that most refugees were decent law-abiding people.

The criminals who came from the port of Mariel created a crime wave in Miami where rapes, assaults, robberies, and homicides skyrocketed. The murder rates continued to double for many years, and the Dade County Coroner's Office resorted to stacking bodies one on top of the other in the morgue. In desperation, they approached the Burger King Corporation seeking a refrigerated truck to store more victims. Families began to arm themselves, and men were giving handguns to their wives and teenage children to carry for protection.

Meanwhile, law-enforcement agencies at all levels were severely undermanned and having great difficulty coping with the situation. A local reporter ran a story about the Miami Police Department's massive hiring campaign. Initially, he wrote, anyone who had used drugs was automatically excluded. Promptly, the criteria dropped to no drug usage in the last ten years, then five years, and then two years. Finally, applicants were being accepted as long as they were not presently under the influence of illegal drugs. The eroding of strict, police selection criteria led to widespread corruption. There were police graduation classes that lost more than half to arrests for criminal activities, primarily drug trafficking and ripping off drug dealers. In the early 1980s, the rule of law in Miami had almost completely disintegrated.

The DEA Miami division had several satellite offices throughout the state of Florida and the Bahamas. The enforcement groups were the principal units for conducting operations and investigating drug-trafficking organizations. I was assigned to the main office in Dade County and given responsibility for enforcement group one. I had exceptional agents including Mark Bumar, Jay Bergman, Al Rollins, Shawn Johnson, Jaime Camacho, Mike Shamas, Art Cash, Tom Scarantino, John Fernandes, Tom Foor, Wendy Lovato, Bobby Martin, Lee Truesdell, Ron Diego, and Mark Cutcliffe. Without question, I had the best enforcement group in the Miami Division. The only other group that came close was the one headed by my close friend, Lou

Pharao, who worked out of the Ft. Lauderdale office. Lou was a highly competent and experienced street agent, who learned the tradecraft on the streets of New York. I respected him, because, like me, he was outspoken and never compromised his integrity to get ahead in his career.

Working in Miami meant little rest and required an enormous amount of effort and commitment on the part of the agents. It was an all-out war against some of the most violent drug organizations in the world. The Colombian traffickers initially used Cuban criminals to handle the distribution of cocaine, but eventually decided they would control all aspects of the drug trade from production, manufacture, and transportation to distribution. The Colombians, through massive violence, rapidly displaced their Cuban associates and sent family members and trusted friends to take over distribution in Miami and other key cities throughout the country. Miami became the cocaine capital of the US, and those who controlled the drug trade in the area were called the Cocaine Cowboys, because their legendary shootouts rivaled those of the Old West. As a result, Miami also became the homicide capital of the US.

It was a problematic time and provided a difficult task for law enforcement. The MO of the various drug-trafficking groups in Miami differed in the way they smuggled drugs. Some preferred to conduct airdrops from twin-engine aircraft, others by landing on clandestine airstrips, but most preferred using a variety of maritime ships. They were strategic and continually developing new and more sophisticated methods to move their drugs into the highly affluent US consumer market.

On one occasion, we received a tip that one group of traffickers was going to use a large rental truck to pick up a significant quantity of cocaine at the Miami International Airport. Allegedly, the cocaine would be arriving as cargo on a Varig Airlines flight from Rio de Janeiro the following day. Our source also provided the license plates of the vehicle being used and the general location of the truck. The information was accurate, and we found it at a local hotel. We made arrangements to conduct a surveillance of the truck, coordinating with the US Customs Cargo Enforcement Team (CET) at the airport.

Our plan included pairing up with Customs agents to facilitate communications on both agencies' radio systems. The following morning, we followed the rental truck to a Varig Airlines warehouse at the airport. Through Customs, we determined the flight from Rio de Janeiro had just landed and Varig personnel were removing cargo from the hold of the DC-10 aircraft. We observed a small cargo train pulling several containers across the tarmac towards the warehouse. The cargo was brought to the rear of the warehouse, and the rental truck was backed up to the front of the building and loading dock. Within minutes, we heard the sound of a large object that had dropped onto something metal and determined that a forklift had unloaded numerous boxes. The rental truck was quickly on the move, and we began to follow. As we continued the surveillance, we began to detect countersurveillance.

We saw the same vehicles as we followed discreetly behind the truck being driven by an older Hispanic man. He began to take evasive maneuvers, but we were able to follow through several winding streets and heavy traffic. The truck drove into an isolated business area and pulled into the front of a long, brick building. A large, silver Mercedes-Benz drove up alongside it and frantically waved the driver of the truck away. The hand gestures of the man in the Mercedes were desperate and wild. The truck immediately backed up and began to move towards a major highway.

Since they had detected surveillance, we conducted a traffic stop, and I questioned the driver, José Machado, a citizen of Uruguay, who indicated his cargo was nothing more than a shipment of shoes. He ultimately provided consent to search the cargo, realizing he was caught. That saved us the time of having to obtain a search warrant. The numerous cardboard boxes all contained kilogram packages of cocaine neatly packaged inside. The total seizure was a little over a ton of pure cocaine, 2,200 pounds to be exact.

At the time, it was the largest seizure of drugs smuggled into the country aboard a regularly scheduled passenger airliner. The Varig flight had originated in Montevideo, Uruguay, but made a stopover in Rio de Janeiro. The traffickers were well aware that cargo coming from countries that are sources for drugs are searched more carefully than those coming from countries that do not produce illegal drugs such as Brazil and Uraguay. It was a common tactic to transship to other areas and then to the US, avoiding intense scrutiny. We seized the Varig aircraft, but it was released when the company agreed to pay a large fine.

The investigation continued for several months, and Varig warehouse employees were interviewed several times. We were able to determine the cocaine was hidden in a container carrying the cadaver of a US citizen who had passed away in Brazil. The warehouse had a camera system that slowly scanned the length of the building. The employees moved the cocaine from one side of the warehouse using a forklift and were able to time the camera in order to avoid being filmed. We arrested several of the airline employees, including Warley da Silva, the person in the Mercedes-Benz who had waved off the driver of the truck. Da Silva was a Brazilian national who had worked for Varig at one time. Seeing an entrepreneurial opportunity, he had turned his attention to compromising other Varig employees in order to assist in the smuggling of cocaine through company aircraft. The investigation was painstaking, but resulted in the dismantling of a significant organization that smuggled huge amounts of cocaine into the US.

Working in Miami was intense, and there were continuous investigative activities or operations taking place. One early morning, I left my house in Coral Springs and got on the Sawgrass Expressway. At a distance, I could see emergency lights flashing from what appeared to be twenty or thirty police cars. As I got closer, I saw a twin-engine aircraft that had landed on the highway just past the tollbooths. The propellers were still turning, but apparently, the pilots had abandoned the aircraft and fled into a large field with tall and thick vegetation to hide in. I was told that the aircraft had been detected by radar as it entered the US and was being pursued by a Department of Customs Blackhawk helicopter. A total of 350 kilograms of cocaine, worth millions of dollars, were found in duffel bags inside the aircraft.

■ ■ ■ ■

In comic relief, the drug trade can also provide some occasional laughs. An old man who lived in a dilapidated trailer in the everglades was arrested for selling cocaine in southern Florida. He was toothless, scraggly haired, very thin, and had obviously seen better days. During the interrogation, he was asked where he had gotten the cocaine. He replied as honestly as he could: that it had been a gift from God. When asked to explain what he meant by "a gift from God," he went on to say he'd been sitting on the porch of his trailer drinking beer one afternoon when two large bales dropped from the sky and landed in his front yard. Obviously, an airdrop of cocaine had taken place, and a geographic miscalculation dropped the bales in his yard. He must have been so drunk that he thought God was blessing him with, of all things, illegal cocaine. God also sent him to prison.

Managing an enforcement group in Miami was rewarding, but making decisions was highly critical, and a wrong call could cost agents their lives. The inability to immediately assess and understand situations during an operation could have fatal consequences. One agent in my group was introduced to a man who said he could provide large amounts of cocaine at a reasonable price. After initial discussions, we agreed to do a *surprise* flash of money. In other words, the trafficker would be shown money without expecting it. Using this tactic, the undercover agent would page another agent, who would drive up in his car and show the money to the trafficker, then leave with the money. This prevented the drug dealer from executing a plan to rob or rip off the undercover agent.

In this instance, the surprise flash went well, and after the meeting, we followed the alleged trafficker, a white male in his early thirties. As we drove, we conducted a license-plate-registration check, which didn't reveal any criminal history. We continued to follow him to the parking lot of a bar, where he met five other white males. I immediately noticed they all had a portion of their shirts sticking out of their pants. This was a warning signal they were carrying weapons. During ongoing counterdrug operations, it was imperative to quickly read a situation and detect a seemingly innocuous detail such as this.

As we maintained surveillance on the group, the undercover agent received a call on his cell phone from the person he had met earlier. The man requested to see the money once again, and I instructed the agent to tell him to get lost. It became obvious they were attempting to structure a robbery from someone they believed was a legitimate dealer of drugs. Many opportunists had moved into Miami to seek their fortunes by ripping off drug dealers. They knew dealers would not report the robberies to the police, so it became a cottage industry in the city.

One of the interesting cases I dealt with in Miami involved boat smuggling. We received information from an informant that a coastal freighter was bringing a large quantity of cocaine into the Miami area. The informant provided a description and name of the freighter with an approximate time frame when it was scheduled to arrive. Later, the informant advised us the Colombian freighter would spend a couple of days on the Miami River before offloading its cargo of cocaine. He also said the entire crew was involved and had knowledge of the smuggling venture.

The Miami River drains out of the everglades and runs through the downtown area. The five-and-a-half-mile-long river flows from the area of the Miami International Airport to Biscayne Bay and for many decades has been a smuggling route for all types of contraband and illegal aliens. Ships using the river were often old and leaked petroleum, causing a nauseating smell of fuel.

We began to coordinate the investigation with the US Coast Guard and provided them with all the relevant information we had developed through our informant. Several days later, the coast guard notified us they had intercepted the freighter in open waters approaching southern

Florida. We were told the ship, along with its twelve-member crew, were being transported to their base in Miami.

We were waiting on the dock in the overbearing heat when it arrived. It was already late in the afternoon. These types of ships have hundreds of locations where large amounts of cocaine can be hidden. Most trafficking organizations hire workers to build secret compartments that are very difficult to locate, so we had many long hours ahead of us. We divided into teams and began the tedious search. The freighter was old and dirty and wreaked in the hot humidity. The wretched smell of petroleum permeated the entire ship. The galley was repulsive with unwashed dishes and utensils, and spoiled food littered the tables and floors. It was a breeding ground for rats and cockroaches. The living quarters were even worse, with soiled clothes and bedding everywhere. It wasn't a pleasant task. The freighter had two large fuel tanks on each side of the ship, and we searched one using long poles that we poked into the murky petroleum. It was beginning to get dark, so we decided to continue the search the following day. The coast guard kept the crewmembers on the ship, since they had no other place to hold them.

Early the following morning, the stench was even worse than the day before, especially the body odor of the crewmembers, which had become almost unbearable. They probably hadn't bathed in weeks and looked like a filthy band of pirates. They were all stripped down to raggedy pants at this point, revealing sun-hardened skin. They truly looked like the cast from the *Pirates of the Caribbean*, and in a way they were, but their treasure was cocaine.

The search continued for many long hours. As the day got hotter, the stench became suffocating. We separated the crew to interrogate them and eventually were able to persuade one to tell us where the cocaine was hidden. During the night, crewmembers had moved the load to the fuel tank already searched, knowing we would not search it twice. It was ingenious on their part. We focused our search there, and fortunately, one of the detained crew volunteered to get into the huge tank to fish out the cocaine with a long stick. It was packaged in kilogram bricks, wrapped with thick plastic tape to prevent the petroleum from damaging the cocaine. The entire seizure came to over three hundred kilograms. Since we could now prove all of the crewmembers had knowledge of and participated in the smuggling of cocaine, the entire crew was arrested and taken into custody.

■ ■ ■ ■

My enforcement group was involved in another investigation of a significant network who wanted to smuggle a large amount of cocaine from Colombia. One of my agents, John Fernandes, met with several of the traffickers who advised him they needed assistance in transporting eight hundred kilograms of cocaine from Colombia into the Miami area. They wanted to hire pilots with the skills to evade radar detection and who also owned a suitable aircraft. We were able to locate two who owned an old, naval Albatross amphibious aircraft we could use in the undercover operation. John acted as the son of the older pilot. The traffickers were elated and decided they wanted the aircraft to land in the waters near the Bahamas. There they would offload to speed boats and move the cocaine into the Miami area. We had no intention of landing in the Caribbean waters, because the situation would be too difficult to control.

I told the two pilots they would be diverting the aircraft to an airstrip in Homestead, Florida. They became apprehensive and said the traffickers would undoubtedly have someone accompany the load as a security measure. Knowing this was most likely the case, I devised a plan for the pilots to purchase two thermoses, and before leaving for Colombia, they were to fill one with coffee and the other with orange juice. I told them to put sleeping tablets in each flask, but to be damned careful not to use a lethal dose. The reason for both was the trafficker providing security on the return flight would undoubtedly like one drink or the other. The idea was to put him to sleep so he wouldn't notice the plane was being diverted until it was too late.

With an armed but sedated trafficker onboard, the pilots felt safer, which gave them more confidence to pull it off. The details began to crystalize as we continued negotiations with the traffickers to tie them into the drug conspiracy. The pilots were told by the traffickers to fly into Aruba and wait until they were instructed to continue onto the north coast of Colombia. Prior to their departure, we coordinated signals and radio frequencies the pilots would use in communicating once they departed Colombia with the cocaine. I also sent one of my agents, Mike Shamas, to Aruba by commercial air, in case the pilots encountered problems and needed help.

Everything was set. The pilots departed Miami and flew to Aruba, which is located twenty-seven kilometers north of the coast of Venezuela and 130 kilometers east of the of the Colombian Guajíra peninsula. A day after they arrived, I received a call from Shamas saying the attorney general there wasn't going to allow the plane to leave, because both pilots had expired licenses and the aircraft didn't have a certificate of airworthiness. Shamas said the AG would allow them to depart only if he received a personal call from the DEA administrator. Not letting a small detail like that derail the operation, I called him, said I was the administrator and would assume full responsibility if the plane crashed in Aruba. It did the trick, and I held my breath the entire time, awaiting word from Shamas that the old, rickety Albatross had safely cleared Aruban airspace.

These were the gambles I took on many occasions to put drug traffickers behind bars. Not everyone was willing to take these risks, but then again, I was not a timid soul. Days later, we received word from the pilots that they were on their way to Homestead with the load of cocaine and a trafficker on board. We contacted the US Customs Service, who launched a Blackhawk helicopter to follow the Albatross as it approached Homestead. My group was in place.

We waited until the plane had landed and taxied to an isolated area of the airstrip. When it stopped, the doors opened, and the first person we saw was the trafficker, slowly swaying and barely able to walk. He was alive, but still heavily sedated, lethargic and completely unaware of what was happening around him. We literally carried him out of the aircraft and loaded him into one of our cars. Once in the backseat, he went back to sleep almost immediately. It took almost forty-eight hours for him to wake up, and when he did, he awoke to his worst nightmare. In the days that followed, we arrested all of the drug traffickers involved. They were tried and given long prison sentences.

■ ■ ■ ■

Crack cocaine was just beginning to be popular in Miami and throughout the US in the 1980s. Drug traffickers had discovered a way to sell a modified version of cocaine hydrochloride to the population of addicts who were seeking an immediate and higher *rush*. Crack is *cocaine base*, one step away from being converted into hydrochloride, the more expensive powder form. The crack dealers in the US received cocaine hydrochloride from Colombia, easily converted it back to cocaine base by a simple technique that involved mixing the hydrochloride with sodium bicarbonate (baking soda), water, and placing it over a heat source. A two-year-old could do the conversion process.

Several years earlier, Colombia had started to suffer from a national epidemic of crack addiction as well. Huge numbers of teenagers were using cocaine base, which they called *bazuko*, and became addicted. Making matters worse, the country was totally unprepared to deal with the addiction problem and didn't have treatment centers or facilities. Many source countries view the illegal drug trade as being a US consumption problem and didn't realize that eventually they too would encounter a significant drug-addiction problem. Drugs don't discriminate.

My group began an investigation on Isaac Hicks, who sold crack cocaine in large quantities throughout Miami. Tom Foor was our case agent who coordinated the investigation with Metro-Dade agents. We began to collect information on the organization headed by Hicks, who was a habitual and career criminal. He was tall, wore an Afro, and had an affinity for flashy jewelry. He had large pendants the size of Western belt buckles, studded with precious stones. One of them had "Mr. Hicks" spelled out in diamonds. He had no intention of keeping a low profile and thought he was invincible.

During an eighteen-month investigation, we executed about twenty search warrants at different residences used by the organization to conduct their trafficking activities. During the searches, drugs, cash and jewelry, as well as several drug ledgers detailing drug transactions were seized. The investigation focused on three houses, including the home of Hicks and his wife, Janet. It was a large, overdone mansion as flashy as he was. One Friday, we watched over three hundred vehicles come and go at the three houses in a three-hour time frame. We executed a search warrant at one, resulting in the seizure of cocaine, packaging materials, cash, and mail addressed to Hicks. Also seized were a rifle, a crossbow, and a fragmentation grenade. As the investigation progressed, we used informants to make undercover purchases and provide valuable information on the organization's activities. Other search warrants resulted in the seizure of more weapons and money.

Hicks and his lieutenants kept ledgers that used a system of color codes and coded notations to record transactions. Different colors corresponded to different quantities of drugs. The investigation against Hicks and his underlings began to solidify. Another search warrant resulted in the seizure of more crack and weapons. But more important, we found a business card in his possession with the same color codes used in a drug ledger seized at another of his houses. He had several sources of supply, and as a result, had become one of the largest crack and cocaine dealers in the Miami area. Like most, he became convinced he was untouchable and could commit criminal acts with impunity. Information developed by different sources indicated Hicks planned to purchase over eighty pounds of cocaine, while another reported seeing over $250,000 stuffed into a large briefcase. The end of the line was near for Hicks and his organization, but he wasn't prepared for what would be final justice.

Surveillance of him and several members of his organization led to the identification of an additional house, where we executed another search warrant. It was cluttered and dirty with trash everywhere, particularly the kitchen. The stove had pots and pans with cocaine residue and was clearly the principal location for the conversion of cocaine into crack. Some of the cocaine had already been converted into the thick and chunky crack. Over twenty-two pounds of cocaine were seized, most of it still in kilogram bricks, with logos on the packages. Other drug ledgers seized indicated the Hicks organization was generating millions of dollars in drug sales each year. Over $33,000 and several weapons were confiscated and close to $500,000 in jewelry. Hicks and members of his organization were arrested and sent to prison, where he learned he had contracted AIDS from his wife and eventually died a horrible death.

In 1990, I was transferred to DEA headquarters in Washington, DC, and assigned to the heroin section, whose responsibility was to support heroin cases throughout the agency. I created Operation Aztec, which served to increase the focus of DEA offices worldwide on the heroin problem. Aztec significantly increased the number of heroin cases in the agency during a time when most of the efforts involved cocaine. My tour in headquarters was very short, because I was promoted to assistant country attaché and sent to Mexico City. I was elated because the assignment would allow me to be involved in field operations again. My greatest reward in the DEA was meeting my wife, Suzanne, who worked in the headquarters graphics section. She assisted the Reagan Administration by developing the well-known JUST SAY NO TO DRUGS campaign promoted extensively by Nancy Reagan. Suzanne created the DEA logo, which has been the proud banner of the agency for over forty years, and a US Postal Service anti-drug-abuse postage stamp.

Several months after I reported to Mexico, I invited her down for a two-week visit. Counterdrug operations are extremely unpredictable, and one was about to make an impact on our time together. We received information from a reliable informant that a DC-6 aircraft would be traveling with a legitimate flight plan from Colombia to the General Juan N. Alvarez International Airport in Acapulco on the Pacific coast. The plane, carrying a load of books, was reported to also be transporting over three hundred kilograms of cocaine. The plan was to airdrop it into the waters off the coast of Mexico. A crew of traffickers in speedboats would retrieve the floating packages and smuggle it inland. Unfortunately, we didn't know the exact time of the illicit operation, nor the location where the cocaine was to be jettisoned into the water. This made it difficult to be proactive and position assets in the area, but we began to closely monitor the daily flight plans destined for Acapulco. Suzanne was staying at the Maria Isabel Sheraton right across the street from the US Embassy. I called her from my office and told her I would see her in about twenty minutes so we could have dinner.

As so often occurs unexpectedly, a few minutes later the MFJP determined the suspect aircraft was headed to Acapulco. We would have a short window of time to intercept it when it landed there. I ran out of the office with one of the Mexican comandantes who was coordinating the operation with me and sped to the Mexico City airport. We called ahead to the pilots of the Learjet, belonging the Mexican attorney general, who were waiting. We jumped into the plane and were given priority for immediate departure. Our flight was short, and as we began our approach to land in Acapulco, the radio traffic from the control tower revealed that the DC-6 was right behind us. On landing, we were met by a large group of MFJP assigned to the area. We waited for less than five minutes and saw the DC-6 land and taxi close to where we were standing. The Mexican police surrounded the plane and pointed AK-47s at the pilots. Five individuals were taken into custody and interrogated on the tarmac, when a search confirmed only packaged books. This meant the load had been dropped into the coastal waters.

Still in my business suit, I accompanied ten MFJP to the local docks, where they commandeered a large fishing boat and placed its captain into service. It was dark as we headed through the bay, which was littered with huge rocks pushing out of the ocean. The captain, who resembled a massive rodent with large teeth and course, spiky hair, ran furiously back and forth along the deck looking for the black rocks to avoid crashing.

We came extremely close to hitting several, and it occurred to me how ironic it would be to survive numerous gun battles only to perish at sea.

The boat moved slowly against each swell, taking over eight hours to reach the area believed to be the airdrop zone. Not realizing how long it would take, the MFJP had not brought any food. Someone in the group produced a large bag of Sanborn's hard candy, each having a raisin in the middle resembling a dead fly. It was the only thing we had, and we fully savored each one. As we searched the waters for any floating bales of cocaine, a US Customs P-3 arrived to provide assistance. They reconnoitered a large area and were unable to detect anything. Before leaving, though, they asked if we needed any other support. I grabbed the radio and jokingly requested an airdrop of food.

After three days at sea, we returned to Acapulco starving. We immediately drove to a hole-in-the wall restaurant and ate everything on the menu. Still in my three-days-at-sea suit, I found a vendor near the beach selling cheap I Love Acapulco t-shirts. I bought several and put one on. One size did not fit all. My suit was beyond help, crumpled, and wet from the spray of the water. We flew back to Mexico City with me feeling bad about having disappeared for three days with Suzanne not knowing what had happened. I knocked on the door, and any anger she may have had went away instantly when she saw how bad I looked. I handed her a bag full of t-shirts hoping to make amends. It worked! She understood the nature of the work and, fortunately, was supportive. Not long after, we were married and embarked on a journey of adventure and intrigue beginning in Mexico.

Chapter 15

From Kilos to Tons

Mike Vigil is a professional in international security matters and an expert in counterdrug operations. He is committed to the development and specialization of complex, security organizations. His knowledge, efforts, experience, and conviction have permitted the creation of better conditions of security in society. He is an obligatory subject-matter expert in the analysis of combating drug trafficking and organized crime.

—Genaro García Luna
Former Cabinet-Level Secretary of
Public Security (SSP) in Mexico

My assignment in Mexico City, the federal district and the capital of Mexico, would be challenging, and now as a midlevel manager my responsibilities would greatly increase. I was pleased to have the opportunity to work in the country's largest city and its most-important political, cultural, educational, and financial center. The population is over twenty-five million people, making it one of the largest cities in the world. It is the eighth richest metropolitan area in the world and has incurred phenomenal growth as well as concomitant environmental and political consequences. By 1980, at least half of the industrial jobs were located in Mexico City. As a result of the uncontrolled growth,

240

the city government could barely maintain basic services. Poor farmers and laborers from the countryside who poured into the city to escape poverty only compounded the city's problems. It is estimated that at least five thousand were arriving in the city each day. Since no housing was available, they took over surrounding lands, creating massive shantytowns that extended as far as the eye could see. This created serious air and water pollution, as well as a sinking city, due to overextraction of ground water.

The drug trafficking in Mexico was flourishing, especially with the demise of some of the more powerful drug lords in Colombia and other South American countries. In the '80s, the United States allocated a significant amount of resources to the Caribbean, then the primary transit zone used to smuggle enormous amounts of drugs into the southeastern part of the US. These resources consisted of aircraft and US Navy ships equipped with sophisticated radar and sensor systems. Those unrelenting attacks on the transportation systems belonging to the Colombians had caused them to shift to Mexico. It was logical that Mexico would become even more prominent in the movement of drugs into the United States; it had a very porous two-thousand-mile border. Also contributing to this situation was the seventy-one-year rule of Mexico by the Institutional Revolutionary Party (PRI). This one-party rule allowed drug-trafficking organizations to grow and become entrenched throughout the country. During that period, the government was centralized, hierarchical, and somewhat tolerant of drug production and trafficking in many regions, especially in the northern part of the country. The effects of widespread corruption created a working relationship between many public officials and the powerful drug traffickers.

In the 1990s, the system began to suffer from instability as the Mexican political power decentralized and the movement toward democratic pluralism began, initially at the local level. It began to move nationwide with the election of President Vicente Fox of the National Action Party (PAN) in 2000. The process of democratization impacted heavily on the balance that had developed between government agencies,

ﬣe Federal Security Directorate, and organized crime. No longer
ᴡᴇʀᴇ many government officials able to ensure the protection of drug
traffickers at the same level and regulate competition among Mexican
trafficking organizations for drug-trafficking routes and geographical
areas (*plazas*). To some extent, the violence during the past ten years is
an attempt by the most powerful trafficking organizations to reestablish
their dominance in different parts of the country.

Many cartels have been severely wounded and crippled by Mexican and
US law-enforcement efforts, leading to major conflict between traffickers
for control of lucrative areas belonging to other criminal groups. As these
organizations began dominating the US drug markets in the 1980s and
1990s, the business became more profitable. This raised the stakes that
also generated the use of wholesale violence to protect and promote market
share. The violent struggle between organizations over strategic routes
and geographic areas reflects those stakes. Many of the most significant
networks are poly-drug, but may specialize in a specific drug. Mexico is a
major producer and supplier of heroin, methamphetamine, and marijuana
and is the most-significant transit for cocaine sold in the US. The poly-drug
nature of these organizations makes them more resilient. They can suffer
drug-and-asset seizures to law-enforcement efforts and easily make up the
losses through the sale of other lucrative drugs.

While in Mexico City, I again had the opportunity to work with
some great agents. Ralph Saucedo, Thomas Telles, Joaquin Legarreta,
my *compadre* Bobby Castillo, Pedro Pena, José Baeza, Bert Flores, Bill
Snyder, Jesse Gutierrez, and Ralph Arroyo were among some of the
best. They were dedicated and experienced agents that formed a strong
nucleus for the complex work required in attacking drug trafficking at
the highest levels. These men were up to the task and highly committed
to dismantling and disrupting the major drug organizations operating
throughout Mexico. This required sacrifice and teamwork. I began to
establish a close, working relationship with our Mexican counterparts,
which wasn't difficult since I knew many of them from my past
assignments along the border and in Hermosillo.

One of my primary counterparts was Mexican Comandante Guillermo González Calderoni, who was operationally capable and commanded respect from all of the Mexican federales. For nearly a decade, Guillermo was one of the highest-ranking commanders in the Mexican Federal Judicial Police and was its top narcotics officer during the administration of President Carlos Salinas de Gortari. He led the operation that resulted in the killing of Pablo Acosta, one of Mexico's most significant drug traffickers. Years later, he also orchestrated the capture of Miguel Félix Gallardo, the godfather of drug trafficking in Mexico.

We jointly managed and coordinated a multiagency operation called the Northern Border Response Force (NBRF). The Mexican government called the operation Halcón (Falcon). Actually, NBRF was a misnomer, because the operation provided geographic coverage to the entire country. We had four Cessna Citation jet aircraft used as interceptors. They were equipped with forward-looking infrared (FLIR) and F-16 radar systems. Two of the aircraft belonged to the US Customs Service and the other two to the Mexican government. US Navy ships along the primary transit zones of the western Caribbean and eastern Pacific provided valuable radar resources. They tracked suspect aircraft heading northbound from South America, primarily from Colombia to destinations in Mexico. Other resources included US Customs P-3s, US Coast Guard aircraft and ships, and fighter aircraft operating out of Southern Command (USSOUTHCOM), which at the time was based in Panama. USSOUTHCOM is one of several geographic combatant commands. Through the US Department of Defense, we were able to obtain over twenty-eight used UH-1H helicopters (Hueys) that were provided to Mexico.

There was an Intelligence Analysis Center (IAC) located in the Embassy that assisted with the collection and dissemination of intelligence and conducted predictive analysis on smuggling operations. Based on information developed on organizations, flight paths, air speed, altitude, and other factors, the IAC could often predict, within fifty miles, where the trafficker aircraft would land. It coordinated all operations with the Joint Interagency Task Force (JIATF) East (now called JIATF South) located in Key West, Florida.

The JIATF is a multiservice, multiagency national task force that conducts counterdrug operations, intelligence fusion, and multisensor correlation to detect, monitor, and hand-off suspected illicit trafficking targets. The 1989 National Defense Authorization Act designated the DOD as the lead agency for the detection and monitoring program targeted against the aerial and maritime traffic attempting to bring drugs into the United States.

Managing the NBRF was complex and required great skill in coordinating operations between US entities and those from Mexico. Initially, there were always issues that erupted and plenty of finger-pointing. The Mexican authorities blamed the US for not having sufficient detection-and-monitoring assets along the transit zones, and the US accused Mexico of not having a viable endgame. In order to make the NBRF a more effective operation, I created a steering committee comprising participating US agencies and, eventually, the Mexican government. The NBRF became highly successful, and coordination between the US and Mexico expanded, which allowed for more impact on the major drug-trafficking organizations smuggling significant quantities of cocaine from Colombia. During the first year of the NBRF, the Mexican and Colombian drug cartels were transporting cocaine aboard twin-engine aircraft primarily to northern Mexico. They left Colombia in the evening hours and landed in Mexico during the early morning. The aircraft were unloaded, refueled, and in the air headed back to Colombia in less than eight minutes. Trafficker ground crews were highly efficient and well armed.

Unfortunately, the UH-IH helicopters we received under the US Department of Defense Drawdown Authority were not the most appropriate. They lacked the speed, lift, and distance capability to be of any significant benefit. We were forced to use fixed-wing aircraft belonging to the Mexican Attorney General's Office (PGR) to conduct what were virtually suicide missions. These planes landed on the clandestine airstrips in hot pursuit of trafficker aircraft in areas infested with armed cartel members protecting their operations. This took some major *cojones,* and we called these aircraft the Flying Coffins. The traffickers normally blocked the airstrips with vehicles or other obstacles to prevent law-enforcement aircraft from landing.

On one occasion, we pursued a suspect aircraft into the state of Michoacán. Once it landed, the traffickers drove a truck onto the field to block the landing of pursuing law-enforcement planes. The PGR King Air made its approach to land at one end of the dirt airstrip and moved down the field at a high rate of speed. The traffickers in the truck waited until the final moment, quickly backed out the way, obviously knowing there would be no survivors, including them, if they continued to block the landing strip. The PGR aircraft narrowly missed the truck by a couple of feet. It was the ultimate game of chicken. We made the arrests and seized 450 kilograms of cocaine and the plane.

We developed a profile for trafficker aircraft coming from the south based on the analysis of numerous air-smuggling activities, which helped us distinguish them from legitimate flights. Traffickers flew at an altitude between eighteen and twenty-one thousand feet, lights out, no flight plan, with fictitious registration numbers. The legitimate registration numbers were removed and fabricated ones placed over them in the event they were seized. This made them difficult to trace. We called them Picassos.

Because I maintained a very close relationship with González Calderoni and other key members of the MFJP, I was always able to obtain authorization to allow US aircraft to enter Mexican airspace in pursuit of a suspect aircraft. It only took one phone call, and the response was always, *"No hay problema, adelante"* (There is no problem, go forward). At times, I was authorized to allow multiple aircraft to fly over Mexico's sovereign airspace. No one could believe I could get this type of permission, since sovereignty issues are extremely sensitive matters, especially to Mexico. Imagine the US authorizing Mexican aircraft to fly into its airspace on an operation. On occasion, the US aircraft pursuing a trafficker aircraft would be dangerously low on fuel, and because of our close relationship I was able to get the MFJP to open an airport in the early morning hours with crews on hand to refuel. I always instructed the US pilots to refuel and leave immediately, because if the local media or oppositional political parties discovered them, it could have resulted in very serious political problems for both Mexico and the US. I highly valued my personal relationships with our Mexican counterparts, because they provided me with many privileges, which I used to expand bilateral operations and investigations.

The NBRF, during the first year, dealt the traffickers severe setbacks as we seized tons of cocaine, numerous aircraft, and made large numbers of arrests. We literally forced them to shift their operations from the northern areas to the southern regions of Mexico. We were involved in NBRF operations almost on a daily basis as the Colombian traffickers began increasing their smuggling operations into Mexico. On many occasions, I went without sleep for three or four days at a time. I would be leaving the embassy in the evening and receive a call that yet another suspect aircraft had been detected and was headed north towards Mexico. Although I had coordinators for these operations, the MFJP felt more comfortable dealing directly with me. I would rush home, have dinner, and coordinate the operation throughout the night until six or seven in the morning the following day; then I'd go to work, only to repeat the process again. As we increased our success rate, the traffickers changed their tactics and began to conduct airdrops over bodies of water; i.e., lakes, rivers, and the Pacific and Caribbean coastlines. Our interceptor aircraft videotaped many of these operations as the large bales, weighing thirty kilograms each, were being thrown out of the planes. Just before the airdrop, they would attach fluorescent light sticks on the cocaine bales, making it easy to retrieve from the water.

One of the mechanisms that greatly assisted the NBRF, was the creation of Mexico's National Intelligence Center, better known by its acronym, CENDRO (Centro de Planeación para el Control de Drogas). CENDRO was a massive undertaking by the government of Mexico.

They selected Jorge Tello Peón, who was highly capable, as its director. He was originally from the Yucatan and an engineer by trade. I assisted Tello Peón in the development of CENDRO as well as a component within the organization named CENDRO 6, which brought together over twenty agencies from the Mexican government. Some of the key players included all branches of the military, federal police, federal highway police, and Customs and Immigration. CENDRO 6 functioned as a national coordination center for operations that facilitated a cohesive working relationship between these agencies on NBRF activities. For example, as we tracked a suspect aircraft, the various representatives would alert their offices in the different states based on the trajectory of the plane. This greatly increased our success rate.

We began to use additional resources including *relocatable-over-the-horizon radar* (ROTHR) to maintain surveillance on aircraft flying at an extremely low altitude of no more than two hundred feet above the water. ROTHR is a unique radar system originally designed to provide tactical warning to military battle-group commanders of air and surface threats at an extended range, allowing time for a responsive engagement. At the time, ROTHR systems were located at Corpus Christi, Texas; Chesapeake, Virginia; and Vieques, Puerto Rico. These systems were put into full-time use for counterdrug surveillance. The ROTHR system in Virginia covers more than 2.2 million square miles of the Caribbean, extending north–south from southern Florida to the north coast of South America, and east–west from the western coast of Central America to the Lesser Antilles. It is a long-range, land-based, wide-area surveillance system that reliably detects aircraft and surface ships off the coastline. It tracks each target's speed, course, and position.

During one operation, we detected a suspect aircraft coming from South America along the eastern Pacific. It was only about two hundred feet above the water. The aircraft was picked up on ROTHR, and as it approached Mexican air space, we lost it on the radar system. One of the pilots of our Cessna Citation aircraft flew an intercept pattern based on the last heading and direction of the aircraft and was able to acquire it on his radar. We followed it to one of the southern Mexican states where it conducted an airdrop into a large lake. CENDRO 6 representatives alerted the military and police in the area, who rapidly responded. They stopped a large truck leaving the scene and discovered over six hundred kilograms of pure cocaine. The success of the operation was part luck, a great deal of skill, and exceptional coordination.

In order to enhance the investigative capability of the NBRF, I developed the First Investigative Special Team (FIST) comprising DEA, MFJP, and ATF agents. This team would deploy to operational sites, once they were stabilized, and exploit all available evidence, such as navigational waypoints of the seized aircraft, radio frequencies, maps, weapons, and other documents. More important, the FIST would obtain serial numbers from various parts of the aircraft. We collaborated with the DEA Phoenix office to trace ownership of seized airplanes through the manufacturers, using the part numbers we provided. The program was called Emerald Clipper.

We determined that the Colombian drug traffickers altered the registration of their planes prior to a smuggling operation in order to conceal any connection to them or their organization. When one of their planes was seized, the Colombians immediately purchased the same type of aircraft, painted it in the same color scheme, and applied the legitimate registration number belonging to the seized aircraft. I named these *replacement* aircraft. This was ingenious on their part. They could bring it into Colombia without paying importation fees while also hiding their criminal activities. Through the NBRF and Emerald Clipper, we provided the Colombian government information on replacement aircraft, leading to the seizure of millions of dollars' worth of trafficker planes.

During one FIST operation, an abandoned electric fuel pump was found near a seized plane. The serial number was traced to a company in Arizona, and the purchaser was quickly identified. He and several others were indicted and sent to prison. They had been involved in smuggling tons of cocaine from Colombia into Mexico and eventually to the US.

The two ATF agents on the FIST, Davy Aguilera and Ismael "Smiley" Rodarte, were great representatives of their agency. Their investigative skills contributed significantly to the NBRF success. We worked well together and supported each other's efforts. I am proud to include them within my circle of close friends.

On another operation, the Mazatlán, Sinaloa, office began investigating several individuals who were planning a large cocaine smuggling venture from Colombia. The Mexican traffickers were seen meeting with a Swedish national who was staying at a local hotel. They were making several trips each day to one of the local docks and boarding two fishing boats called the *Mardoqueo* and the *Daniel Torres*. I traveled to Mazatlán to help coordinate the operation, since it would undoubtedly require NBRF resources.

On arrival, I met with José Menéndez, the resident agent in charge. I knew José from my days in Miami and respected his ability as an investigator and undercover agent. He was tireless, dedicated, and could always be counted on when the chips were down. José briefed me on the situation and reported the two fishing boats had departed several days earlier. They were still conducting surveillance on several of the traffickers who remained in Mazatlán, including the Swede and another person who worked as a bartender at an exclusive restaurant. The descriptions of the *Mardoqueo* and *Daniel Torres* were sent to the JIATF West in Alameda, California.

Within a few days, both ships were located near the Galápagos Islands, a huge staging area for maritime smuggling operations. These famed Pacific islands are part of Ecuador and located about 972 kilometers west of the country. The group consists of fifteen main islands, three smaller islands, and 107 rocks and islets. Drug traffickers loitered in the area as though fishing, to eventually rendezvous with other ships and receive large cargos of cocaine and other drugs.

We received word both ships were headed north along the Central American coastline and were being careful to stay in international waters. A navy ship was tracking the two boats, and within a day, a US Coast Guard cutter had joined the surveillance. I was with José in the downtown area of Mazatlán, coordinating the operation with the MFJP, when I received a telephone call from the commanding admiral of JIATF West. He wanted to intercept the *Mardoqueo* and the *Daniel Torres* as soon as possible, since they were in danger of losing them. I respectfully rejected the idea, because we would end up with nothing more than one load of cocaine and insignificant crewmembers. On the other hand, if the Mexican authorities didn't seize the cocaine, we wouldn't have a case against the key players in Mazatlán.

The admiral warned, "It's on your head then."

I responded by telling him I would take my chances, and hung up. I knew if something went wrong, I would take a huge hit that could negatively impact on my career. As I said before, taking risks didn't bother me, and if I stood on righteous ground, I was willing to make a decision and stand by it.

José and I were at my hotel discussing the evolving operation and planning for all variables—such as the arrests of all individuals involved, the potential transfer of the cocaine to speed boats, and the need for surveillance in sovereign waters—any of which might come into play as we moved forward. We made sure the MFJP in Mazatlán were kept abreast of the operation and that we could count on them to take action when the time came.

My cell phone rang and a representative from JIATF West reported the two fishing boats were rapidly approaching Mexican national waters and the pursuing coast guard cutter would lose them unless they were given permission to enter them. I made an urgent call to Alejandro Alegre, who worked as Tello Peón's deputy, and explained the situation. He replied he would get a response for me in less than twenty minutes. Fifteen minutes later, Alegre called and authorized the coast guard ship to enter Mexican waters. I passed the information rapidly to JIATF West, who seemed incredulous that the Mexican government had given me permission to enter their sovereign waters.

Information during the evening hours flowed between the DEA, MFJP, and JIATF West. The coast guard reported the *Mardoqueo* had anchored a few miles from the coast of Mazatlán and the *Daniel Torres* continued to travel north towards the Sea of Cortez. We alerted the Mexican navy and provided them with a description of the fishing boat. Meantime, the MFJP obtained a small boat and began moving towards the *Mardoqueo*. They eventually reported boarding and taking everyone into custody. In the city of Mazatlán, arrests were being coordinated and executed—including of the Swede, who was detained as he returned to his hotel room.

In the morning, the MFJP comandante came to the DEA office and reported they had been unable to find any cocaine after an exhaustive search. I told the comandante he should focus his interrogation on the bartender who had been identified during the early stages of the investigation. The comandante agreed, returned to the boat, and apparently punched the bartender in the chest. He then immediately pointed to some large and heavy metal plates in the hold of the ship. I hadn't meant for the comandante to interrogate the bartender with that level of enthusiasm, but I had to admit it proved highly effective.

We removed one of the plates and found a small hole that had been cut to allow access to the bowels of the boat. We had one of the smaller MFJP agents squeeze through into the compartment. He stuck his head out saying it was filled with tons of cocaine. Each bale, at twenty kilograms apiece, had been formed to fit perfectly through the hole. It took hours to offload approximately seven tons of cocaine, piling it up like a small mountain on the dock.

Later, the Mexican navy intercepted the *Daniel Torres* close to the state of Sonora. It was brought to Mazatlán, and another seven tons of cocaine were discovered in a large, false compartment in the stern of that ship. The total seizure was worth billions of dollars. We discovered the cocaine belonged to the Cali Cartel headed by Gilberto and Miguel Rodríguez Orejuela. The Mexican government was very proud of the overall results and underscored how great things can be accomplished through international cooperation and some risk-taking.

■ ■ ■ ■

Not everything was serious. One morning at a Country Team meeting in the embassy, the head of the commerce section reported the Mexican government was gravely concerned about the extinction of the sea turtle. He went on for half an hour explaining new laws being implemented to prevent overfishing and impose criminal sanctions. An hour after the meeting, Tom Telles and I decided to visit Rodolfo León Aragón, the director general of the MFJP. León Aragón was commonly known as El Chino (the Chinaman). He was half Chinese and originally from the southern Mexican state of Oaxaca.

We drove to the central offices of the MFJP, a few miles from the embassy on Avenida Reforma. The deep-purple-colored building stood out from the others, reinforcing my opinion that there is very little subtlety in Mexico. We were escorted into León Aragón's office, where he sat with his ostrich cowboy boots propped on top of his desk. Next to him was a large, silver bowl of hardboiled eggs. We watched as he banged each egg on the desk to remove the shell, before devouring it. He offered us some, explaining they were sea-turtle eggs and very healthy. He had at least thirty in the bowl. The irony hit me that after sitting through a lengthy discourse earlier in the morning, I now watched him pop one egg after the other in his mouth with apparently no concern about the demise of the sea turtle. Before leaving, he gave us a container of tamales from Oaxaca. When we returned to the embassy, Tom came to my office and showed me one of the tamales he'd begun eating. He was a little puzzled because the meat was white and full of scales. I told him the tamale looked like it was made with iguana meat. This made him gag, throw it in the garbage can. and rush out of my office. I was just grateful he'd eaten one first and saved me from a Qaxacan culinary experience.

■ ■ ■ ■

The conflict between two powerful drug factions, the Tijuana Cartel headed by the Arellano Félix brothers and the Sinaloa Cartel headed by Joaquín "El Chapo" Guzmán, had escalated into a full-scale war. It was a battle over lucrative geographical areas and control of the drug trade in Mexico. Ramón Arellano Félix hired members of the violent Logan Heights street gang in San Diego to travel with him to

Guadalajara to hunt and kill Guzmán. They were in Guadalajara over a week and had not been able to locate him. Ramón decided to end the operation and was at the airport with his group of assassins waiting for a flight to Tijuana. Many of them were outside of the airport with their weapons, which included AK-47s. They had the appearance of Mexican federal police and were communicating with cell phones and handheld radios.

By sheer coincidence, Guzmán had decided to travel to Puerto Vallarta and headed to the same airport. As he approached in a small sedan, one of the assassins saw him and yelled at the others to alert them. They rapidly began to unlock the safeties of their weapons and focus on Guzmán, while they also scanned the area for his security detail. As they began to prepare for the kill, Cardinal Posadas Ocampo drove into the airport to pick up the Vatican Nuncio in Mexico, Girolamo Prigione, who had meetings planned in Guadalajara.

The cardinal was in a white Mercury Grand Marquis and dressed in black. The assassins, believing he was part of Guzmán's security, began shooting at the cardinal and his driver. He was shot fourteen times in his chest, stomach, and legs. His driver was ripped apart by six rounds from an AK-47. Both men died slumped against one another. Guzmán and his escort, despite a heavy barrage of hot lead, returned fire, and innocent bystanders could be heard screaming as bullets began to explode in every direction. The mayor of Arandas, Jalisco, was also killed as he drove into the airport, when several bullets pierced the windshield of his car, striking him in the face. He died instantly.

Guzmán and a couple of his men raced into the terminal and dove into an opening of one of the baggage conveyer belts giving them access to the runways. They quickly vanished, and airport security could not explain how they had been able to get into one of the most secure areas and get away. In a matter of ten minutes, seven people lay dead, including two of Guzmán's bodyguards. Amid the carnage and chaos, Ramón and his killers were able to board the fight with their weapons and return to Tijuana.

It was never proven, but I'm positive they had false Mexican police credentials, which most traffickers are able to obtain, allowing them to carry weapons onto commercial aircraft. The killing of the cardinal led to many conspiracy theories, most of which claimed the government had killed him because he was going to expose corruption. The truth of the matter is he was at the wrong place at the wrong time.

Many of the Arrellano Félix brothers went into hiding after that tragic incident, and Ramón was killed in a shootout with police in Mazatlán. Benjamin, the patriarch of the cartel, was captured by the Mexican military in Puebla after living under an assumed identity. While in custody, he stated Amado Carrillo Fuentes, known as the Lord of the Skies for his air-smuggling operations, had introduced his brother Ramón to MFJP Director León Aragon. Carrillo told Ramón that León Aragon could be very useful in his ability to travel anywhere in the country without problems. He had been in charge of Mexico's federal police for two years at the time. Allegedly, Ramón and León Aragon had developed a close relationship.

According to Benjamin, shortly after the killing of the cardinal, he received a call from León Aragon urgently requesting a meeting. Benjamin said they met at the Tijuana airport and he was told they were in serious trouble for killing the cardinal. Benjamin responded by saying they weren't responsible. He claimed to be in Tijuana at the time and that his brother Ramón had already boarded the airplane in Guadalajara when the shooting took place. He also said León Aragon told him that, in order to help him, he would need $10 million in cash and six residences where he would execute search warrants. These were needed to create the appearance that operations were being conducted against the Tijuana Cartel to appease the public outcry. Benjamin said he would determine which residences would be provided and address the issue of the money. León Aragon agreed, then made a telephone call to a person he identified as the Attorney General of Mexico Jorge Carpizo MacGregor. Benjamin reported he overheard him say everything had gone well and, after ending the call, that the attorney general had instructed him to move forward with the plan. Benjamin alleges that $10 million was paid and the addresses of six residences were provided. During a meeting with León Aragon sometime later, he told me he had executed several search warrants in Tijuana but was unable to locate any of the Arrellano Félix brothers. What they found was a collection of expensive women's clothing. He said he called the local female federal prosecutor, telling her to take whatever she wanted.

Guzman was captured in 1993 in Guatemala while arranging the logistics for a multi-ton cocaine delivery from Colombia. Soon after his arrest, he was extradited to Mexico where he was sentenced to a twenty-years for drug trafficking. In 2001, he bribed prison guards who smuggled him out of maximum-security prison in Guadalajara known as Puente Grande in a laundry cart. He eluded authorities, despite a bounty of five million dollars, for thirteen years by hiding in the rugged mountains in his home state of Sinaloa. On February 22, 2014, the Mexican marines, with intelligence support from the DEA, Immigration and Customs Enforcement (ICE) and other U.S. agencies, began a series of raids in Culiacan, Sinaloa, on known safe houses used by Guzman. On the raid of one targeted residence, the marines knocked down the reinforced door only to find that Guzman had escaped into a tunnel hidden beneath a bathtub. The tunnel led to the city's drainage system. His close confidants did not have time to escape and were captured. After intense interrogation, they disclosed that he had fled to Mazatlan. The next day, in the early morning hours, the marines kicked down the door to a condominium on the fourth floor of the Miramar beachfront resort and arrested Guzman and one of his body guards. He was still in bed with an AK-47 assault rifle next to him. He did not have a chance to reach for it. His much younger beauty queen wife, Emma Coronel, and his twin daughters, were with him, but were later released.

■ ■ ■ ■

At a Country Team meeting, Ambassador James Jones wanted to focus on US interests in the country. The meeting went on for hours, discussing trade and other economic programs as the top US priorities. Counterdrug efforts were placed as number seven of eight. I argued that it would be a grave mistake not to make drug trafficking a higher priority, because the problem would only worsen and the Mexican drug-trafficking organizations would become more powerful. I presented a strong case and persuaded him to change it, but only to number three on the list. Unfortunately, there were too many competing interests within the embassy and US policy in general. The decision did not adequately recognize how drug trafficking posed a national security threat to Mexico and other countries throughout the world. Its impact was highly corrosive on the political and economic systems of many countries and augmented the recipe for massive corruption. I often reflect on those meetings and wonder if the current situation in Mexico would be as dire today if the entire issue of the drug trade had been made the top priority during those early years.

Instead, the push was for expanded trade between the US and Mexico, creating the North American Free Trade Agreement (NAFTA). The goal of NAFTA was to eliminate barriers to trade and investment between the US, Canada, and Mexico. The implementation of NAFTA brought the immediate elimination of tariffs on more than half of Mexico's exports to the US and more than one-third of those from the US to Mexico. Within ten years of the implementation of the agreement, all US/Mexico tariffs would be eliminated, except for some US agricultural exports to Mexico, which were to be phased out within fifteen years. Most US/Canada trade was already duty free. During the initial negotiations of NAFTA, numerous congressional delegations came to Mexico City on fact-finding missions. One of these delegations met with Mexican President Carlos Salinas de Gortari at Los Pinos, the equivalent to our White House, to discuss final details of the treaty. During the meeting, one of the congressmen told Salinas de Gortari he didn't consider Mexico to be a true democracy, since the PRI had been the only party in power for decades. Salinas de Gortari asked the delegation to accompany him to the Hall of Presidents where he showed them a painting of Benito Juarez, a former president of Mexico and full-blooded Zapotec Indian from the state of Oaxaca. He asked the delegation if the US had ever had a minority as president. Obviously, this happened years before the election of President Obama. There were no further comments from the delegation on the issue of democracy in Mexico.

The NBRF continued to be a success, but began to face difficulty when the most powerful and cunning drug trafficker in the history of Mexico, Amado Carrillo Fuentes with his Colombian sources of supply, began to use French Caravelle and Boeing 727 commercial jet aircraft to transport cocaine into Mexico. The traffickers had become well aware of the NBRF and developed a strategy in an effort to outrun and outgun it. They purchased used aircraft having much greater speed than the NBRF Cessna Citations we were using in Mexico. They removed the seats and would typically place ten to fifteen tons of cocaine onboard. It was late summer when we began to develop information that Amado was in the process of collecting money from his clients so he could send a partial payment to his sources in Colombia. We knew he needed at least $40 million from drug sales in the US—he was expecting a delivery of fifteen tons of cocaine.

Tracking these planes with the intention of making arrests and seizures became a weekly ritual. One evening several weeks later, we detected a large, commercial aircraft approaching Mexico along the western Caribbean. We identified it as a 727 and determined it didn't have a flight plan, making it highly suspicious. One radar system after another tracked it, primarily from US Navy ships positioned strategically along the Central American peninsula. We ordered our aircrews to quickly get into the air and maneuver themselves ahead of the target, based on nothing more than the trajectory. The plane finally slowed its speed and began to descend south of the city of Chihuahua. CENDRO 6 began coordinating with the police and military in the area.

The plane landed in the desert, sending a huge cloud of dust high into the air, which was visible on the sensor systems in one of our Cessna Citations. As soon as the 727 landed, several figures were seen placing railroad ties on the improvised airstrip to prevent the law-enforcement aircraft from also landing. The FLIR system was able to identify over seventy traffickers guarding the area, all carrying long weapons, most likely AK-47s.

The area was remote and security forces were having a difficult time locating access roads. The Policia Federal de Caminos (Federal Highway Police) wrecked four vehicles attempting to drive through the terrain in the dark. In this case, they were fortunate not to have made it to the trafficker-controlled site, because they would have been massacred, being severely outnumbered and outgunned.

The 727 offloaded its cargo of cocaine and replaced it with the $40 million, refueled, and was gone in less than fifteen minutes. This was critical information and showed the traffickers had become very proficient and agile in their air-smuggling operations. We attempted to follow the trucks, but by that time, our aircraft was very low on fuel; we had to discontinue the operation.

Another 727 landed at an airfield used by the Mexican airline TAESA near the town of Lagos de Moreno, in the central state of Jalisco. TAESA employees at the field told Mexican police that drug traffickers waiting for their jet forced the ground crew to light the runway and let the traffickers go after unloading their cargo. TAESA denied its employees were involved in the drug operation. The incident heightened suspicions that cocaine was being moved on planes or airfields used by the airline company founded by Carlos Hank Rohn, the eldest son of one of Mexico's most powerful politicians, Carlos Hank González. There were many allegations of family ties to the drug trade, although they were never proven.

A month later, a Caravelle jet landed on the airstrip of an old mining company near the desert town of Sombrerete, in the north-central state of Zacatecas. As the plane touched down, its landing gear was severely damaged, causing the pilots to abandon it and flee. We were able to coordinate a fast response from the MFJP, who reported seizing two and a half tons of cocaine. Later, we discovered the police had actually stolen most of the load. Days after the operation, US authorities along the border made several seizures of cocaine with the same markings and packaging materials as the ones seized in Sombrerete. An internal investigation by the PGR resulted in the arrests of several Mexican federal agents. Based on previous operations, we surmised that over six tons of cocaine had been on the plane. In five years, the NBRF was responsible for over 140 metric tons of cocaine, hundreds of arrests, and hundreds of millions of dollars in seized aircraft, including their duplicate *replacements* in Colombia.

González Calderoni, one of two top commanders in the MFJP, who had served for ten years, eventually fell from grace in the Mexican government and was accused of corruption. He knew many of the darkest secrets of the Mexican government. He fled his country and came to the US just before he was charged with corruption and the torture of prisoners. González was one of the highest-ranking officials to publicly discuss political espionage conducted by Mexico's PRI governing party. After four years of exile in McAllen, Texas, he began to turn against his old confidants and publically disclosed the murky and dangerous subculture of his domain for more than a decade. He admitted a Mexican drug trafficker was one of his sources and bragged about making large cash payments to Raúl Salinas de Gortari during the presidency of his brother, Carlos Salinas de Gortari. He reported telling the president about these allegations.

His most explosive accusation was that Luis Medrano, a high-ranking member of the Gulf Cartel, confided to him that he had paid Raúl a large sum of money for political assistance in buying two Mexican seaports. Medrano wanted to purchase the state-owned businesses that administered the ports of Salina Cruz, on the southern Pacific coast, and Coatzacoalcos, on the Gulf coast. The deal never materialized, but Raúl negotiated with Medrano and promised to use his influence on the cartel's behalf.

In a meeting with President Salinas, US Ambassador Jones discussed González's allegations: "González has so much bad stuff on your administration that it could bring down your government." The Mexican leader, reportedly, "did not flinch."

González also alleged that Raúl Salinas, director of a food commodities agency, requested he intercept the telephone calls of Cuauhtémoc Cárdenas, the leftist presidential candidate who was challenging his brother for the presidency. González conducted the illegal intercepts and delivered the tapes to Raúl throughout the campaign. Just weeks after he became president, Carlos Salinas sent military troops to arrest Joaquín Hernández Galicia, the powerful boss of the Mexican oil workers union. Javier Coello Trejo, a deputy attorney general, ordered González Calderoni to interrogate Hernández and force him to implicate himself in the stockpiling of illegal arms, by signing a confession. It took fourteen hours of psychological pressure and water-boarding before he signed the confession. His only sin was to allow union members the right to vote as they wished in the 1988 elections that Salinas, the PRI candidate, narrowly won. Hernández was sentenced to thirty-five years in prison.

González also alleged that Coello Trejo ordered him to arrest Miguel Félix Gallardo, Mexico's biggest trafficker, who had eluded capture for many years. The order came just before the US was to certify Mexico's anti-drug cooperation, which could involve economic sanctions or, at the very least, cause a political embarrassment. González asked, "Why do you want to catch him now when you didn't want to arrest him before?" Coello Trejo told him, "The certification is coming."

Félix Gallardo was tracked down in Guadalajara by wiretapping the telephones of family members and associates. He offered $7 million for his release, and when it was refused, he resorted to death threats. González countered by telling Félix Gallardo he would be the one killed if it were disclosed that he had ordered the deaths of close associates who were perceived as threats, information revealed in the wires. After his capture, González was invited to Los Pinos, where President Salinas thanked him and also gave him a bonus of $100,000.

Prior to his leaving for the US, he told me of his plans to live in McAllen, Texas. I warned him it was too close to the border and he'd be an easy target for anyone who wanted to kill him. I asked him to reconsider and go to an area where he could easily hide. He was a close ally of the DEA's, and I did not want him in any danger. He refused to listen and moved to McAllen, where he opened a trucking company. As he was leaving the office of his attorney, accompanied by a friend, a lone gunman casually walked up to his Mercedes-Benz and fired a single bullet through the window. It ended the life of a most-colorful and capable Mexican commander. The well-dressed assassin never glanced at the friend with González and slowly walked away. That homicide has never been solved.

■ ■ ■ ■

One of the principal targets of the DEA in Mexico at the time was Juan García Ábrego, the leader of the Gulf Cartel. García Ábrego began his career as a criminal under the tutelage of his uncle, Juan Nepomuceno Guerra, the head of a criminal organization operating along the US–Mexico border. Guerra mentored his nephew in mastering a wide range of criminal activities, especially drug trafficking. García Ábrego initially began smuggling marijuana into the US and established close ties with Colombian cocaine sources of supply in Cali and began trafficking tons of cocaine, allowing him to amass a fortune. He developed a large organization with trusted associates who specialized in transportation, distribution, money laundering, and security.

As with most criminal organizations, he insulated himself by dealing with only a few principal lieutenants who carried out his orders. His two most trusted underbosses were Óscar Malherbe and Luis Medrano, who carried out orders, including murder, with ruthless efficiency. Medrano and Malherbe enlisted the services of a number of other individuals, including Jaime Rivas Gonzales, Tony Ortiz, Tomas "Gringo" Sanchez, and Juan Ibarra, to transport cocaine into the United States and then smuggle the proceeds into Mexico. García Ábrego didn't have qualms in using violence on anyone who threatened his criminal empire or angered him. A former Mexican police officer, who later became a drug trafficker, had a heated argument with García Ábrego and days later was shot in the back at Guerra's Piedras Negras restaurant. Through time, García Ábrego expanded his political influence by corrupting members of the Mexican police and high-ranking political figures. He negotiated with his Cali sources to get a percentage of the cocaine he was funneling into the US rather than a commission of $1,500 per kilo. That agreement came at the price of guaranteeing all shipments from Colombia to its ultimate destination. If the cocaine shipments were lost or seized, he still paid for them.

García Ábrego used money from his drug operation to purchase large ranches in Soto La Marina, an area south of Matamoros. Malherbe and Medrano arranged for loads of cocaine to be flown to these ranches and from there to Matamoros. García Ábrego began to stockpile tons of cocaine in various warehouses along the US border and smuggle it to various distribution points such as San Antonio, Houston, Dallas, Chicago, New Orleans, Los Angeles, Phoenix, and Oklahoma City. Based on reliable information, the DEA estimated García Ábrego was making hundreds of millions of dollars every year. He began to use his brother Humberto to launder the vast amounts of money and engage in wholesale corruption by bribing government officials. An astute businessman, he attempted to keep violence to a minimum, because it was bad for business. On the other hand, he knew he had to protect his territory from encroaching traffickers wanting control of his drug routes.

A rival drug trafficker, Casimiro Espinoza, unwisely began his move on the Gulf Cartel's area of operation, and García Ábrego ordered his murder. The attempt failed, but he was injured and taken to a local hospital. The next day, several gunmen shot their way into the Raya Clinic, looking to finish the job. In what sounded like a military battle, hundreds of rounds were fired, and several innocent people were killed, including a man and his child, a security guard, and a bedridden woman. Espinoza died the following day as a result of several gunshot wounds inflicted while in his bed. Eventually, García Ábrego was indicted in the US on drug trafficking charges and money laundering. At the time, the Mexican government was not extraditing its citizens, but we were able to locate a birth certificate indicating he was born in Paloma, Texas, making him a US citizen. This made things easier, once he was apprehended, to get him out of Mexico.

The Monterrey DEA office had primary responsibility for the investigation of García Ábrego, and the Mexican government assigned Eduardo Valle Espinosa "El Buho" (The Owl) to work with us on the operation. He was known as the owl because he wore oversized glasses and was short and chubby. Valle had been a student activist, reporter, and author; and was hired by the Mexican Attorney General's office as a consultant on drug-related matters. It was a perplexing assignment, since he knew nothing about this specialized field. Two outstanding agents, José Baeza and Larry Hensley, worked tirelessly on the investigation, but found they couldn't rely on Valle because he was usually drunk. To rectify the situation, I met with René Paz Horta, head of Mexico's National Institute to Combat Drugs (Instituto Nacional para el Combate a las Drogas or INCD) to request that Horacio Brunt Acosta replace Valle.

Brunt was the head of the INCD's intelligence section and a seasoned investigator; I knew we could rely on him to pursue the investigation aggressively. Since I had a good relationship with Paz Horta, he agreed to make the reassignment within a week. Brunt became a strong ally of the DEA, and we began pursuing the upper hierarchy of García Ábrego's organization. We arrested José Luis Sosa Mayorga a.k.a. El Cabezón (Big Head), who coordinated drug flights into Mexico from Colombia, and Adolfo de la Garza a.k.a. The Eraser, one of the Gulf Cartel's principal enforcers. Medrano and Malherbe were also captured, forecasting the end for García Ábrego.

During the manhunt for García Ábrego, a historical event occurred in Mexico. President Ernesto Zedillo, who succeeded Salinas, named an attorney general from the PRI's main opposition party, the National Action Party (PAN). This was the first time in history someone from the PAN had held such a high government post. Antonio Lozano Gracia, the new AG, was young, intelligent, and charismatic. Shortly after he took office, I attended a management conference in Guadalajara with all DEA supervisors in Mexico. I had just finished dinner with Bert Flores, another good agent nurtured on the streets of Chicago, when my cell phone rang.

The caller identified himself as the Executive Secretary of the Attorney General and said Lozano Gracia wished to speak with me. I was a little surprised, because I had never met the new attorney general. A minute later, Lozano Gracia came on the line and told me he knew I was someone who could be trusted and wanted to meet with me as soon as possible. We made arrangements to meet the following week when I returned to Mexico City.

Several days later I went to the main PGR offices. The building was large with more security than Fort Knox. I passed through tight security, which included several searches and metal detectors. One of the many attractive secretaries at a large reception area informed me the attorney general was waiting. She took my passport, gave me a security badge, and escorted me to the office of Lozano Gracia. The AG approached with a large smile on his face and shook my hand profusely. I took an instant liking to him—many attorney generals who came before him were arrogant and nothing more than bureaucrats—he was very down to earth and genuine.

He invited me to sit on one of the large leather sofas and asked if I would like something to drink. I asked for a glass of Teohuacan—that sparkling water that serves several purposes in Mexico. He thanked me for meeting with him, saying he had heard from many members of the PGR and federal police that I was highly trusted and had provided invaluable assistance in developing many of the institutions and operations in Mexico. He explained further he wanted to work closely with the DEA on attacking organized crime in Mexico. He knew he would sooner or later come under attack by PRI members and needed to move quickly in dealing with many issues. He was a man surrounded by many political enemies waiting in the wings to strike. We developed a close relationship based on mutual respect and trust and knowing the realities.

The FBI had agents assigned to foreign countries as liaisons to build relationships with host country security and intelligence agencies, but they were not operational. They exchanged information dealing with counter-intelligence and terrorism. It is a fine line, but they are able to do it through executive order and by U.S. Attorney General Guidelines. In foreign countries, they are referred to as Legal Attaché's The FBI office in Mexico City had a tendency to make allegations against the Mexican counterparts who worked more with the DEA than with their agency, but conveniently ignored allegations of corruption against those counterparts who worked closely with them. Eventually, the FBI began to make accusations that Brunt was being paid $500,000 a month by García Ábrego for protection. If this were true, why would Brunt have arrested the key members of García's organization? It didn't make sense but obviously involved ulterior motives.

The FBI continued with the allegations, finally convincing the US ambassador to take a letter they had authored requesting Lozano Gracia remove Brunt from his position, the position my DEA office had requested he fill. They maintained that "because of corruption," despite lacking a shred of evidence or proof, he be removed. I found out through the ambassador's secretary that he had delivered the letter that day, and I called Lozano Gracia to make an appointment to see him within the hour. During this meeting, I told him it would be a great mistake to remove Brunt, because our joint efforts had destroyed much of the Gulf Cartel's infrastructure. He didn't hesitate and said that, based on my recommendation, he would keep him in his current position. We had a long conversation about his concerns for and dedication to making his country secure from the destructive forces of drug trafficking.

We continued the meticulous tracking of all available leads and information from informants, which led us to a walled ranch house in Villa Juarez just south of Monterrey. For hours, sixteen Mexican agents crouched along the wall while one of them watched the movement in the house. They were tense, because they would have to rely on the element of surprise to ensure their survival. García Ábrego was finally spotted near a window, and the order was given for the assault.

They sprinted towards the house with the only sound being the crunching of gravel against the soles of their boots. The agents could literally hear the pounding of their hearts and took quick short breaths as adrenaline pumped through their bodies. It was dark when they violently crashed through the front door and pushed through with the barrels of their AK-47s pointing straight ahead. The onslaught caught García Ábrego and his two bodyguards by surprise. He ran out of the house into the backyard, brandishing a handgun in his right hand, and dove into a hole, refusing to surrender. He was surrounded.

In the end, common sense prevailed, and he tossed his weapon into the dirt, stood up, hands in air. He had gained weight and appeared tired. Being one of the most wanted fugitives had taken a toll on his health. He had not lost his arrogance, however, and said, "You are all going to be hearing from me." He was smug and probably believed he would soon be released because of his political connections. It was midnight when I called the ambassador to advise him we had captured García Ábrego. My second call was to DEA headquarters, where everyone was ecstatic. After arriving in Mexico City, García Ábrego was shocked he was going to be expelled to the US because of his Texas birth certificate. In a fit of rage, he lost his composure and snarled, "You are all dead men."

The next morning, the ambassador held the daily Country Team meeting. He routinely went around the table counterclockwise, asking each agency head about any significant events that had occurred the day before. I sat at a strategic location, giving me the opportunity to speak before the FBI legal attaché was given his turn. I provided details of García Ábrego's capture and added the operation had been accomplished with Brunt, despite the malicious reporting that had accused him of taking bribes from the drug lord. The FBI legal attaché turned beet red and got the message loud and clear.

A day later, an attorney representing García Ábrego approached Brunt and offered $10 million for his release. It was rejected. During the several days it took to prepare the legal paperwork for his expulsion to the US, I contacted the Houston DEA division to advise them García Ábrego would be transported in a PGR aircraft. I gave them the approximate time of arrival and details regarding his transfer. At the airport, he refused to get into the aircraft and had to be carried onboard. He knew life as he'd known it was over, but he was going to make it difficult to the very end. The small group of DEA agents who arrived at the Houston airport to take him into custody were stunned to find thirty FBI agents all dressed in baseball caps and raid jackets displaying the letters FBI. I was astonished when I saw the front page of *Time* magazine with García Ábrego surrounded by FBI agents. Everyone involved knew who had been responsible for the capture.

During his trial, several former members of the Gulf Cartel testified they had assisted him in smuggling as much as fifty tons of cocaine into the US. In the end, the drug kingpin received eleven life sentences.

Janet Reno, the US attorney general, had developed a close professional relationship with her Mexican counterpart, Lozano Gracia. Reno, in my opinion, was one of the better attorney generals. She was courageous and had the moral integrity to stand up for what was right. She came to Mexico City for meetings with US agencies and also with the Mexican government. Lozano Gracia invited her and several of us to lunch at the Hacienda de los Morales, one of the most spectacular restaurants in Mexico City.

The hacienda formed part of the lands conceded to conquistador Hernán Cortés by the king of Spain. The first mulberry trees were planted there for the production of silkworms and have endured for more than four centuries. The hacienda dates from the sixteenth century and is a magnificent structure which has played host to illustrious visitors throughout its history.

On arrival at the restaurant, we were seated at a large table surrounded by security personnel. I was seated directly across from Ms. Reno. The waiters began to deliver plates filled with corn tortillas, guacamole, and *gusanos* (worms) from the maguey cactus. The large worms were sautéed in soy sauce and are considered a delicacy. Every head turned in her direction to see her reaction. She calmly picked up a tortilla, scooped up a large spoonful of worms, topped it with guacamole and began eating without flinching. She instantaneously earned the respect of all the Mexican dignitaries at the table. The next appetizer was *escamoles*, large ant eggs, which she ate as well. The Mexican officials still talk about Reno and the respect they have for her.

Two years later, President Zedillo removed Lozano Gracia from his position due to nothing more than politics. It was a tragic loss, because he was a dedicated attorney general and a loyal ally of the US, as well as a great patriot of Mexico. In a poll of Mexican journalists, academics, and analysts published by the newspaper *Reforma*, Lozano Gracia ranked fourth among twenty-three senior government officials in terms of his ability to do his job, while President Zedillo ranked eighth.

The DEA continued working in Mexico without many formal restrictions other than our own internal policies and procedures. The Mexican government knew we carried weapons, but was unwilling to give us formal authorization. It would have put our lives in imminent danger to be prohibited from having them. This working arrangement could have drastically changed when four men, who identified themselves as members of the Mexican Judicial Police, abducted Dr. Humberto Álvarez Machaín from his home in Guadalajara. He was the physician who had injected DEA agent Camarena with stimulants to keep him conscious during the brutal interrogation leading to his death several years earlier after being kidnapped. They were not police officers, and the impersonation was a ruse to facilitate the abduction. The men were gruff bounty hunters acting under the direction of the DEA. Machaín was bound, gagged, and driven to a neighboring state, held overnight in a cheap hotel, and in the early morning, forced to board a small, private plane that took him to El Paso, Texas, into the hands of waiting DEA agents.

The DEA had been frustrated by Mexico's failure to arrest Machaín after his earlier indictment in Los Angeles. Statements from several witnesses revealed he was present when Camarena was being subjected to inhumane beatings. We do not take lightly the killing of one of our own and will take great lengths to capture and bring to justice those responsible. As a result, the DEA conceived the plan and paid this group of Mexican nationals to kidnap Machaín and transport him to the US. This clandestine operation aroused Mexican furor and indignation, and even more so when the United States Supreme Court subsequently ruled the abduction did not affect the trial court's jurisdiction to try the case. The US Supreme Court ruled they are not concerned how an individual came before a US court, as long as it did not "shock the moral conscience." This standard would be violated in instances where the individual was tortured, but barring that situation, the fugitives were fair game.

There was a backlash against the DEA when the Mexican government declared it would no longer cooperate in bilateral counterdrug efforts with the US. Weeks later, they reconsidered, but in order to calm the continuing uproar in Mexico, the PGR insisted they would begin imposing rules restricting the activities of DEA agents operating in Mexico. Tello Peón was designated to establish what would become known as the Rules of the Game. I met with him for several weeks to negotiate these rules.

The discussions were long and intense. I fought hard against any major restrictions, because they would have disastrous consequences to our operations in one of the most critical source countries. And worse, other Latin American nations could follow Mexico's lead in hindering our activities. It was a difficult time, and I worked tirelessly on this issue. I respected Peón's situation as well, since he had to contend with serious political fallout. The entire country was expecting the DEA to be seriously curtailed or even expelled. In the end, my close relationship with Tello Peón and many other key contacts within the Mexican government paid off.

The agreed upon *rules* capped the number of agents the DEA had in Mexico to those that existed at the time. This didn't matter to us, because there was no intention to increase personnel in the near future. They designated half a dozen cities where DEA agents could live. This was also not a problem, because they were the locations where we already had agents permanently assigned to US consulates. Another rule was that we pass all useful intelligence to Mexican authorities. Again, not an issue, since this was interpreted as tactical intelligence, which we passed routinely. They also required we notify them of any trips taken to other areas in Mexico, which again was not a severe rule. For anyone not intimately involved in the process or having knowledge of DEA's operations, the Rules of the Game sounded harsh on the surface, a political win for Mexico, but were actually very innocuous. We knew it was in the best interests of both Mexico and the US to continue bilateral efforts. Many years later, Mexico allowed the DEA to open more offices and increase the number of agent personnel.

It is important to maintain a level of perspective on what occurred with Machaín. Had the Mexican government kidnapped an American citizen, regardless of whether he was a criminal, the US would have definitely been more than indignant and applied extremely severe sanctions on Mexico for years. We got a slap on the wrist. In the end, a federal judge in Los Angeles ordered the release of Machaín on a directed verdict of acquittal and did not allow the jury to decide. In other words, he was of the opinion the government had failed to prove its case. The decision shocked everyone, but unfortunately, the die was cast, and nothing could be done. Machaín returned to Mexico and never paid for his involvement in killing of one of our agents. It was a bitter pill to swallow.

One of my objectives in Mexico was to develop innovative strategies to attack the powerful and sophisticated drug-trafficking organizations and get the various Mexican agencies to work together in a cohesive manner. In furtherance of this plan, I met with Adrián Carrera Fuentes, who had replaced León Aragon as the director general of the MFJP. Carrera Fuentes had no police experience. He had been a former warden of a large prison in Mexico City, where he conducted a lucrative business selling food items and favors to prisoners who could afford them. Despite his limited expertise, I was determined to engage him in our mission. I proposed a large-scale operation that required the resources of the Mexican military, federal, state, and municipal police; and federal prosecutors. The operation, lasting several weeks, was designed to seal off entire geographic areas to drug-trafficking organizations. It would initially focus on a single Mexican state and then expand to include multiple states. Carrera Fuentes warmed to the idea and supported the plan. We implemented the initiative in the northern Mexican state of Sonora, and I named it Operation Cobra.

We planned for several weeks, and early one morning, thousands of military and police personnel, equipped with a multitude of armored vehicles, helicopters, and enough weapons to start a small war, rolled into Sonora as most people still slept. They quickly moved into predesignated positions and established roadblocks at chokepoints on all major roads leading into and out of the state. Roving patrols covered the areas with no established roads but could be navigated by land vehicle. The army conducted surveillance on clandestine airstrips to prevent their use by drug traffickers. Police personnel were provided with information on known-trafficker residences, warehouses, and ranches, which would be raided. We also used US Customs Service P-3 aircraft to fly along the border in an effort to detect trafficker planes landing in Mexico close to the US border.

A command center was established at one of the local MFJP offices, providing necessary communication and coordination between the military and the police. The center would also be responsible for sending additional personnel to critical events, and helicopters were made available for this purpose. The entire operation sealed off the state of Sonora, and nothing moved through the area without us knowing about it. Numerous seizures and arrests were reported by both the military and police, but the true success story was in the coordination and collaborative efforts by the principal Mexican security agencies towards a common objective. President Salinas de Gortari was so impressed by the operation and its results that he offered it to other state governors, where operations were also highly successful.

■ ■ ■ ■

Each year, the DEA participated in the International Drug Enforcement Conference (IDEC) initiated in 1983. Originally, the IDEC only included Mexico, Central and South America, and the Caribbean. The country hosting IDEC assumes the presidency of the conference, while the DEA administrator is the permanent copresident. The conference usually has one or two representatives from each country.

During IDEC, the representatives exchange ideas and are then divided into regional groups to discuss issues of mutual importance. The first few conferences I attended seemed to lack operational focus by those in the DEA who helped organize it. When the regional groups were formed, the foreign counterparts were provided a list of general operational goals—for example, impede the movement of precursor chemicals to drug-trafficking organizations. The DEA policy dictated that its representatives couldn't participate and were to act as silent observers. I didn't agree because it was demeaning for the counterparts to be spoon-fed counterdrug strategy for their respective countries. I also thought it prohibited bilateral planning necessary for successful operations and initiatives between participating countries. As a result, the police officials in the working groups suddenly became attorneys arguing over using "shall" instead of "will." Eventually, I had an opportunity to change the culture of the IDECs when I attended one with Enrique Arenal, the head of intelligence for the MFJP who also worked for Adrián Carrera Fuentes.

During the first day of the conference, Arenal told me he wanted to be the secretary of the IDEC, a prestigious and coveted position. I had solid rapport with the high-ranking police representatives from the countries that attended IDEC and met with the officials from Panama and Costa Rica. I asked Panama to quickly nominate Arenal when it came time to elect the secretary. I told the representative from Costa Rica to second the motion before anyone could recommend anyone else. Arenal was made secretary, giving me the platform to change the back-slapping, hand-shaking nature of IDEC to one of an effective operational-planning conference and allowing for significant and global impact against the drug trade.

When we broke into the regional planning groups, I was more than ready. Arenal now owed me a favor, and I graciously asked him to support and push for a multinational operation, initially among Mexico, Guatemala, and Belize. My idea was to conduct an operation involving the three countries and then move to incorporating all of Central America. It would have a domino effect, and once the other Central American countries observed the success of the initiative, they would readily participate. I wanted to ensure the operation was successful and move to a much-larger regional operation, eventually including the Andean Ridge countries. He agreed to support my idea, and later we put it in motion. Arenal came to me again during the conference to tell me he had conferred with his superiors in Mexico City and they wanted to host the next IDEC. I structured the recommendation and lobbied for support among the various countries and was able to garner votes. Mexico easily won the presidency for the following IDEC.

Returning to Mexico City, I began to plan the initiative I called Operation Triangle. I coordinated with the DEA country attachés in Guatemala and Belize and invited them to travel to Mexico City with their top-ranking police commanders. The MFJP hosted the operational meeting. We agreed on a highly structured strategy to attack drug trafficking in all its manifestations and share information. The three countries worked well together, resulting in numerous seizures and arrests. More important, Guatemala later allowed MFJP agents and Mexican helicopters to fly into Guatemala in support of a counterdrug operation. This is exactly what I was hoping for, and Operation Triangle exceeded my expectations. President Clinton later wrote a letter to the DEA administrator complimenting the agency on Triangle. Subsequently, I developed Operation Unidos I, which involved Mexico and all seven Central American countries. Later, I implemented Unidos II, which was even more expansive, with Mexico, Central America, and all Andean Ridge countries participating. The operations required continuous communication and coordination by many DEA country attachés and participating governments. These multinational operations were possible through coordinated efforts and focused mutual objectives.

General Barry McCaffrey, director of the Office of National Drug Control Policy, during a speech in Mexico City, complimented Mexico on their efforts in combating international drug trafficking and recognized the country for:

> Participation in three, major, regional combined-counterdrug operations, Operation Triangle, Operation Unidos, and Operation Cobra, which have involved other Central American nations and resulted in multiton cocaine seizures.

Additionally, the US Department of State in its "International Narcotics Control Strategy Report" included the following:

> DEA initiated Operation Triangle, a multifaceted tri-national approach, involving the countries of Mexico, Guatemala, and Belize. This DEA concept, announced and coordinated at the IDEC conference, is the first stage of the Mexico/Central American Regional Counter Narcotics strategy. Operation Triangle was to simultaneously target and arrest drug traffickers, seize illegal drugs and weapons. This operation also included the location of and destruction of illicit crops and clandestine airfields. Participating Mexican agencies included the Mexican Federal Judicial Police, National Institute for the Combating of Drugs (INCD), Mexican Army, Navy, and Air Force, the Federal Highway Police, as well as state, local and municipal law-enforcement

agencies. Mexico's seizures alone included 1,506 kilograms of cocaine, 15 tons of marijuana, 36 kilograms of opium, 2,000 kilograms of methaqualone, 3 maritime ships, 13 weapons, and 27 arrests. Another unprecedented achievement exhibited was Operation Unidos, a ten-day simultaneous regional enforcement operation involving Mexico and all countries of Central America (Panama, Belize, El Salvador, Guatemala, Honduras, Nicaragua, and Costa Rica).

This broad enforcement operation was designed to immobilize major trafficking organizations by targeting and securing all available smuggling routes, eradicating illicit crops, and destroying clandestine airstrips. During this saturation enforcement effort, Mexico alone seized 4,837 kilograms of cocaine, 36,321 kilograms of marijuana, 119 kilograms of marijuana seed, 13 kilograms of amphetamine, 2 aircraft, 145 vehicles, 6 maritime ships, 200 weapons, and 2 tons of munitions. In addition, 109 fugitives were arrested and 15 clandestine airstrips destroyed. It is important to also note that 1,428 fields of opium poppy were destroyed, equaling an area of 182 hectares that could have produced an estimated yield of 2,190 kilograms of opium and 916 marijuana fields destroyed, equaling an area of 88 hectares that could have produced and estimated yield of 106 metric tons.

As evidenced by the seizures and arrests, Operation Unidos can be considered one of the most significant regional successes in counterdrug efforts. Operations Triangle and Operation Unidos are unprecedented in Mexico's counterdrug efforts, especially in terms of the massive logistics and international cooperation required to implement them. One of the most important drug seizures was by the Mexican navy when 1,125 kilograms of cocaine was confiscated as a result of a firefight with drug traffickers trying to cross the Usumacinta River from Guatemala into Mexico.

The *Los Angeles Times, Nov. 20, 1996, Mark Fineman* reported on Unidos II and stated the following:

> For the second time in a year, Mexico has joined almost a dozen Central and South American nations in an international counter-narcotics blitz, cracking down on land, air, and sea routes between Colombia and the southern U.S. border to intercept an annual pre-Christmas rush of tons of cocaine and marijuana headed for the United States. Mexican law enforcement officials confirmed here Friday that Mexico and eleven other countries from Bolivia to Belize are sharing intelligence in an operation that began November 4. The effort has netted nearly two tons of cocaine, 45 tons of marijuana, 300 drug traffickers, 120 weapons, four boats, and an executive jet. U.S. anti-drug agencies are helping to coordinate the operation.
>
> The largest single seizure came after a predawn air chase over the Mexican state of Sinaloa on Thursday, when Mexican drug agents scrambled five airplanes and a helicopter to force down a jet that was tracked by international radar from Cali, Colombia, into Mexican airspace. It was carrying a ton and a half of cocaine.
>
> The U.S. Drug Enforcement Administration says those drug mafias use Mexico as a transit route to supply up to 75% of the cocaine sold in the United States. "This operation was a great success," Lozano Gracia said of Thursday's seizure. "The ability to react quickly was fundamental."

Mexican officials said their fast reaction resulted directly from the multinational operation (Unidos II): The jet was tracked by radars in several countries, including the United States, from the moment it took off, until Mexico intercepted it. In official documents explaining the operation, dubbed "Unidos II," the Mexican government said "The battle against narcotics trafficking is the responsibility of all countries—those that are used to produce and traffic drugs and those that consume them." This operation is similar to a ten-day multinational crackdown (Operation Unidos I) a year ago that U.S. officials proclaimed "an unprecedented success.

Counternarcotics officials said then that their blitz was planned for November because the drug cartels try to produce and distribute narcotics stockpiles before they cut back at year's end. "The trafficking organizations tend to wind down and go home for the holidays," one U.S. official said, "But they try to flood the market first so everyone can have a white Christmas." Officials in the United States called last year's crackdown by Mexico and all seven Central American nations the biggest multinational anti-narcotics operation in history. This year the operation was expanded to include the South American nations of Bolivia, Colombia, Ecuador, and Peru—the world's principal cocaine producers. But Mexico, as the main transport route between the producers and the U.S. market, clearly made the largest contribution to the operation.

The coordination and cooperation was extraordinary, and I give a lot of credit to everyone who played a role and made the operations a huge success. The enormous amounts of money being generated from the illicit drug trade prompted drug traffickers to use different methods of laundering to conceal its origin and sometimes transporting bulk currency to their major sources of supply. The Mexican drug traffickers had developed reliable ways of getting millions of dollars to their Colombian sources and were ingenious in the tactics they used in handling the money.

I received information from a reliable source that a large amount of money was being shipped to Colombia secreted in air-conditioning units. The source indicated the air-conditioning units were currently at the Mexico City airport awaiting transport aboard a Mexican commercial aircraft.

I immediately called Armando Subirats Simón, INCD director of Air Interdiction, who had replaced González Calderoni. Subirats Simón was an aeronautical engineer by trade and had become a great friend of mine, which allowed for a very close working relationship. We had regular meetings and planned operations almost on a daily basis. More so, he was highly competent and available no matter the time of day. I passed him the information regarding the air-conditioners and said it was from a reliable source. I explained the units were packed with US currency. I conveyed a sense of urgency, because I believed they could be leaving the country within hours. I asked him to contact Mexican Customs at the airport and check all manifests for air-conditioning units destined for Colombia.

Later that afternoon I received a telephone call. It was Subirats Simón, who excitedly told me they had located thirteen air-conditioning units and found a small mountain of US currency in large denominations. The units were destined for Bogotá. A check of the manifest identified the shipper, and a group of MFJP was on its way to execute a search warrant at his residence. A raid at the suspect's home revealed other air-conditioners waiting to be loaded with money from drug sales, and it was apparent they had been using this smuggling method for some time.

The next day, I was invited to the INCD for a press conference. The stacks of money, which totaled $6.3 million, were neatly placed on tables. Several members of the MFJP brandished machineguns, wore black uniforms, and stood guard over the money. The room was full of senior officials from the INCD who were ecstatic over the seizure for several reasons. In Mexico, the police are given a certain percentage of the money they seize as a reward. It was another success story all the way around.

■ ■ ■ ■

Mexico is a country of conspiracies, and my assignment there provided me with an invaluable window to see exactly how they worked and the key players involved. On a hot day, when the pollution in Mexico City was unusually high, one of the most powerful political figures of the PRI stood in front of a party building one block from the Avenida Reforma. Francisco Ruiz Massieu was in great spirits and would soon become the PRI majority leader in the Chamber of Deputies. He had served as the governor of Guerrero and was the ex-brother-in-law of President Salinas de Gortari. He had married Adriana, the president's sister, but after a few years, the marriage disintegrated and the divorce had created bitter feelings with the Salinas family. He only had a few more seconds to live.

A skinny, twenty-eight-year-old bean farmer stood nearby. He quietly approached the politician and fired a bullet into his head. Ruiz Massieu died instantly in a pool of blood. The amateur assassin, Daniel Aguilar Trevino, had never met the man he killed and only knew him from magazine photos. He had never been to Mexico City; he lived in Corralejo, a fifteen-hour drive from the city. Although Aguilar Trevino was completely unknown, he was quickly apprehended. The assassination sent reverberations throughout the country.

I was at the US Embassy just a mile from where Ruiz Massieu was killed and heard the news within minutes from contacts in the MFJP. Within two weeks, PRI Deputy Manuel Muñoz Rocha was linked to the killing but disappeared and could not be found by federal authorities. Aguilar Trevino confessed to the shooting and named his accomplices, who were also arrested. Ruiz Massieu's brother, Mario, the deputy attorney general, was put in charge of the investigation. He was responsible for making Carrera Fuentes the director general of the MFJP and gave orders to do what was necessary to bring those responsible for his brother's murder to justice. Carrera Fuentes put Arenal in charge of interrogating suspects and converted an office at MFJP headquarters into a torture chamber. Less than a month later, Mario resigned his post and publicly asserted he had proof that high officials in the PRI were blocking his investigation.

In a conversation with Carrera Fuentes, he told me Mario wanted him to also publicly denounce PRI officials, but he refused. He said it would be political suicide and parted ways with Mario. Three days later, Mario was arrested in Newark, New Jersey, boarding a flight to Madrid. He was in possession of $46,000 he had not reported, as required by US law ($10,000 or more when entering or leaving the country). Subsequently, $17 million was found in US bank accounts belonging to Mario. In a turn of events, the Mexican government charged him with impeding his brother's investigation. The US government declined to deport him to face charges in Mexico. He later committed suicide at his home in New Jersey, where he was under house arrest rather than stand trial on money-laundering charges. Arenal was dismissed from the MFJP and sent to jail for a short time for human-rights violations for his torture of suspects in the Ruiz Massieu investigation. Carrera Fuentes was later charged with corruption and taking millions of dollars from drug kingpin Amado Carrillo Fuentes.

Carrera Fuentes admitted that his relationship with Carrillo Fuentes began when he was a prison warden where the "Lord of the Skies" was serving a prison sentence. Allegedly, the international trafficker offered him wealth beyond his imagination once he was released from prison. After he became the director general of the MFJP, he met with Carrillo Fuentes at a restaurant in downtown Mexico City. Carrillo Fuentes offered him millions if he was willing to protect his criminal activities and ensure the tons of cocaine he was importing from Colombia were not seized. He accepted the offer and admitted giving Mario Ruiz Massieu at least a million of those dollars. MFJP Director General Carrera Fuentes was sentenced to six years in prison.

Almost a year and a half after Francisco Ruiz Massieu was brutally assassinated, Raúl Salinas de Gortari, the older brother of President Carlos Salinas de Gortari, was arrested for masterminding the killing of Ruiz Massieu. President Zedillo ordered his arrest three months after succeeding Salinas. The new prosecutors appointed by Zedillo based the arrest on the facts uncovered through their investigation. After a four-year trial marred with intrigue and political sparring, Raúl Salinas was convicted of ordering the murder of Francisco Ruiz Massieu and sentenced to fifty years in prison.

The verdict shattered the armor of a political system operating with impunity. Under Mexico's judicial system, there are no jury trials or courtroom cross-examination of witnesses. The trial against Raúl Salinas was a written record of close to 140,000 pages on which federal judge Ricardo Ojeda Bohórquez based his decision. After Judge Ojeda signed the verdict and sentence, he sent his clerks to the Almoloya, Mexico's most severe maximum-security penitentiary, to notify Raúl Salinas as he stood at the bars of his prison cell that he had been sentenced to fifty-years. Raúl was in complete shock and unable to speak. He slumped against the bars.

The case was tantamount to a Mexican *telenovela* (television soap opera) filled with over-the-top drama. The conviction destroyed the reputation of Carlos Salinas, who had been hailed as a visionary and reformer during his six-year administration. In humiliation, he left Mexico for Ireland to live in exile. I saw photos of him sitting on a park bench in Dublin reading newspapers with a not-surprising look of dejection.

Several months after the arrest of Raúl Salinas, Swiss authorities advised us they had arrested Raúl's wife, Paulina Castañon, and his brother-in-law, Antonio Castañon, in Geneva. Both appeared at a local bank attempting to make a substantial withdrawal. Paulina introduced herself as the wife of Juan Guillermo Gómez González and presented her Citicorp-issued power-of-attorney under the phony name and a passport with her husband's picture and fake identity. They were attempting to withdraw over $84 million from an account owned by Raúl Salinas under his alias. Bank officials became suspicious and told Paulina, the third wife of Raúl Salinas, the withdrawal could not be made immediately because the bank computer was down. She was asked to return the following day. Paulina was unaware that Swiss authorities had been monitoring the account closely after noticing suspiciously large money transfers. Part of the account's deposits had been wire-transferred from Mexico to the US through Citibank, and from there to Europe. The following day when Paulina and Antonio returned to the bank, Swiss authorities were waiting and they were taken into custody. Their arrest led to the discovery of a vast fortune spread throughout the world and totaling hundreds of millions of dollars, even though Salinas never officially received an annual income of more than $190,000. He was responsible for managing a Mexican food bank, nothing more. The Swiss authorities forwarded a facsimile of the passport in Paulina's possession in the name of Juan Guillermo Gómez González. The photo, however, was unmistakably that of Raúl.

I arranged a meeting with high-ranking officials from the Office of the Mexican Attorney General. I briefed them on the details regarding the arrests in Geneva and showed them a copy of the false passport belonging to the brother of President Salinas. They exhibited disbelief that Raúl Salinas had such a large fortune hidden in Swiss bank accounts. A coordinated investigation between the DEA, Mexican Attorney General's Office, and Swiss authorities was initiated to investigate the massive fortune accumulated by Raúl Salinas. It revealed Citibank in New York was responsible for funneling well over $100 million into the European banks of Banque Pictet, Citibank Zurich, Julius Baer Bank, and Banque Edmond de Rothschild. The accounts were opened under the fictitious names of Juan Guillermo Gómez González and Juan José González Cadena as well as companies such as Novatone, Trocca Limited, and Dozart Trusts.

In a subsequent letter, Raúl Salinas explained he had used different names to open the accounts because he was unfamiliar with the Citibank system and therefore used fictitious names and companies to avoid a political scandal. Salinas also denied any involvement in drug trafficking. Mexican authorities believed the money was either from drug trafficking, or at the very least, from corruption and commissions Salinas charged businessmen for contracts with the administration headed by his brother. Salinas offered the flimsy explanation he had decided to organize an association of investor friends and began to construct mechanisms for putting together a financial portfolio which after his brother's administration ended, would allow for the assets to be repatriated to Mexico for investment projects.

Salinas alleged that Citibank in New York devised the entire strategy, naming Amy Eliot as the person who was in charge of accounts from Mexico. He also stated Eliot was free to execute these movements to include the opening of accounts under names not stipulated by Salinas. He indicated the decision to move the funds was based on the fact that Mexican authorities were aware of the existence of the fake passport. Throughout the interrogation, Salinas denied the funds were his and insisted his role was only to manage the accounts. The investigation also brought into question Citibank's practice to accept deposits from foreigners incapable of justifying the source or size of their assets.

One late evening while at home, I received a call from the PGR informing me that Swiss authorities needed information on Salinas's involvement in the drug trade or they would release the funds from the frozen accounts. I asked if it could wait until morning, but they insisted they needed it that same night. It was midnight, but I drove to the embassy.

In my office, I prepared a document detailing information that DEA had on Salinas. I knew the potential for it leaking from the PGR to the press was highly likely, so I didn't use DEA or Embassy memorandum forms bearing any formal letterhead, because of potential retaliation from the Mexican government. I used a simple white sheet of paper and scribbled an unintelligible signature that didn't resemble anything like mine. Various informants had provided the information contained in the document, whom I obviously didn't identify.

I left the embassy and drove to the PGR, where they were waiting for me. They reviewed the information and thanked me for the quick response to their request. We sat in a small group and discussed details of the ongoing investigation and the impact it would have on their government. I left in the early morning hours. Sometime after I had left Mexico, the memorandum did leak to the media, and the attorneys representing Salinas made several attempts to interview me. Their efforts were futile.

The *New York Times* in an article dated Dec. 23, by Sam Dillon reported:

> Salinas's alleged ties to narco-traffickers have been remarked almost as often as his questionable business dealings, read one cable sent to Washington. After Raúl Salinas was arrested, the acting head of the Drug Enforcement Administration in Mexico, Mike Vigil, sent a memo to the Mexican Government detailing what American officials knew of Salinas's links to narcotics. It reads: "A source of information who was a personnel friend of Juan García Ábrego reported that Salinas was a principal backer of a project to establish businesses in Salina Cruz, Oaxaca, which would facilitate the movement of drugs from the Pacific to the Gulf coast, and vice versa." Other sources of information have made similar reports.

Eventually, the government of Switzerland transferred over $74 million from the $110 million in frozen bank accounts held by Raúl Salinas to the government of Mexico. The Swiss Justice Ministry reported that the government had demonstrated that the funds had been misappropriated. The Salinas family would not receive any of the frozen funds. After serving ten years in prison for the murder of Ruiz Massieu, Salinas was acquitted by a Mexican court and subsequently released from jail.

Chapter 16

Massacre on the Plain of the Viper

Mike was head of the DEA International Operations at a time when a joint worldwide drug-enforcement effort was lacking. His leadership was instrumental in the organized effort to link and combine drug intelligence. His model of multinational operations and the global Centers for Drug Intelligence (CDI) is used today. He made a difference.

—Rob Silano
DEA Special Agent (Ret.)

One of the greatest tragedies in the history of bilateral efforts between the US government and Mexico occurred during a counterdrug operation in the state of Veracruz on the southwest coast, east of the Yucatán peninsula. The consequences would create a wide divide between the Mexican army and the federal police that would impact on Mexico's future ability to wage an effective campaign against the illicit drug trade.

The Mexican Secretary of Defense, based on the prolific use of trafficker aircraft in smuggling cocaine into the country, issued a directive to the army to occupy, destroy, and secure the 634 clandestine airstrips that had been detected in the country. Actually, there were thousands more, taking into account that traffickers were landing on

285

isolated roads, pastures, along the beach, anywhere that had a flat surface. In compliance with this directive, General Alfredo Morán Acevedo, commander for the sixth military zone, ordered some of his troops to maintain surveillance of thirty clandestine airstrips. The Secretary of Defense, General Antonio Riviello Bazan, named Morán Acevedo the commander of the military zone and replaced General Vinicio Santoyo Feria. Morán Acevedo had previously been the military attaché to Brazil. It was a time when Morán Acevedo wasn't required to make difficult decisions or effort in the field.

Based on the orders of Morán Acevedo to destroy a clandestine landing strip, Lieutenant José Alfredo Coronel Vargas, along with fourteen other soldiers, deployed to a location known as *el Llano de la Vibora* (the plains of the Viper). The area consisted of several agricultural fields, many of which were fenced with barbed wire. The group of soldiers concealed themselves in a cluster of trees surrounded by the sprawling pastures and passed the hours by making small talk and telling personal stories. The soldiers were young and came from poor families. Many enlisted in the army to escape extreme poverty; it was the only alternative for most of them.

One evening, as the sun disappeared over the horizon and darkness enveloped the area, the soldiers watched headlights of a vehicle slowly moving in their direction. They were cautious because they didn't know if the large truck belonged to a local farmer but questioned what a legitimate farmer would be doing in that area at almost midnight. The soldiers quietly moved towards the truck with their weapons ready for any potential confrontation. When the truck was about twenty meters away, they motioned for it to stop. Against the bright lights, the soldiers observed two men jump from the truck and run. They fired several rounds at the fleeing suspects, but none found their mark. Lieutenant Coronel Vargas ordered his men not to pursue them for fear of an ambush. The soldiers also saw a second vehicle that seemed to be following the truck. It stopped for a few seconds and then sped away.

When they thought it was safe, the soldiers approached the three-and-a-half-ton Ford. They discovered eight metal barrels, each containing about two hundred liters of aviation fuel. They also found fifteen smaller containers, with approximately sixty liters of fuel in each, and an electric gas pump. Inside the cab was an AK-47 assault rifle with two full magazines and several lamps commonly used to illuminate landing strips for trafficker airplanes landing at night.

In the early morning hours of the following day, the NBRF began to track a suspect aircraft traveling from South America along the eastern Pacific coast of Central America. It was not traveling at a high rate of speed, and we assumed it was a single-engine. What made it suspicious was that it didn't have a known flight plan and was flying only a few thousand feet above sea level.

I immediately contacted Comandante Armando Arteaga to alert the aircrews and enforcement teams and put them on standby. The launching of the aircrews that would ultimately intercept the trafficker aircraft was a matter of timing, and we had to calculate the projected trajectory and speed of the suspect plane. Arteaga contacted Comandante Eduardo Salazar Carrillo in Mérida, Yucatán, telling him to prepare his interdiction crew to leave for the local airport. He and other Mexican federal agents were staying at a small, low-rent motel near there. All of the agents—Roberto Javier Olivo Trinker, Juan José Arteaga Perez, Ernesto Median Salazar, Oscar Hernandez Sanchez, Miguel Marquez Santiago, Francisco Zuvire Morales, and Abel Angel Acosta Pedroza—quickly dressed and loaded their weapons, most of which were AK-47s. They were brave young men that I had come to know well and considered close friends. They knew the great risks they were taking but did their jobs with heroic courage and valor.

As the suspect aircraft approached the Gulf of Tehuantepec near the coastline of the southwestern Mexican states of Oaxaca and Chiapas, I spoke with Comandante Arteaga; the decision was made to launch the two Cessna Citation aircraft based in Mérida, Yucatan, and Tapachula, Chiapas. One of the Cessna Citations belonged to the

Mexican government and the other to US Customs. The latter would take the handoff from a P-3 aircraft that was tracking the small plane now identified as a Cessna 210 Centurion with registration number XA-LAN painted on its fuselage. Operations in Mexico were complicated in that it has a coast-line on the Pacific and the Caribbean. Each required a different strategy taking into consideration the resources and necessary Mexican infrastructure in the various geographic areas.

We conducted a check and determined the registration was fictitious and actually belonged to a Learjet. Shortly after the Cessna Citations were in the air, I opted to launch the two PGR King Airs also stationed in Mérida and Tapachula. Comandante Salazar and the other federal agents quickly boarded the King Air in Mérida, painted in the standard blue-and-white PGR colors. The Cessna Citations, which were faster and had sophisticated radar and sensors, would intercept and track the suspect aircraft. They would also guide the King Airs with the agents to the landing site of the trafficker plane.

The mission of the King Air interdiction crews was to land behind the suspect aircraft, if possible, to allow the agents to effect arrests and seizures. These operations were dangerous, especially when dealing with vicious drug traffickers willing to protect their operations at all costs. The agents were able to intercept the suspect aircraft a few miles south of Tuxtla Gutierrez heading east across southern Mexico. The crew of the PGR King Air was given the flight path of the plane and fell in behind the pursuing Cessna Citations. At the helm of the King Air carrying Comandante Salazar's group were two veteran pilots, Jesus Rodríguez García and Jorge Héctor Orring Urista. The pilots had spent years with the PGR and had a close working relationship with the agents led by Comandante Salazar.

A few minutes past six in the morning, the suspect aircraft began to circle the Llano de la Vibora in the state of Veracruz. It overflew the area for almost forty-five minutes looking for signs of the ground crew that would assist with refueling and other logistics. The trafficker pilots must have become suspicious, but they had crossed the line of no return and were running out of fuel. Our Cessna Citations maintained an altitude of ten thousand feet, where they maintained surveillance of the trafficker aircraft.

I kept in constant, minute-by-minute communication with Comandante Arteaga. We had coordinated many of these operations previously and worked extremely well with one another. At fifteen minutes before seven, the trafficker Cessna Centurion began to rapidly descend. It was at this time that our Citations observed the Ford truck, partially hidden in the trees. They were unaware it was now in the custody of the Mexican Army. They communicated this sighting on a designated radio frequency also used by PGR flight crews. Just minutes before seven, the suspect aircraft landed in a north-to-south direction. It came to a stop two hundred meters from where the soldiers were hiding. The pilots, a male and female, casually walked to where the fuel truck was parked and caught sight of several soldiers near the tree line. They immediately turned and began to walk in the opposite direction. The soldiers didn't fire or try to impede their escape.

Eight minutes after the Cessna Centurion landed, the King Air transporting Comandante Salazar and the group of federal police also landed and stopped at least three hundred meters from the small aircraft. The soldiers were over five hundred meters away from the PGR aircraft. The US Customs aircraft began to film the activities on the ground using a forward-looking infrared (FLIR) system.

Now on the ground, the federal police quickly exited their aircraft, and Comandante Salazar ordered his men to advance towards the abandoned trafficker aircraft in two columns. The agents arrived at the aircraft and began to look through its windows. In less than thirty seconds, under a barrage of high-velocity rounds, the agents fell to the ground to make themselves less of a target. They fired several rounds to cover Comandante Salazar as he ran back towards the PGR aircraft. The two PGR pilots left their plane on hearing the volley of gunfire that echoed off the tall trees. They ran in a crouch to a nearby ditch that was only fourteen inches deep and dove in headfirst. Between the sounds of automatic gunfire, the police would scream, *"Policía Judicial Federal!"* The soldiers would yell, " *Ejército, identificarse!"* (Army, identify yourself!) Unfortunately, the distance was too great, and they couldn't hear each other.

Comandante Salazar didn't stop running until he reached the ditch where the PGR pilots were taking refuge. The remaining agents maintained their positions with chests pressed against the moist grass. From the ditch, the comandante called out the call signs for the seven agents who were pinned down near the suspect aircraft. All of them responded. They were still alive *at the moment.* Through the use of a handheld radio, Comandante Salazar was able to establish communication with one of the PGR aircraft flying over the area. Desperately, he asked them to contact the PGR offices in Mexico City and request they immediately contact the commander of the sixth military zone and have them cease-fire. He used his code name Gamma 10.

The information was passed to Moisés García Flores, the executive secretary to the Director General for Interception. He quickly called the central office of the Federal Judicial Police in Veracruz and made contact with one of the duty agents. She was shocked and understood time was of the essence. She was able to communicate directly with Morán, who she later described as being completely arrogant. Morán would not give the cease-fire order, since the individuals had not identified themselves as agents.

He defied all common sense and logic for a field commander. An experienced person would have ordered a cease fire and made a determination of the facts before letting the situation result in the tragic loss of life. Morán abruptly terminated the conversation with the duty agent by telling her he was on his way to the area with two more platoons of soldiers. García Flores received a call from the duty agent relating the conversation between herself and Morán. He then *personally* called Morán and, again, asked him to stop his men from shooting at the federal police. Incredibly, Morán refused a second time to order a cease-fire and stated he personally was taking an additional one hundred soldiers to the area. His last comment was, *"No se en que va parar todo esto"* (I don't know how all of this is going to turn out). The die was cast, and he was about to consummate the senseless, brutal massacre of agents in the service of their country.

The soldiers continued to fire on the federal police, despite the fact the agents had never demonstrated any aggression. Comandante Salazar removed his white t-shirt and placed it on the end of the barrel of his AK-47 and waved it in the air as a sign of surrender. This provoked even more intense fire. An hour after the shooting started, the agents had not yet suffered a loss. Morán arrived at el Llano de la Vibora forty minutes after his conversation with García Flores. He ordered over one hundred soldiers to surround the agents, and then in an act of complete insanity, gave the order to fire. There was no chance of escape much less survival of the ferocious attack.

After fifteen minutes, Comandante Salazar no longer heard the voices of his men in the open field. An eerie silence enveloped the area, and Salazar heard the approach of soldiers. He yelled they were federal police and not to shoot. He heard two shots and hugged the ground.

The pilots of the second PGR King Air determined they would also land and attempt to diffuse the deadly situation on the ground. Another team of federal police led by Comandante Luis Rivas was on the aircraft and were veterans in counterdrug operations. The plane, with bold and visible letters "PGR," landed and came to a stop. The pilots opened the door and immediately came under fire from the army. The pilots and the group of five agents took cover behind the aircraft. One of the pilots ran into an area with thick large bushes and weeds. From there, he observed the soldiers approach the agents and the other pilot, pointing their weapons in a menacing way.

The agents later testified the soldiers took their PGR credentials and continued to insult and abuse them. One of the officers demanded the agents use his handheld radio to instruct the two Cessna Citations flying above to land. He also wanted to know what the crews of the two aircraft had observed regarding the confrontation. The agents refused to have the aircraft land and told the officer the frequencies of the aircraft were different from his radio. He hit the agents on their heads with a metallic object and pointed his handgun, threatening to execute them. From his distant hiding place, the PGR pilot saw the motionless bodies of seven agents. They were all dead.

Morán ordered a group of soldiers to establish a perimeter around the area, not allowing anyone to enter or observe the scene of the massacre. He also instructed another group of soldiers to collect the weapons of the dead agents and remove the contents of the trafficker aircraft, which included approximately 370 kilograms of cocaine. It also contained a large, plastic fuel container with hoses leading to the aircraft's fuel system, the tactic used by traffickers to extend their distance capability. The PGR pilots and agents still alive were taken into custody by the military and later released. Comandante Salazar told me the only thing that saved the rest of the PGR personnel at the Llano de la Vibora was telling the soldiers that the Cessna Citations were filming the entire scene.

The conflict between the Mexican Army and the PGR continued over the seven dead agents. The army insisted on taking the bodies to a military hospital located in the center of Veracruz. The PGR responded with decisiveness and adamantly said they had instructions to oppose taking the dead agents to a military hospital and would use force to comply with the order. An agreement was finally reached that autopsies would be conducted at the Institute of Forensic Science.

That same day, Comandante Arteaga and I discussed the investigation being conducted on the killing of the agents. He indicated an objective investigation was being conducted by the PGR, but they urgently needed the FLIR tape from the US Customs Cessna Citation. It would be used as evidence, and the attorney general wanted to review it. I contacted the Customs attaché at the embassy and requested the tape. He indicated it had already been sent to Washington, DC, for review by Customs leadership. I was infuriated that a valuable piece of evidence needed for the rapidly unfolding investigation in Mexico was now out of the country when time was so critical. The attaché didn't seem concerned with the urgency of the Mexican government.

It finally arrived in Mexico City several days later. I met with the Customs attaché behind the embassy to retrieve it and give him a piece of my mind for jeopardizing an ongoing investigation. He still didn't understand the relevance of the tape.

I encountered this reversal of roles continually during my foreign assignments. Many US agencies lost sight of the fact they were there to support the host government. All too often, they expected these governments to support *their* agendas. This shortsightedness surfaced in many forms. I repeatedly witnessed US agencies demand actions that they would never consider if the situation were reversed. Case in point was a request by Customs to fly their P-3s into Mexico with impunity. Yet, when a Mexican helicopter erroneously strayed slightly into US airspace, it generated an angry diplomatic note of protest.

Still outraged by the removal of the tape, I was finally able to deliver it to the PGR and again met with Comandante Arteaga. He had confronted Morán, who arrogantly remarked, "*Eso es lo que pasa cuando se meten con nosotros*" (That is what happens when you mess with us). Morán claimed mistaken identity during an investigation by Mexico's National Commission of Human Rights (CNDH).

The Commission interviewed everyone involved, but the most damaging evidence comprised the statements of the surviving PGR agents, the FLIR tapes, the two telephone calls from the PGR to Morán that his men were firing on federal agents, and more significantly, the autopsy reports. The evidence showed that many of the seven agents were killed at close range. One was literally stitched with bullets from head to waist at a distance of a few feet. Another was shot in the head at close range with a handgun. One agent was still alive when he was forced to open his mouth for a bullet to be fired through the upper part of his mouth into his brain. In the end, Morán, General Humberto Martinez Lopez, and many other military personnel were sent to prison for many years. There is considerable speculation as to what motivated the massacre on the plains of the viper. It is my opinion, Morán was incompetent and arrogant but wanted to prove his prowess as a field commander. It had tragic and deadly consequences. Most of those involved believe the military was protecting the drug operation, but one thing is certain, Morán Acevedo was drunk with power and had crossed the line into the realm of insanity.

Comandante Salazar came to see me at the embassy and told me plainclothes military personnel had been following him. He said they were attempting to develop disparaging information in order to discredit him. He was a capable field commander, who fortunately survived the massacre. He and I had been friends for several years, and I made sure the PGR took care of him. The massacre on the plain of the viper further inflamed a substantial distrust between the military and the federal police. It continues to exist today, and it greatly detracts from effective coordination and communication between these two entities that are at the forefront of Mexico's counterdrug efforts.

Chapter 17

The Devastating Heroin Flood in Texas

Special Agent Michael S. Vigil, DEA (Ret.), never substituted words for action or sought acclaim while he methodically pursued the most dangerous, merciless, and vicious drug traffickers worldwide and brought them to justice. His conspicuous and visionary leadership was compelling; his invincible determination was inspirational; and his indomitable sense of purpose was unavoidable. It was my genuine privilege to observe his courage and calmness under fire, his grace under pressure, and his decisiveness in decision-making. I am grateful to have had the real fortune to learn and practice the best principles and techniques of international drug enforcement under the tutelage of this legendary agent and winner of the prestigious Top Cop award.

—William J. Walker
Special Agent, Deputy Assistant
Administrator, DEA (Ret.)

After six and a half years in Mexico City, I was transferred to Dallas, Texas. Another transfer meant sadness to leave many good people but excitement to meet new ones. Before leaving, I was given a great *despedida* (going away party) attended by many high-ranking Mexican officials. They brought a large mariachi band telling me to keep them for as long as I wanted. They played into the early morning hours and sang "El Rey." It is still my favorite song, and when I hear it, I'm always reminded of Mexico. Those memories will serve me for several lifetimes, but I was looking forward to new experiences and challenges. The exposure to different assignments, without question, greatly broadened my experience and capabilities. It increased my ability to quickly make critical decisions and develop effective strategies.

Many within the agency suffered from *decision paralysis* and were apprehensive about dealing with controversial issues. They had limited exposure and lacked the most fundamental principles of leadership and management. Leadership is the ability to make informed decisions and not be afraid of controversy. On a daily basis, I made calls knowing they would come back to haunt me because of those in the agency who were risk-averse. I protected my subordinates from those who had never done anything of significance in their careers and were so eager to attack those who did. William Wallace, one of the leaders of the Scottish wars for independence, once said, "Men follow leaders, not a rank." This statement succinctly describes leadership at its best. It was well-known in the agency who had been tested in the field of battle and who had compromised their integrity for promotions. I proudly accept the words of my great friend, Lou Pharao, who said, "Mike never kissed ass to get ahead."

Johnny Phelps was the SAC of Dallas whom I had worked with previously in Colombia. He had paid his dues on the streets and spoke fluent Spanish. He expected a lot from his subordinates but was more than fair if you did your job. I had studied the situation in Dallas and knew it was a significant transshipment area for drugs being smuggled across the border from Mexico. Drug-trafficking organizations took advantage of the interstate system and massive airport to move their products to other parts of the country. However, as with all transshipment areas, some of the drugs remained there and created significant issues with drug addiction and associated crime, including violence.

I wanted to hit the ground running and began contacting some of my informants in Colombia and Mexico to begin developing cases for the enforcement groups under my command. There were some great agents in Dallas such as Mischa Harrington, Jesús Gallo, Joe Rodríguez, Keith Bishop, Bob Shannon, Dave Cordova, Rick Smith, Clay Morris, Vic Routh, and task-force officers from the Dallas Police Department, Kenny LeCesne and Kim Sanders. I worked with these agents in developing investigations and strategies to enhance the productivity of the division. As a matter of course, I maintained contact with a number of highly reliable informants who were capable of providing valuable information on drug-trafficking organizations at the international level.

Managing informants has become a dying art in the past ten years, because the agency has unfortunately put its emphasis on wiretaps to the detriment of other investigative tools and methods. Informants are an important resource and can provide insider information about an organization and facilitate the penetration by undercover agents. Informants have diverse personalities and require expert handling to harness and focus them on operational objectives. They also require nurturing, cajoling, and motivation, with constant communication to enhance their potential capabilities. I found, after many years, my experience enabled me to determine whether they were giving me valuable information or fabricating, and I never felt it necessary to put a single informant on a polygraph, as is commonplace today.

I spoke with an old informant in the Mexican state of Sonora, who told me he was in contact with a significant heroin trafficker looking to sell half a pound of high-quality heroin. The trafficker had, apparently, recently sold several kilos of heroin and wanted to sell the rest before buying more opium for conversion into heroin at one of his labs. The informant was to tell the trafficker he had a buyer in Dallas but that he would have to deliver to him there. A day later, he called saying the trafficker was willing, so I purchased two airline tickets for them to travel to Dallas. The informant called me from Mexico just before they boarded their flight and provided me with a description of the trafficker and what he was wearing. He also said the trafficker had taped the heroin to his body in order to smuggle it through US Customs.

I gave the case to Joe Rodríguez who was a good undercover agent and spoke fluent Spanish. Arrangements were made for other agents to conduct surveillance as Joe met with the informant and the trafficker at the airport. As often happens, not everything goes smoothly, regardless of how well you plan these operations. Although the informant and trafficker had reservations on the same flight, they were put on different flights because of overbooking. The informant arrived first. He said the trafficker should be on the next flight from Tucson.

They had decided to fly from Hermosillo to Tucson and then on to Dallas. This meant a delay, but there was concern because the trafficker didn't speak English. The agents and informant waited at the airport several hours when he finally arrived and was taken to Joe's vehicle, where they negotiated and examined the heroin. After getting sufficient incriminating statements, surveillance agents roared in to make the arrest. The trafficker was completely surprised and was sent to prison for several years.

■ ■ ■ ■

Removing drug dealers from their livelihood of selling drugs and engaging in reckless violence was rewarding and made us feel we were upholding our sworn duty to protect and serve. The Dallas office also initiated Operation META, which targeted large-scale methamphetamine traffickers tied to the Amezcua brothers in Mexico.

The Amezcuas were undoubtedly some of the largest and most prolific traffickers in the world. They were known as the Colima Cartel and operated primarily out of Guadalajara, Jalisco. José de Jesús Amezcua headed the criminal network with his brothers Adán and Luis acting as his principal lieutenants. They purchased ton quantities of ephedrine, the primary precursor used in the manufacture of methamphetamine, from Germany and several other countries.

In order to put it into perspective, the price of a kilogram of ephedrine or pseudoephedrine (used in over-the-counter cold medication) was about sixty dollars and, once converted into methamphetamine using many different chemical processing methods involving sodium hydroxide, anhydrous ammonia, iodine, red phosphorus, and acids, the traffickers sold it for $18,000 or more. The profit was astronomical and worth the risk to many, including the Amezcuas. They were flooding the US market in what could only be described as a blizzard of *ice* moving across the US from west to east. Through a more organized and sophisticated operation, the Colima Cartel was able to take the business from outlaw motorcycle gangs and independent traffickers, who once dominated the meth trade by purchasing ephedrine and pseudoephedrine from Mexican suppliers. The Amezcuas smuggled tons of precursor chemicals imported from different countries such as China, Germany, and India, through the Mexican port of Veracruz by boat and then transported it overland to areas in central and northern Mexico, where they controlled *super labs*.

As the operation gained momentum, I was able to get other DEA offices involved, and it quickly expanded into a multijurisdictional investigation. We worked with the FBI, ICE (Immigration and Customs Enforcement) and state and local agencies in seventeen different US cities and nine states. We identified key individuals in the organization and their modus operandi through extensive physical and electronic surveillance. The coordination became more difficult as the investigation continued to grow. It required constant communication by the various case agents and supervisors. We identified a female in Atlanta whose telephone toll records revealed she was calling a number used by the Colima Cartel. She was identified through ongoing wire intercepts and communications with other significant targets. We pushed the office to quickly initiate a wire intercept on her telephone, but they were slow in moving forward with the affidavit. I felt a wire on her number would have led to a US indictment of the leaders of the cartel. Unfortunately, circumstances intervened, resulting in the premature action of having to bring that entire operation to an end. The DEA Los Angeles office discovered a large lab operating near a daycare center and another close to an equestrian center where riding lessons were being given to children. There was enormous concern that the highly toxic and volatile chemicals used in manufacturing methamphetamine could potentially cause a massive explosion with great loss of life. After a discussion with several federal prosecutors, we decided to move against the criminals tied to the conspiracy and seize the labs we had identified.

Operation META was still a huge success that resulted in the arrest of a hundred members of the organization and the seizure of 133 pounds of methamphetamine, 1,765 pounds of marijuana, and 1,100 kilograms of cocaine along with the destruction of several labs. In a press conference, Attorney General Reno stated, "The operation was dangerous; it was difficult; and it took meticulous planning and coordination ... And to the merchants of meth, we make this pledge: Your days are numbered. We will not tolerate your threat to our children and our neighborhoods." Later, the Mexican government arrested the Amezcua brothers and put them in prison effectively ending their reign. Justice may be blind, but its sword cuts a wide swath.

Keith Bishop was the principal agent on this investigation and was working almost twenty-four hours a day. His stamina came from his days with the Denver Broncos where he was a star, offensive guard. One particular morning, he came to my office to explain his concern about an altercation he'd had on the highway as he headed into work. Another driver, suffering from out-of-control road-rage, made obscene signs at Keith and threw a cup of coffee at his car. He pulled in front of Keith to block him. As Keith got out, I can only assume the man quickly came to the realization he had made a serious error in judgment. Keith is a huge man and has hands the size of a catcher's mitt. Foolishly, the man charged Keith, who effortlessly picked him up like a rag doll and slammed him into the ground. The local police who came to the scene, saw Keith, looked at the other combatant and were ready to diagnose the enraged driver as insane. I laughed and told Keith not to worry about it. He knew that I'd take care of any fallout that might occur. The incident never surfaced again.

The traffic in Dallas was routinely horrible. As I drove to work one day, I turned on the local news channel. Normally, my radio was always on an oldies station, since music always relaxed me and took my mind away from the pressures of the job. The newscaster reported the tragic death of the eleventh high-school student in Plano, Texas, to die from a heroin overdose. According to the news report, heroin abuse in Plano had become an epidemic, and the local hospitals were being *flooded* with incidents of overdoses. This was shocking news, since Plano was one of the most affluent cities in the US and, at one time, rated the eleventh-best area to live in the country, according to *CNN Money Magazine*. It was not a surprise to me, however, that Mexican brown powder and black-tar heroin were now flooding many areas of the country.

During the remainder of my commute, I formulated a strategy to address the situation in Plano. Rushing into my office, I told my secretary, Liz Sotomayor, to contact Bruce Glasscock, the Plano chief of police and get a meeting for later that day. I called the demand-reduction coordinator, Paul Villascuesa, and told him not to go anywhere, because we'd be leaving soon and I would brief him in the car. I was in a hurry, and he knew it was an important and urgent situation. Within minutes, Liz had arranged the meeting with the chief, so Paul and I were on the road to Plano in less than an hour.

In the meeting, I told the chief we were aware of the significant heroin problem in Plano and wanted to assist him in developing a criminal case against the responsible traffickers. Chief Glasscock was a professional and well liked by both federal and local law-enforcement officials. He truly cared about making Plano as safe as possible for all of its citizens. I recommended the development of a twin-pronged approach in which we would create a multiagency task force consisting of federal, state, and local law-enforcement agencies with dedicated prosecutors. The task force would develop and share tactical information from all appropriate sources that would be used to generate operational activity. Additionally, we would develop prosecutable cases, deciding whether to take them federal or local depending on which would have the most impact. The second prong would be an aggressive demand-reduction program to educate parents, students, and teachers about the dangers of heroin abuse.

Most teenagers in Plano didn't know they were taking heroin. They believed it was a *designer drug*, because the sources of supply and street distributors didn't call it heroin. It was referred to as *chiva*, which in Mexican trafficking jargon means heroin. It is highly addictive and dangerous. Plus, heroin and other illegal drugs, unlike those manufactured by the pharmaceutical industry, don't have quality control on dosage or purity levels. As a result, it was the equivalent of playing Russian roulette each time they ingested or injected the heroin into their system. In Plano, chiva became the *in thing* used by the young people who came from affluent families and had easy access to money.

I told Chief Glasscock the DEA would fund the entire operation and would contact other police departments in the area to create the informal task force. I advised him that Dave Cordova would do the undercover work, since he had worked in Mexico with me and understood how Mexican drug traffickers operated. Dave was another great agent and fluent Spanish-speaker. The chief agreed with the plan, so we moved forward.

I immediately started coordinating with other law-enforcement agencies, as well as federal and local prosecutors. They were all more than willing to work together and assist the city of Plano. I told Paul to work with the Plano police department demand-reduction personnel and structure a town-hall meeting for the citizens to discuss the heroin problem. Dave was taken away from some of his other responsibilities in order to focus on penetrating the sources of supply.

The entire operation was in full swing within days. We held the town-hall meeting in a large auditorium, where approximately fifteen hundred people from Plano attended. There was a panel comprised of law enforcement, parents whose children had died from heroin overdoses, and prosecutors. The interaction with the attendees was strong and positive. We explained the effects of the drugs, treatment options, and the need to educate children at an early age. It was disturbing when we discovered the local hospital had been inundated with over a hundred overdoses, not all fatal, but clearly revealing a massive problem. Terrified teenagers anonymously dropped off friends who had overdosed in front of the emergency room and immediately left.

We determined the heroin being distributed was *black-tar*, named for its thick and tar-like consistency. The Mexican drug traffickers in the area handled distribution like a pizza-delivery business. Local teenagers called or paged the dealers, who quickly delivered the heroin to the buyer. It wasn't long before we had penetrated the criminal organization through several informants we recruited.

We identified Ecliserio Martinez García as the head of the network, and his subordinates, the Meza brothers, and Santiago Mejia, who was barely seventeen years old. Ecliserio was born and raised in a poor, mountainous village in the southern Mexican state of Guerrero, with poverty so great it was difficult to survive, much less lead a fruitful existence. In order to seek a better life, he and his wife came to the US, illegally crossing the Rio Grande River near Laredo, Texas. They made their way to McKinney, about fifteen miles from Plano, and moved in with another couple also from Guerrero.

Ecliserio, no stranger to the drug trade, had seen the large opium-poppy cultivations along mountain streams and small valleys in his home state. He also knew chemists who processed the raw opium into brown or black-tar heroin. He had the connections and determined that Plano was ripe for establishing a heroin market, since there was one already established for cocaine and marijuana. He began to smuggle heroin directly from clandestine labs in Guerrero via different couriers by placing it in the hollowed-out heels of men's shoes. Ecliserio and his organization distributed heroin with an extremely high purity level. It went straight from the lab into the arms of the Plano teenagers, who didn't have the tolerance to withstand the purity.

During an undercover meeting with Ecliserio, Agent Cordova was told they were aware their heroin had killed several high-school students in Plano but really didn't care. The statement underscored the callous attitude that drug traffickers have about the lives they destroy. Our strategy worked, and within six weeks, we had made several undercover purchases of heroin from the principal traffickers, including Martinez García and the Meza brothers. We indicted twenty-nine individuals on federal conspiracy and distribution charges. The operation was successful only through the coordinated efforts of all participating agencies that led to the indictments and subsequent prosecutions, effectively ending the heroin *massacre* in Plano.

The Anti-Drug Abuse Act of 1988, created the High Intensity Drug Trafficking Areas (HIDTA) program. It provided assistance to federal, state, local, and tribal law-enforcement agencies and was designed to facilitate cooperation among all agencies to enhance intelligence sharing and coordinated activities. Many years had passed with no one making the effort to get HIDTA designation for north Texas. In 1997, I determined the area needed the valuable funding and resources that came with HIDTA and began to develop a strategy for implementing the program under the authority of the Office of National Drug Control Policy (ONDCP).

Initially, I met with the police chiefs throughout the area to get them onboard. I explained the valuable funding and resources it would bring them and the other police departments and federal agencies. They realized any available resource would help them address the drug problem in their jurisdictions. I also met with the US Attorneys' Office to gain their support as well. After several months of painstaking work, the North Texas HIDTA came into existence and encompassed the counties of Dallas, Tarrant, Collin, Denton, Kaufman, Navarro, Ellis, Johnson, Hood, Parker, and Smith.

That effort paid huge dividends. It continues to facilitate the coordination and cooperation between area law-enforcement agencies through development of a centralized operations facility, housing many of the joint investigative, administrative, and intelligence initiatives. The comingling of experienced officers and agents from numerous agencies at the facility has resulted in the sharing of valuable operational information between the task forces, as well as long-term cooperative relationships that will benefit law enforcement in the future. The Regional Intelligence Support Center has been described as a model for other HIDTA investigative support centers.

Importantly, it also enhances officer safety by providing de-confliction services for all area law-enforcement operations. *De-confliction* is the coordination of all agency operations in the area. This process assists inadvertent conflict during operations that could have tragic consequences—as seen between the Mexican military and federal police in Veracruz. The North Texas HIDTA currently has forty federal, state, and local law-enforcement agencies participating in the program. It developed the first multiagency regional drug strategy to attack the identified threats by targeting the most significant drug, violent-crime, and money-laundering organizations in the area. This strategy has produced significant results with the prosecution and dismantling of major cocaine, heroin, and methamphetamine trafficking organizations, as well as the arrest of numerous individuals engaged in drug-related firearm trafficking and other violent crimes.

Chapter 18

Unlikely Partners

Michael S. Vigil has a global perspective of drug trafficking and its relationship to terrorist organizations. Furthermore, he has developed and worked closely with the Haitian National Police on many significant initiatives such as the implementation of the bilateral operation between Haiti and the Dominican Republic called Operation Genesis. He was also the architect of numerous major multinational counterdrug offensives such as Columbus, Liberator, Conquistador, and others that were hugely successful. He is a visionary and one of the greatest strategists that we have been honored to work with throughout the years.

—Mario Andresol
Former Director General of
the Haitian National Police

While having lunch with the US Attorney in Dallas, I was called by the DEA administrator and informed I was being promoted to the Senior Executive Service (SES), the most coveted position within the federal government. My role and responsibilities had changed during the past years, and I had become increasingly more of an executive-level manager. Based on my extensive operational experience in the field, I fully understood the issues faced by agents on a daily basis and the support they needed. I am a firm believer in "you can't lead from where you have never been."

The SES promotion gave me command of the Caribbean Division. I felt a sense of accomplishment and had worked very hard to reach this career objective. My promotion had been earned, while many others had been promoted based on politics and cronyism. Very early in my career, it became apparent that in order to rise in the ranks, I would have to do four times the work of those who compromised their integrity to get ahead. I took pride in my work and had great confidence in overcoming obstacles to implement innovative strategies and tactics. The Caribbean would be a formidable area for developing effective counterdrug strategies where I could continue using my broad expertise on operations and intelligence.

My area of responsibility consisted of one million sixty thousand square miles, with a total population of about forty million people. Additionally, it had a total of thirty countries and seven thousand islands. The jurisdiction of the DEA division also included Guyana, French Guyana, and Suriname on the northern coast of the South America continent. The Caribbean has always been an important transit zone for drugs, particularly cocaine, destined for the US and Europe. The drugs were transported using a wide variety of routes and methods. Go-fast boats, small launches with powerful motors, cargo freighters, fishing boats, and containerized cargo ships were the most common conveyances for smuggling ton quantities. Twin-engine aircraft with extended fuel tanks were also used effectively to transit the Caribbean into the southeastern area of the US. The Caribbean also plays an important role in the laundering of drug profits and many countries have extensive offshore banking systems that facilitate the practice. Many criminal organizations prefer to move drug money through bulk shipments, avoiding an incriminating trail of financial records.

My headquarters was located in San Juan, Puerto Rico, which was used by many international drug-trafficking organizations as a major point of entry for drugs being smuggled into the United States. Puerto Rico's three-hundred-mile coastline, the vast number of isolated cays, and six million square miles of open water between the US and Colombia, make the region ideal for a variety of reasons. It's only 360 miles from Colombia's north coast and eighty miles from the east coast of the Dominican Republic. Puerto Rico is easily reachable by twin-engine aircraft carrying payloads of 300–500 kilograms of cocaine. The go-fast boats make their roundtrips to its southern coast in less than a day. Colombian traffickers have made it into one of the largest staging areas in the Caribbean for illicit drugs destined for the US market. Although Puerto Rico is still a self-governing commonwealth, once the drugs enter its territory, they are for all intents and purposes in the US. Individuals traveling from Puerto Rico into Miami or other US points of entry are not subject to searches.

Many Caribbean countries have sparse resources, uncontrolled coastlines, and air space that facilitate exploitation by international drug traffickers. Haiti, for example, which forms the island of Hispaniola along with the Dominican Republic was ripe for exploitation because of geography, poverty, government paralysis, a disbanded parliament, dysfunctional criminal justice system, an unprotected coastline, and an understaffed and inexperienced police force with limited resources. During the Duvalier regime, corruption was rampant, and public officials received large payoffs from drug traffickers to protect their operations. When "Baby Doc" Duvalier left, the Colombian organizations were already poised to take advantage of the chaos and expand drug-trafficking operations in the country.

My division had an effective core of agents with a strong work ethic and boundless energy. The men who come readily to mind are Jim Akagi, John Rende, William Walker, Tom Detriquet, Jim Mavromatis, Fernando Feliciano, Gary Davis, Pat Stenkamp, Carlos Ramirez, Ray Ollie, Jim Agee, Virgilio Ayala, Leduc Obas, Brad Sosnosky (Mongo) and Efrain de Jesús. The building *housing* the DEA offices in San Juan, however, was a disaster. It was poorly maintained and not secure. The entrance to our parking lot was next to a busy intersection, which enabled drug traffickers to park across the street to observe DEA personnel entering and leaving. To make matters worse, the building was next to a housing project populated by some of the most violent local drug dealers on the island. The entire building was decayed and dilapidated. The interior carpets were saturated with mildew, and most of the doors had to be opened without the luxury of a doorknob. There were no doorknobs, just holes.

Just two months after I arrived, a category-four hurricane, George, slammed into the island, causing major devastation. It dealt a severe blow, leaving most of the island without power and water for weeks. The one-hundred-mile-an-hour wind gusts blew several large metal panels off what passed as a roof. Water poured into many of the top floors, ruining computers and office furnishings. But in this catastrophe, I saw an opportunity to move out of our miserable office space.

I contacted the GSA Regional office in New York and requested an immediate inspection. In less than a week, a team came to assess the damage. They saw firsthand several of many large rats that drowned during the storm, along with aggressive mold and a disgusting stench that permeated the air. It didn't take the team long to see the dire need. We were more than pleased to begin our move out of the building within a few weeks in, what GSA called, a *constructive evacuation*. We were then relocated into a more suitable, modern building in Guaynabo.

From my experience in leadership, I knew the people on my team were my greatest resource. Understandably, they were of the utmost importance to me, and I was concerned because the morale in the office was already low prior to my arrival. Contributing factors were primarily quality-of-life issues, such as inadequate public services, totally unreliable utilities, and limited accessibility of medical care. The high cost of living, an exclusionary social structure, limited availability of appropriate schools for dependent children, and the high incidence of crime created difficulty and stress to each family. Before I did anything else, I wanted to address these problems.

I contacted the military-base commanders in San Juan and Fajardo to gain commissary privileges for my personnel. The request was fast-tracked and approved. Conveniently, each year I received $5 million in discretionary funding, which I used in part to pay for the education of children belonging to DEA employees in Puerto Rico. The most appropriate school was at the Ft. Buchanan military base that charged $10,000 a year per student. The investment in my team was more than worth the funding. Morale improved significantly, and I turned my focus to the task facing us.

■ ■ ■ ■

The transit of illegal drugs throughout the Caribbean created unique challenges to law enforcement. One of those was an intelligence void concerning trafficking organizations operating in the region. Another was ineffective, almost nonexistent, cooperation among law-enforcement agencies. To enhance the communication and coordination between the key countries and islands in the Caribbean, I developed and implemented a comprehensive system for sharing information called the Unified Caribbean Online Regional Network (UNICORN).

The encrypted system was the first of its kind in the region and allowed the various countries to communicate on international drug trafficking throughout the region. It also encouraged a more structured methodology to dismantling transnational organizations using a cooperative approach to operations. Through expansive information sharing, we were able to identify and exploit the vulnerabilities of these networks and dismantle them in a systematic manner. My technical group traveled to the different countries to install the system and provide training. Ernesto Garay, a talented intelligence analyst, and the intelligence group continually collected and shared relevant information with participating countries. The UNICORN system was the first step in developing a comprehensive regional strategy in counterdrug operations.

After initiating UNICORN, I focused on the island of Hispaniola, particularly Haiti. It had become the most critical area in the Caribbean for drug-trafficking activities by Colombian and Dominican criminal networks. Haiti is on the western part of Hispaniola, the second-largest island in the Greater Antilles. It is the third-largest country in the Caribbean, behind Cuba and the DR. The Dominican Republic shares a 360-kilometer border with Haiti, and for decades there was conflict between the Haitians and the Dominicans. When Rafael Trujillo was elected president of the DR in 1930, he defined the country as a Hispanic nation—Catholic and white—as opposed to Afro-French Haiti. Trujillo portrayed Haiti as both a threat and the antithesis of the Dominican Republic and dreaded the growing influence of Haitian culture.

This fear led him to conduct a policy of *Dominicanness*, which ultimately resulted in the killing of thirty thousand Haitians. It is rumored he sent the Haitian government a bill for $30,000—a dollar a head—to bury them. Trujillo initiated Operation Perejil, which resulted in the killings of thousands of Haitians and dark-skinned Dominicans living on the border between both countries. Like the Old Testament *shibboleth*, these people were asked to pronounce the word *perejil*, believed to be difficult for French-speaking Haitians because of the *r* and the *j*. Everyone who failed was summarily killed. I mention these facts to highlight the resentment and political issues that made cooperation between both countries extremely problematic.

In order to effectively confront the drug trade there, I had to overcome decades of conflict and horrific violence that had driven a huge wedge between two great peoples sharing the same island. The only way I could possibly accomplish this goal was to leverage the personal relationships I had been able to develop with Pierre Denize, head of the Haitian National Police, and Vice-Admiral Luis Humeau Hidalgo, who headed the Dominican National Directorate for the Combating of Drugs (DNCD). Both men were committed to fighting the trafficking of drugs in their respective countries and worked closely with the DEA. I initially met with Denize, who commanded over six thousand Haitian police officers. Denize's stylish suits hung well on his tall, lean build, and he spoke rapid, flawless English, learned while living in New York. He reported to his cousin, Robert Manuel, the Secretary of State Security in the Haitian Justice Ministry. They worked well together, and Manuel supported Denize in his efforts to stabilize Haiti which no longer had a military.

During our meeting, Denize was reluctant to participate, but I was determined and pressed the issue. I finally convinced him the Colombian traffickers were a distinct and inevitable danger to his country and its citizens. He understood my argument and agreed to the joint operation with the Dominican Republic. His only caveat was that the Dominicans would have to come to Port-au-Prince to plan the operation. He did not want to travel out of the country. I was agreeable to his request. To grant it, however, I would have to convince Admiral Humeau to meet with Denize in Haiti.

The admiral was a genuine gentleman and a dedicated ally of the DEA. In fact, the DR was our strongest partner in the Caribbean. In my discussions with him, I explained the conflicts of the past should not hamper efforts to strengthen the island of Hispaniola against violent drug traffickers and their malevolent criminal activities. He was well aware how drug-trafficking organizations were exploiting Hispaniola as a transshipment point for tons of cocaine. He realized it was time to work closely with Haiti and agreed to travel with me to Port-au-Prince. Several weeks later, we had a historic meeting in Haiti, and both Admiral Humeau and Director General Denize were gracious and cordial as we began to plan a joint operation that I appropriately named Genesis.

Our planning session lasted the entire day, and we developed a comprehensive strategy using a large map placed on a sizable conference table. We agreed to launch counterdrug operations in both countries and along the common border area. We would also direct efforts and resources against some of the major criminal networks operating on the island. The UNICORN system would act as the principal component for sharing information and coordinating the entire operation. The Dominicans invited members of the Haitian National Police to work with their police and customs authorities on the Dominican side of the border that extends 360 kilometers. We agreed to initiate Operation Genesis in November and I would return to Puerto Rico to coordinate the participation of the US Coast Guard, which would play an important role along the southern waters of Hispaniola. At the end of the planning session, Humeau and Denize shook hands and wished each other the best of luck, parting as friends.

Operation Genesis, within a week, garnered several hundred kilograms of cocaine throughout Haiti and the DR. The Haitian National Police also arrested the family of a significant Colombian drug lord, but the charges were weak. The Dominican government had a more viable case against them, so the Haitian police drove them to Malpasse, the principal border-crossing point, and turned them over to the Dominican police. Later, the Haitians requested assistance from the Dominicans on a serial killer who fled Haiti to avoid apprehension. The Dominican authorities located the suspect as he was about to board a flight to the US in Santo Domingo. They reciprocated and turned him over to the Haitians. Operation Genesis resulted in the unprecedented exchange of information and greatly enhanced cooperation between the DR and Haiti.

As a result, the Haitian National Police assigned an officer and also an experienced analyst to the DNCD in Santo Domingo to facilitate operations and the exchange of information. Four more Haitian National Police officers were stationed at Dominican border-crossing points. DNCD officials, on the other hand, were assigned to the Haitian National Police headquarters in Port-au-Prince, as well as several Haitian border-crossing areas. The exchange of information was further expedited by the UNICORN system, which facilitated database checks of suspicious persons and vehicles being stopped and examined. The information was sent to my intelligence group who performed criminal checks. The long-term objectives for Operation Genesis exceeded all expectations, and decades later, both Haiti and the Dominican Republic continue to work together on counterdrug operations. In essence, the successful operation overcame the conflict and distrust in Hispaniola that had generated fertile ground for international drug traffickers. For that, I am deeply gratified for the significant role I played in Genesis.

The Dominican DNCD conducted numerous extralegal wire intercepts, but at the time did not have the necessary legislation, at the federal level, to make them legal. The intercepts served a very important purpose by targeting major drug-trafficking networks and immobilizing them in a top-to-bottom approach in which the upper hierarchy and the lower-level members would be arrested and successfully prosecuted.

Unfortunately, wire intercept evidence from a foreign country cannot be used in US courts unless they are court authorized. This was critical, since US-based indictments were key objectives if a particular country didn't have adequate laws to prosecute. In order to overcome this legal issue, I eventually made contact with the chief local prosecutor in Santo Domingo. At the federal level, no laws existed permitting the use of wire-intercept operations, but I wanted to explore the possibility of using local laws to legally sanction them. The young, dynamic prosecutor promised to research the matter and contact me in less than a week with either positive or negative news.

Five days later, he called and said they found an existing law that could be broadly interpreted to allow court-authorized wire intercepts capable of withstanding legal scrutiny. I contacted the Department of Justice in Washington, DC, to convene a meeting to discuss strategy on the use of evidence gleaned from court-authorized intercepts in the DR. The local prosecutor and I traveled together and met with DOJ officials in a daylong discussion. In the end, we concluded the law would be invaluable and US prosecutors could use the information on prosecutions in the US. It was a great coup, making the DOJ attorneys elated over the outcome. The process and ensuing investigations rapidly yielded a tremendous amount of evidence, resulting in numerous indictments in the US. This also had a significant impact on many transnational criminal networks operating on the island of Hispaniola.

■ ■ ■ ■

The DEA held a regional meeting with many of the heads of police forces in the Caribbean to discuss threat assessments of drug-trafficking organizations operating in the region. I broached the need to work together on a joint, regional operation that would have a discernible impact on the drug trade. Most of the representatives supported the idea, but the British representative in the Cayman Islands argued against it. His arguments were totally illogical, but the Brits were routinely obstructionists, especially if an operation was not their idea or did not give them a lead position. They followed this pattern in other operations I would initiate in other parts of the world. Their negativity resulted in a domino effect, causing police representatives from many of the Caribbean nations not to participate, relegating the discussion to nothing of relevance. At the end of the day, I met with all of my country attachés and explained we were not going to accept no for an answer. I instructed them to meet individually with their respective police counterparts and convince them to support the proposed initiative to create a more cohesive operational environment throughout the Caribbean. It was simply a divide-and-conquer tactic. The idea worked.

We moved forward with a solid plan to get Caribbean countries communicating and working together on common objectives. At a later planning session in Santo Domingo, I presented a comprehensive operational strategy for the initiative that I named Columbus. The operation would include fifteen countries, primarily from the Caribbean, including Suriname, situated on the northern part of the South American continent. It was multifaceted and focused on air, land, and maritime interdiction, drug eradication, and attacking large-scale drug-trafficking organizations. I determined that Santo Domingo would serve as the northern command center and Trinidad would be the one in the south. Participating countries agreed to place representatives at the command centers during the twelve-day operation. They would report arrests and seizures directly to their representatives, which would be consolidated by the command centers. The UNICORN system would again be used to facilitate the exchange of actionable intelligence. The arrests and seizures would, however, be secondary to the following principal objectives:

1. The development of a cohesive cooperative environment among source and transit countries.
2. Disruption of drug-trafficking activities in the region.
3. The consolidation of counterdrug efforts in the Caribbean.
4. The continued development of a comprehensive regional strategy.
5. Expanding the sharing of information between countries.

During Operation Columbus, the participating countries reported an excess of twelve hundred arrests, and the seizure of nine hundred kilograms of cocaine, thirty-eight weapons, twenty-six vehicles, twenty-seven maritime ships, three clandestine laboratories, one aircraft, and more than half a ton of marijuana. It became evident during this unprecedented operation that a coordinated effort among countries was necessary to have an effective impact against transnational criminal organizations.

A US official from another agency later reported the operation had caused the price of cocaine to rise by 15 percent indicating reduced availability. Davis Douglas, an assistant police superintendent in Trinidad, stated, "All the police in the nation were involved."

Beres Spence, Jamaica's chief of narcotics said they arrested 655 drug traffickers. He added, "I wish that I could do this every day."

Pierre Denize and the Haitian National Police arrested major cocaine kingpins Edme Noel, Thibauld Emmanuel, and Wista Louis, responsible for smuggling tons of cocaine into the US.

Every participating country reported significant results, but more important, they begin to share information with one another. The wave of raids served as the first major test of controversial *ship rider agreements* that allowed US ships and aircraft to chase drug smugglers into the national waters and airspace of other countries. Norman Henslee, commander of the US Coast Guard's Caribbean fleet, reported that a US Navy ship chased a drug boat into the waters of Jamaica, whose government had previously argued that such an act would violate their sovereignty, before reluctantly signing the pact. The success of Operation

Columbus showed that countries were becoming more receptive to ship riders and developing much broader and effective collaboration. The significant results and effectiveness of Columbus peaked the interest and motivated other countries to participate in multinational operations.

A few months later, to broaden the scope of Operation Columbus, I initiated Operation Conquistador, involving twenty-six countries from the Caribbean, Central and South America. Many capable and outstanding DEA country attachés and US Coast Guard officials embraced the initiative. Again, all participants met in Santo Domingo to develop a comprehensive plan. Everyone was enthusiastic, and after witnessing the previous success, the British representative from the Caymans actually participated. He also expressed anger he had not played a role in Operation Columbus. I reminded him that it was he who tried to impede it. But we shook hands, and the past became irrelevant, with the future of collaborative efforts in counterdrug operations being the only thing that mattered to me. In the planning, we again established two command centers in Trinidad and Santo Domingo, which participating countries would staff with personnel. I noticed how small and impoverished countries, when allowed to participate, would, as they say, *kick ass*. Pride and motivation are a powerful force that will not be denied or impeded.

An article appearing in the *Los Angeles Times* on March 30, 2000 by Mark Fineman captured the essence of Operation Conquistador:

Operation Aimed at Drugs for U.S. Is Cited as Model

Caribbean Basin: Dozens of nations join effort to cut off flow of narcotics from Colombia, netting five tons of cocaine and 2,331 suspects, DEA says.

Drug-enforcement officials Wednesday unveiled the results of what they called the biggest international effort ever to stem the tidal wave of Colombian drugs flowing through the Caribbean to U.S. shores. Dubbed "Operation Conquistador," the seventeen-day crackdown that ended Sunday involved 26 Caribbean and Central and South American countries, the U.S. Drug Enforcement Administration said. Agents throughout the region seized more than five tons of cocaine, 120 pounds of heroin, 2,331 suspects, 13 boats, 170 boats, 83 weapons, 17,340 rounds of ammunition, and more than two million dollars in property, the DEA said.

But DEA Special Agent Michael Vigil, who heads the agency's Caribbean operations, said its greatest success was cooperation among enforcement agencies from more than two dozen nations through which an estimated one-third of the cocaine sold in the U.S. passes. "Obviously, it's not going to stop the trade, but what we want to do is run these operations continually to keep the drug dealers off balance," Vigil said in a telephone interview from his base in Puerto Rico, where he announced the operation.

But the whole reason for these operations is to get these countries to work together and share information," he said. "And they really went out with hurricane force this time."

Even anarchic and impoverished Haiti, which has become the region's biggest transit point for Colombian cocaine headed north, contributed "enthusiastically" to the operation, Vigil said.

The fledging U.S.-trained Haitian National Police, which was sharply criticized in a recent State Department report for corruption and lax drug enforcement, staged searches throughout the capital, Port-au-Prince, making arrests and seizing 40 pounds of cocaine. They added that National Police Chief Pierre Denize is committed to the drug fight in Haiti and that the operation had at least a temporary chilling effect on the drug trade there and throughout the region.

Other nations with checkered reputations in the drug war also participated with surprising zeal, Vigil said. In the South American coastal nation of Suriname—whose former dictator, Desi Bouterse, was convicted on cocaine charges and sentenced in absentia to sixteen years in jail by a Netherlands court—police arrested one hundred suspects and staged nearly three thousand searches of residences, boats, aircraft, and vehicles during Conquistador.

But the most compelling evidence of the operation's immediate impact appeared to be in the marketplace. In Puerto Rico, a key cocaine gateway to the U.S. mainland, DEA intelligence agents say the price of the drug soared since Operation Conquistador. A kilogram of cocaine that sold for between eight thousand to fourteen thousand a month ago is now fetching as much as twenty-four thousand dollars.

Several months after the culmination of Operation Columbus and Conquistador, I was in Haiti with Pierre Denize addressing the movement of drug profits from Haiti to offshore banks in Panama. Couriers were transporting millions of dollars on commercial flights, and the Haitian National Police were powerless to take action, since no laws existed to allow seizure. Haitian law is based on French law, so I suggested they research even antiquated legislation that might give them authority to seize the money and use it to train and buy equipment for the police. Denize, much to his credit, hired three legal scholars, who spent months doing intensive research and finally discovered a law that could be used to confiscate the money legally and subsequently forfeit it to the Haitian government. As a result, the Haitians began seizing tens of millions of dollars at the Port-au-Prince International Airport. It was a significant blow to drug traffickers operating in Haiti and a great benefit to the Haitian National Police, who could use it to buy needed equipment.

On another occasion while in Haiti, I received a call from Frank Marrero, a staff coordinator at DEA headquarters who was another agent who had proven his worth on the streets of New York and throughout his career with the DEA. Frank said that DEA's Office of Congressional and Public Affairs had received a call from representatives of the National Association of Police Officers' (NAPO) *Top Cop* committee who had heard of Operation Columbus and wanted the DEA to recommend me for their Top Cop award. The request was forwarded to Frank for action.

I told Frank I had never heard of it and was not really interested, but he persisted, saying it was a very prestigious award. I finally agreed and told him to respond as long as I could accept it on behalf of the entire Caribbean Division. I discovered the NAPO TOP COP Award is the most prestigious award in law enforcement. Former presidents, attorney generals, dignitaries, and celebrities from the television and movie industry attend the ceremony. Since NAPO launched the awards program in 1994, the TOP COP awards have paid tribute to outstanding law-enforcement officers across the country for actions above and beyond the call of duty. Each year, thousands of nominations are submitted from federal, state, and local law-enforcement agencies. After careful review, a committee consisting of law enforcement members, celebrities, politicians, and other dignitaries select the top ten submissions who will each receive the award. Many of the submissions not selected for the TOP COP award receive honorable mention recognition during the ceremony.

I didn't hear anything for several weeks and then received a second call from Frank that I had been selected as a recipient. Frank said I would be notified by NAPO regarding the details of the ceremony. NAPO representatives contacted me and requested news videos and articles they could use in developing a video to be shown during the ceremony, which would be held at the historical Warner Theater in downtown Washington, DC. The theater, originally named the Earle Theater, was built in 1924 as a movie palace presenting live vaudeville and first-run silent movies. It is a beautiful, ornate theater complete with a large balcony, box seats, sweeping curtains, and antique chandeliers. Its impressive spectacle set the stage for an incredible weekend.

Prior to the ceremony, the ten Top Cops were given a special tour of the White House. As we walked through the Red Room, I looked out across the front lawn where the press and dignitaries generally congregate, thinking of how many times I had been on the outside looking in from the street. The following day, Vice-President Al Gore met with us at the hotel. We followed him into a large conference room where the media was waiting with dozens of film crews. The vice-president congratulated the Top Cops for our efforts in protecting the country against crime and terrorism.

That evening, there was red-carpet electricity at the Warner Theater as hundreds of people began to fill the seats. Lynn Russell, anchor for CNN, was the master of ceremonies. The event began with theatrical pomp and ceremony. Attorney General Janet Reno presented awards to those who received honorable mention for their heroic actions. After her presentation, celebrities from various law-enforcement television programs presented the main awards with the same mix of special effects and pageantry as an Academy Awards production, followed by a high-action video about each award winner, designed and produced professionally by experts from the movie industry. The visuals and sound design were at a par with Hollywood. The stars of *Law and Order—Special Victims Unit* Mariska Hargitay and Christopher Meloni presented me with my award. I accepted for all DEA agents who risked their lives on a daily basis, and I paid homage to my father, calling him a true American hero for his exceptional military service during World War II. The ceremony was followed by a lavish reception, giving everyone the opportunity to mingle and take photographs. To my amazement, the celebrities wanted to be photographed with the recipients, saying, "We just play the role. You all are the real heroes."

POLICE Magazine, Nov. 26, 2000, reported:

Napo Honors Top Cops

Officers from ten agencies were proclaimed tops in their field this August at the National Association of Police Organizations (NAPO) Seventh Annual TOP COPS Awards. This gala event featured several luminaries who play law officers on television.

According to Jody Couser, nearly 1,200 people filled the DC Warner Theater to applaud the TOP COP winners. Vice-President Gore, who attended, pledged his continued support for law-enforcement officers and paid tribute to the TOP COP Award winners.

■ ■ ■ ■

Several months later, I began planning the largest multinational drug operation in history, involving thirty-six countries from the Caribbean, Central and South America, and Mexico. It required meticulous planning to develop a strategy with clear and viable operational objectives. I wanted the command centers to again be located in Trinidad and Santo Domingo. It was important for participating countries to report activities, i.e., arrests, seizures, and other relevant information, to their representatives at the command centers. The individual countries would relay overall statistics and successes directly to their representatives, and therefore the reporting would not be from the DEA. High-ranking police officials were pleased with the results of Operations Columbus and Conquistador and looked forward to working together again.

I named it Liberator in honor of Simón Bolívar. Representatives from the Andean nations thanked me for naming the operation after one of their most significant historical figures. This small token would be highly motivating in order to honor their beloved Bolívar. The plan was to conduct the operation for a period of twenty-four days. It involved the US Coast Guard and the police forces and military from the participating countries in what would be the largest counterdrug operation ever undertaken. Security forces, which would play a role, numbered in the tens of thousands in what was described as one of the largest operational coalitions in history.

The *Ottawa Citizen*, Oct. 1, 2000, reported the following:

2,876 People Nabbed In Monster Drug Bust
36-Country Sting Largest of its kind in History

During the operation, speedboats were chased, complete with volleys of bullets similar to the opening sequence of a James Bond movie, this time in the Orinoco delta as a backdrop rather than London's docks. Helicopters, naval ships, fixed-wing aircraft with sensors and radars were used to support the operation. Cocaine laboratories were destroyed, illicit drug crops were eliminated, assets derived from drug profits were seized, and drug traffickers were arrested. Many of the operational activities occurred in snake-infested and hostile terrain, but the participating countries were not deterred and swept through the region like an avenging storm.

Over 39,000 searches were conducted during the operation. The operation netted approximately 2,876 arrests, 20 tons of cocaine, 94 cocaine laboratories, and the seizure of $42 million in assets. The operation has been heralded as beginning a new era in international cooperation."

The operation succeeded because of the exceptional cooperation of the participating countries. They recognized the need to be flexible on sovereignty issues, which many times in the past had acted as a barrier to counterdrug operations. The best judges for the impact of Operation Liberator and the other operations were the countries themselves, and all, without exception, were gratified with the results and lasting strategic relationships, coordination, and communication they produced. These were the true and most-important benchmarks of Columbus, Conquistador, and Liberator.

The development of multinational operations is a difficult and complex endeavor. They require the delicate maneuvering and handling of cultural, political, religious, and economic considerations, which can easily hamper the forward movement of any operation. Inevitably, you have to overcome internal obstacles made by incompetent and envious elements attempting to impede rather than support. It also requires each country to be individually approached and convinced of the value of dedicating large amounts of resources, including manpower from their police and military organizations. I believed a blanket approach proved overly complicated, because one dissenting voice could create a negative domino effect. Also key are one's credentials and personal relationships with high-ranking counterparts, who ultimately make the decision on participating or not. The proposed strategy has to be extremely transparent and take into account the resources of each country. The coordination and strategy development require massive efforts, involving months of meticulous planning. Equally important are the establishment of communications and information platforms for the sharing of tactical, strategic, and operational intelligence. The development of command centers is also critical, which greatly facilitate and enhance coordination and communication.

■ ■ ■ ■

We targeted a violent drug-trafficking network headed by Miguel O'Connor Colón, who was smuggling large quantities of cocaine and heroin from Colombia in twin-engine aircraft. The drugs were air-dropped off the coast of Puerto Rico to waiting high-speed boats. The code name for the investigation was Chupa Cabra meaning goatsucker, which was

O'Connor's well-deserved nickname. He had gained prominence and consolidated his power after Tomás Arroyo Colón was arrested on federal drug charges. We identified at least twenty distribution points throughout Puerto Rico being supplied by his organization and, through the skillful use of undercover agents, were able to penetrate many of them.

O'Connor was a feared psychopathic killer who had no empathy for even members of his own gang. One day, while driving through an area controlled by his organization, he saw one of his men asleep instead of watching for police activity. He ordered gasoline poured on him below the waist and ignited the saturated clothing with a cigarette lighter. The gang member barely survived and was left horribly disfigured. In one year, O'Connor and his subordinates were responsible for the brutal murders of thirty people, including rival drug dealers. Many victims were shot over one hundred times with machineguns. People became so intimidated by the level of violence, they never went outside, becoming prisoners in their own homes. The organization was so brazen, they sold drugs openly and threatened to kill anyone who denounced them. After nine months, we were able to develop a strong prosecutable case against the entire organization through undercover buys, surveillance, and information provided by informants.

During the investigation we worked closely with the FBI, the US Marshals Service, the US Immigration and Naturalization Service, IRS, ATF, US Coast Guard, and the Puerto Rican police. Building complex investigations involves strong coordination with the US Attorneys' Office, who will prosecute the cases. It is a "hand-to-glove" process where evidence should be presented to a jury in a logical, systematic manner, and must be easily understood.

A day before the arrests, we assembled over three hundred federal, state, and local agents to plan the arrests of the criminals who had terrorized the island of Puerto Rico for so many years. Very early the following morning, in a synchronized effort, we arrested forty individuals without incident. The day after the arrests, I was leaving my apartment, and one of the security guards told me I had arrested his son in the operation. As a parent, he was deeply concerned, but it revealed how insidious the problem had become and the fact that our security was constantly at risk.

The Washington Times published an article with the following quotes:

"Today's arrests illustrate effective cooperation between law enforcement," said Attorney General Janet Reno in a statement. The collaborative effort demonstrated during this operation sends a strong message to those who choose to engage in trafficking that their illegal operations will not be tolerated."

"There is no doubt this was the most violent organization we have seen in Puerto Rico over the past ten years and the arrests will mean a significant drop in both the distribution of drugs and the level of violence," said Mr. Michael Vigil, Special Agent in Charge of the Caribbean Division. "They were not afraid to machinegun people in public places, shooting some of their victims as many as a hundred times, and many in the community did not feel safe." He said the O'Connor Colón gang caught the eye of agents because of the tremendous profits it was generating at numerous distribution points on the island and because of the blatant level of violence associated with the gang, including the assassination of rival gang members in public executions. Mr. Vigil said each of the twenty-plus drug-distribution centers produced daily drug sales of between twenty and fifty thousand dollars and that 40 percent of the drugs were being sold to buyers in Puerto Rico. The other 60 percent was shipped via aircraft to several US cities, including Boston, New York, Chicago and Miami. "We will respond above and beyond the call of duty to rid Puerto Rico of drug trafficking and related violence," said Mr. Vigil. "Its citizens are deserving of this tireless effort."

Chapter 19

Global Operations

Mike Vigil is a hero to the country of Afghanistan and the entire region. He was responsible for developing Operation Containment and other programs that have greatly assisted many countries, including Afghanistan. He is an internationally renowned expert in counterdrug operations and is highly respected by many nations in the world. He is one of the true great warriors and my country has deservedly made him an honorary General.

—General Mohammad Ayoub Salangi
Deputy Minister of Interior, Afghanistan

After two years as the SAC of the Caribbean Division, I was promoted to Chief of International Operations. It would require another move back to Washington, DC. This was my eleventh move, far more than most agents incur, but each transfer greatly expanded my knowledge, skills and experience. It was time for other interesting challenges and the politics of DEA headquarters. As the chief of international operations, I supervised all DEA offices worldwide, *excluding* those in the United States. This included Europe, Latin America, Africa, Central Asia, the Middle East, and Central and Southeast Asia, with over a thousand personnel. It was a considerable responsibility, but I was aware it was fertile ground for developing innovative ideas and programs. I had a great team of agents, such as Frank Marrero, Frank Mazilli, Dave Lorino, Gary Sheridan, Rich Daniels, Tony Greco, Jimmy Coppola, John Emerson, and many others. The politics at headquarters was usually stifling, but I was able to overcome the obstacles standing in the way of my operational objectives. I never took no for an answer and would seek ways to move around or over impediments.

One of my first priorities was to regionalize our international operations. Foreign offices were under the command of country attachés and were responsible for at least one but, in most cases, multiple countries. Many of the country attachés were GS-14s (a first line management level) who experienced continual encroachment by personnel from the US military and State Department. One of the most significant violators of jurisdiction was the Department of Defense's Southern Command (USSOUTHCOM), which was then based in Panama but has since moved to Florida.

The DEA is the lead agency on counterdrug efforts with USSOUTHCOM acting as support, but somehow they had managed to reverse the roles. They often developed counterdrug strategy in direct conflict with ours and never asked us to participate or coordinate the strategies to ensure a common and cohesive focus. Furthermore, it sent confusing signals to our foreign counterparts. Being very rank conscious, the State Department and the military generals attempted to circumvent and disregard our country attachés on a regular basis. I personally intervened to prevent this from occurring.

It was also important that all foreign offices were operating cohesively and developing regional operations that could be meshed into global strategies. Because of these two factors, I began a series of meetings with my section chiefs to begin creating *regions* and to decide which geographical areas would come under each region. I instructed them to obtain feedback from the country attachés, but ultimately the final decision would be mine. In the end, I divided the DEA offices into the Andean Region, the European Region, the Far East Region, the Middle East Region, the Southern Cone Region, and the Mexico/Central

America Region. Senior Executive Service managers would supervise the regions as directors, and the country attachés in each region would report to the regional directors. Once this regionalization plan was implemented, the encroachments by other agencies virtually came to a halt. It also acted as the catalyst for advancing and implementing effective global operations.

■ ■ ■ ■

On September 11, 2001, the US suffered a significant and well-planned attack. Terrorists using hijacked commercial aircraft flew them into the World Trade Center towers in New York City like missiles, with deadly accuracy and massive destruction. I was in my office at DEA headquarters watching the events unfold in New York City on television. Half an hour passed after the initial attacks, when I heard what I thought was a loud sonic boom. The windows and building shook. The central DEA offices in Washington, DC, are located directly across the freeway from the Pentagon. Seconds later, I heard people screaming from the other side of the floor that a plane had just hit the Pentagon. I rushed over and saw thick, black smoke billowing from the west side of the Pentagon. It was severely damaged by the impact of American Airlines flight 77, causing one section of the building to collapse.

As the aircraft approached the Pentagon, its wings knocked over light poles and its right engine smashed into a power generator before slamming into the building, killing all fifty-three passengers, five hijackers, and six crew members. The plane hit the first floor of the Pentagon. The front part of the fuselage disintegrated on impact while the mid and tail sections kept moving for another fraction of a second. Debris from the tail penetrated deepest into the building, breaking through 310 feet of the outermost building's five rings. The DEA's two buildings were immediately evacuated, and most of the personnel congregated outside in the large courtyard. Police sirens penetrated the morning air, and military personnel from the Pentagon began pouring onto the various, nearby streets, some covered in soot and others streaming tears. It was a morning most Americans will remember forever. The destruction and loss of innocent lives were horrific, and it struck a chord that terrorism had definitely become more sophisticated and a danger to the continental United States.

The US response was swift, and the Taliban regime in Afghanistan was quickly toppled. The situation in Afghanistan became much more complicated, however, than just conducting a regime change. The US and coalition partners would contend with the potential unleashing of a torrent of opium and heroin on the world. The Golden Crescent region consisting of Afghanistan, Pakistan, and Iran is a major source for opium and heroin. Years of warfare in Afghanistan, including the Soviet invasion and occupation throughout the 1980s and the civil strife of the 1990s, decimated the country's economic infrastructure. In the mid-1980s, Afghanistan produced increasing quantities of illicit opium, and by 2000 accounted for over 70 percent of the world's supply, supplanting Burma (Myanmar) as the leading producer. A drought in Burma contributed to the situation in Afghanistan.

As a result of the Taliban's taxing and controlling poppy cultivation during their rule, which culminated in a ban during 2001, cultivation and production had declined to only sixty-three tons, significantly below what it had been in previous years. Exploiting the chaotic situation following the collapse of the Taliban regime and the initiation of a coalition military action in the fall of 2001, Afghan drug traffickers encouraged farmers to resume opium-poppy cultivation.

In 2002, despite a renewal of the poppy ban in January and a modestly successful eradication campaign in April of that year, Afghanistan, once again, resumed its position as the world's leading producer of illicit opium and heroin. By this time, it was the source of 92 percent of the global supply for these dangerous and highly addictive drugs.

The large-scale production of opium is not only a significant threat to Afghanistan's future and the region's stability, but also has worldwide implications. Clandestine laboratories in the country convert the opium into high grade heroin. Because Afghanistan doesn't produce the precursor chemicals required for the conversion process, they are smuggled into the country from Pakistan, India, the Central Asian countries, China, and Europe. The largest processing labs are primarily located in the south, with smaller laboratories in other areas, including the eastern Nangarhar Province. In the past, many heroin labs were located in Pakistan, particularly in the Northwest Frontier province, where there is little government control. During the Taliban regime, they relocated to Afghanistan to be closer to the source of opium.

Shortly after the regime change in Afghanistan, I began to develop a multinational strategy, knowing massive amounts of opium and heroin would begin to flood the region and move quickly into Western Europe. I also knew it was critical to move swiftly and effectively. First, I would need a country in the region willing to host a multinational conference and, at the same time, be politically acceptable to other countries participating in the operation.

I selected Turkey. It is a secular but Muslim country and, for the most part, had good relationships with other nations in the area. Now I had the task of convincing them to serve as host for the planning conference. Prior to leaving for Turkey, I met with the DEA administrator to brief him on my plans. At the meeting were other senior executives, one of whom mentioned we should include Britain, claiming they had a large presence in Central Asia and the Balkans. I knew this not to be the case, but it got the attention of the administrator, who was immediately sold on the idea. I had learned from past experiences that their inclusion would only cause the usual impediments, but I was confident I would overcome them.

In early November 2001, I was on a plane to Ankara, Turkey. It was a long trip of over eighteen hours but gave me time to begin developing my approach in getting this complex project off the ground. On arriving, I was met by DEA personnel and, an hour later, settled into a hotel room in the downtown part of the city. The next day, I met with the director general of the Turkish National Police at his office. He was an older gentleman and enthusiastically embraced hosting the conference.

He also offered the use of the Turkish International Academy against Drugs and Organized Crime (TADOC) to train the police officers of countries who would be participating in the regional initiative. With Turkey onboard, we had only to set the dates for the conference.

At three in the morning, I was awakened by a telephone call from headquarters advising me a meeting would be taking place in London with various British agencies, including the MI6 intelligence service. I was told the Brits had some ideas regarding a strategy for attacking the heroin and opium being produced in Afghanistan. I knew better but made arrangements to travel that afternoon to London. Once there, I met with the DEA representatives from headquarters and our British colleagues. Incredibly, they literally discussed the weather for an hour, and on several occasions, I made futile attempts to steer the discussion to something more substantive. The Brits had nothing, as I had suspected all along. The meeting was all fluff and a waste of time. I returned to Turkey the following day after losing three days of valuable time.

The Turkish National Police were a different story. They were a no-nonsense organization, and it didn't take long to meet with all of the key players and solidify an agreement that the Turks would host the planning conference in Istanbul, one of my favorite cities in the world.

After returning to DEA headquarters, I continued to plan with my section chiefs in selecting the countries critical to the overall success of the operation, which I name Containment. I selected the name based on the focus of the strategy, which was to contain the movement of heroin and opium being produced in Afghanistan. A total of twenty-six countries were identified, including the Central Asian states, India, Pakistan, Turkey, the Balkan countries, Russia, China, Germany, and the United Kingdom. We worked through the various country attachés to extend an invitation to the countries. Iran had actually agreed to participate until President George W. Bush made the comment they were part of the "Axis of Evil."

Regardless, the other countries remained ready to participate. It was a matter of encouraging them to put aside political differences and work towards a common objective, a coordinated attack on a problem that threatened their respective nations. Within two months, DEA country attachés and high-ranking representatives from the many countries converged on Istanbul. I still recall walking into the hotel where the conference would be held and greeted by a huge banner displaying the DEA logo and the symbol of the Turkish National Police. I met with several foreign representatives that evening, and each expressed appreciation for the invitation to attend this historic meeting.

The conference room was huge and had a long table in front set on an elevated platform that served as the dais. The next morning, several ranking Turkish officials welcomed everyone and gave speeches from a podium and expressed how honored they were to host the historic event. The various representatives from other countries read lengthy speeches and comments. When it was my turn, I left the raised dais and stood directly in front of the representatives and addressed them from the heart. I told them we stood together as one and their countries and humanity would reap enormous benefits by the sacrifices they would all be making during the operation. The connection was made. They all understood.

Throughout history valued leaders have stood directly in front of their troops just before a battle. With the force of their personality, they melded their troops together for a common cause. What I was doing was part of their culture. As I praised and encouraged them, I began to see a fire ignite in their eyes. We connected as brothers on the same field, fighting the same fight together.

Interestingly, a year later at an IDEC conference in Bolivia, the Greeks who had attended that conference in Istanbul, presented me with a marble sculpture of *Winged Victory*, a second-century statue honoring the Greek Goddess Nike (Victory). It conveys action and triumph. One of the Greek generals had carried it by hand from Athens and given it to me with a few simple words: "You are just like us." It was a great honor, and I will always carry those five words with me until my I take my last breath.

The first day of the Operation Containment conference, the delegation from India asked for assistance from the Pakistani government in securing their common border area. Because of a deep-rooted and intense conflict between both countries over the Kashmir region, everyone held their collective breath, waiting for the Pakistanis to reply. India and Pakistan have fought at least three wars over Kashmir, including the Indo-Pakistan Wars of 1947, 1965, and 1999. The tense moment was dissolved when the Pakistani general replied; "We will gladly help you in securing the border area." That minor interaction set the stage for the entire successful initiative. In the evening, I went to my room and began putting the final touches on the Operation Containment strategy.

The following day, after every country had given their presentations, I approached the key representatives, asking them to meet me in a smaller conference room. I presented my strategy in detail, which included targeting the most significant drug-trafficking organizations in the region; controlling and managing common border areas; preventing the illegal importation of precursor chemicals, especially acetic anhydride; tracing the money derived from illicit drug profits; and expansive interdiction efforts. This tactic—to present, agree, and commit to the strategy prior to the general assembly—would eliminate any obstacles. The principals embraced the strategy, and experience indicated the remaining participants would also readily accept it. Early the next morning, I asked the Turkish representatives to put the entire strategy on PowerPoint to be shown on a large screen. As I stood in the conference room prior to that day's discussions, I watched the delegations exchanging ideas with great levity and good spirits.

It was interesting that being together for just a couple of days had created such strong bonds and friendships. It was rewarding to see the interaction and participation of these countries that had put aside political issues to address a common threat. As anticipated, I didn't receive opposition to the strategy—other than one British representative, who I quickly brushed aside. The die was cast, and there was nothing they could do to further impede the strategy.

The German delegation offered to connect the intelligence center in Bucharest, Romania, to the Balkan Information System (BIS) used by thirty-three European countries to share drug-related data. The Romanian intelligence center would function as the principal component for the sharing of information during Operation Containment. The Russians also would allow linkage to their GAIZ system for criminal intelligence. Everyone played a significant role.

That evening, I hosted a wine and beer celebratory party for the participants. The Russian generals brought ten bottles of vodka and wanted to drink a toast with me using water goblets filled to the top with straight vodka. We crossed arms and drank the entire glass. I repeated this six times and was surprised I was still standing. The Russians were also impressed I could keep pace, but that night, I apparently went to bed with all my clothes on and left the hotel room door ajar. I had removed my suit jacket, but my tie was still on, and in the morning, my head felt like a large sledgehammer had battered it.

We said our farewells with each one excited to be fully engaged in this historic operation. Before leaving the hotel, the Turkish government presented me with a beautiful, handmade lantern with Arabic scripture as a token of their respect.

During the first month of the operation, a total of 1,005 kilograms of heroin, 250,000 tablets of amphetamines, 352 kilograms of opium, 125 kilograms of hashish, and 1,500 metric tons of precursor chemicals were seized. Operation Containment exceeded all expectations and was wildly successful. Prior to the operation, only 407 kilograms of heroin had been seized during a ten-month period. During the first nine months of 2004, seizures under Operation Containment had skyrocketed to 14,932 kilos of heroin. The following year, over 577 arrests were made, a 16-percent increase over 2004; 248 heroin conversion labs were seized, approximately twenty-three times the amount seized the previous year; almost forty-four tons of opium gum, over seven times the amount seized in 2004; and fourteen tons of precursor chemicals, over four times the amount seized the previous year. In a short time, there was a 2,826-percent increase in the seizures of heroin over those seized before Operation Containment was launched!

It was recently touted by the DEA administrator as being one of the most successful initiatives ever developed by the DEA, creating more stability in the region and unprecedented cooperation and coordination in counter-narcotics/terrorism efforts. This operation continues to be funded by the US Congress to this day and will continue to be in the foreseeable future, since it has allowed fledgling democracies to develop and diminished drug profits from supporting terrorist activities in that part of the world.

In order to enhance our global reach and have greater impact in Afghanistan, it was critical to create a DEA office in that country. This would allow the DEA to develop investigations and coordinate operations such as Operation Containment against some of the largest traffickers in the world. It would also allow us to work with the US Embassy Country Team in developing the capabilities of the Afghan National Police by providing valuable training and equipment. I contacted Jeff Stamm, my country attaché in Pakistan, instructing him to travel to Kabul and determine the feasibility of establishing an office there. Jeff had been in the region for quite a while, and I could count on him to provide me with an objective assessment.

He called me a week later to say the building where the US Embassy had been located had structural damage due to mortar shells and military-grade weapons. He had been inside and watched as a Northern Alliance soldier, who had helped overthrow the Taliban, approached a civilian on the sidewalk in front of the embassy and shot him in the chest at close range with an AK-47. We understood the risk, but it was the nature of our business. As soon as the embassy was reestablished, I opened the DEA office that has now become a regional office having the largest DEA presence in the world.

■ ■ ■ ■

One of my other projects as chief of international operations was to create Regional Drug Intelligence Centers. I have always been an advocate of creating large coalitions and implementing multinational initiatives to aggressively attack drug trafficking and all its negative manifestations. The key factor for this type of frontal assault has been—and will continue to be—the expansive sharing of information between countries throughout the world. It is imperative that mechanisms for the exchange of information continue to be developed and evolve to meet current and future requirements to stem drug trafficking, which is now synonymous with terrorism and insurgent activities. I began to mull the idea over in my mind to create that strategy, since I was now in a position to do so.

One day I went to lunch with Michael McManus, one of my section chiefs, and began to explain my idea. He always jokingly told others not go to lunch with me, because I conceptualized strategies and then enlisted them to work with me on the implementation. We began developing the strategy for regional drug intelligence centers, which we named the Centers for Drug Information (CDIs). Initially, I wanted to establish them throughout Latin America and the Caribbean, but eventually move to globalization. In the early development phase, I designated Mexico City as the regional center for Mexico and all seven Central American countries, the Dominican Republic for the Caribbean, Colombia for the Andean Ridge countries, and Bolivia for the southern cone nations. I knew from the beginning a plan this creative would be riddled with political obstacles.

Internally, those who lacked vision would undoubtedly attempt to derail it. I would also have to convince the individual countries to accept the primary regional center locations and, more important, persuade them to expand the sharing of sensitive information at a much broader level. Funding for the project had to be obtained, because the DEA's budget could not support it. Only two agencies had large enough checkbooks to support the intelligence centers, State and the DOD. It would not be an easy task, since their budget allocations are designated at least a year in advance. The protocols for sharing information were extremely critical and would have to be crystal clear, otherwise the initiative could easily fail. The countries needed to understand the policies governing the exchange of information and then commit to them. I was fortunate that an IDEC was imminent and would be held in Santa Cruz, Bolivia. It would provide me the opportunity to meet and lobby the various countries. These forums had become highly useful to me, since they were a viable platform to initiate international counterdrug programs.

During the IDEC conference, I met with the representatives from Latin America and the Caribbean. The heads of police forces in Central America had concerns that Mexico would not share information with them if the regional site were in Mexico City. I advised them that Mexico had agreed to do so and would not be a problem. They trusted me and agreed to participate in the initiative. The other countries also agreed to work together and fully share drug-related information. During IDEC, the ranking police representatives provided briefings and status reports on their counterdrug-trafficking activities. They reaffirmed their support for the CDIs and the major benefits that would be derived in dismantling drug-trafficking organizations operating in their areas. This gave the initiative the vote of confidence required to begin moving forward.

The DEA administrator was not initially supportive of the CDIs, but after seeing the show of support, he held a press conference during IDEC saying he fully supported the project. Lt. Colonel John Carroll, US Marine Corps, military liaison to the DEA, also worked on the project and provided significant contributions. Eventually, the CDIs took shape, and funding was acquired from the DOD. The program immediately began to assist foreign law-enforcement organizations in the sharing of information and coordination of law-enforcement operations.

The system offers standardized reporting forms, data storage in a central, relational database with search capabilities, passport and fugitive database, real-time chat, and other analytical tools. The CDIs rapidly expanded worldwide, currently having over a thousand users in fifty-eight countries that include a South Central Asia Regional Center in Kabul, Afghanistan; a Southeast Asia Regional Center in Bangkok, Thailand, and a West Africa Regional Center in Accra, Ghana. An automated online language-translation feature serves to minimize language barriers for a majority of the participants. This secure system allows the users to share information on drug movements, seizures, drug traffickers, alien smuggling, money laundering, weapons trafficking, clandestine laboratories, terrorism, and smuggling of precursor chemicals.

The CDIs have been instrumental in dismantling international drug-trafficking networks and disrupting smuggling and distribution activities. Without question, the system has become a significant weapon for many countries in a global effort against the major funding source for terrorist networks. This program continues to be funded and will be expanding to many other countries in Africa, Southeast Asia, and Europe. Through the CDIs, the DEA is also strengthening partnerships with foreign law-enforcement counterparts to maximize the impact of worldwide counterdrug operations. In the end, the initiative was not a bad idea to have been developed during a quick lunch.

Each year, I had a number of interesting visitors. One of them was definitely Nicolai Petrushev, who replaced Vladimir Putin as head of the Federal Security Service, formerly known as the KGB. Petrushev assumed the position in 1991 when Boris Yeltsin promoted Putin to acting prime minister. He was already a seasoned, veteran spy master and loyal to Putin. Petrushev was born in Leningrad and graduated from the Leningrad Shipbuilding Institute where he worked as an engineer. He joined the KGB in 1975 and worked in the counterintelligence section of the KGB Regional Directorate for the Leningrad region. He was later appointed Minister of State Security for the Republic of Karelia. Petrushev holds the rank of general of the army and has a PhD in law. He was on a state visit to the US, and the DEA was on his list of agencies to meet with on matters of interest to his country.

I hosted a lunch for him in my conference room. He had a very large entourage of Russian officials and US State Department personnel who were tasked with making sure his visit went well and no problems loomed on the horizon. Petrushev was a tall, stately man with blond hair and crystal-blue eyes. He could easily play the role of the quintessential KGB agent in a James Bond movie. He smiled, and we exchanged greetings through an interpreter. We enjoyed lunch and discussed the global problem of illicit drugs and transnational crime. We both agreed that coordination and communication were the key elements to developing a coherent counterdrug strategy.

Within the Office of International Operations, the section which dealt with foreign visitors maintained a supply of nice gifts for high-ranking visitors. Before his arrival, I had selected a porcelain eagle and a beautiful clock encased in mahogany. After lunch I presented him with both gifts, but he was unimpressed and handed them to his aide. Just at that moment, I remembered a decanter of Bacardi rum given to me when I left the Caribbean, which I had stored in the bottom drawer of my desk. I slipped back into my office, brought it back to the conference room, and handed it to Petrushev. He looked very carefully at it, then leaped out of his chair and gave me a huge Russian bear hug. That bottle of rum helped cement our relationship with Russian officials in the area of combating the drug trade. Sometimes the smallest things moved the cause forward.

The position of chief of international operations provided me with the opportunity to travel to a great number of countries carrying the DEA banner and to make the agency the strong and global leader of counterdrug operations. Even the Chinese government recognized this and presented me with the *key to the city* of Shanghai. On a trip to Berlin, Bob Mangiamele, another exceptional agent and the country attaché for Germany, Czech Republic, and Poland met me at the airport. He had done a great job establishing strong relationships with his counterparts in all three countries. We decided to have dinner, and I was looking forward to having some typical German cuisine. Surprising me, Bob drove into an Italian restaurant parking lot, claiming it had the best Italian food in Berlin. We walked in and you would have thought the Godfather had entered. The owner personally greeted him, followed by all the chefs, and finally the elderly matriarch who, of course, was dressed in black. He was right, the food was phenomenal, but the next day, I forced him to take me to have some schnitzel.

My primary goal in traveling was to established global coalitions and long-lasting friendships with the highest levels of government in many countries. The current prime minister of Bulgaria, Boyko Borisov being one. I was visiting Sofia, Bulgaria, on another matter but made it a point to visit Boyko at his office. We hugged each other and sat down to chat. His English was broken, but I understood the message he was attempting to convey. He told me the Bulgarian media knew I was in the country and wanted to interview me. I had been there previously and had given a press conference with Boyko and the former prime minister, in which I praised the counterdrug efforts and activities of the Bulgarian police. Boyko requested I return to his office the following Monday at three in the afternoon, where the media would be waiting.

When I returned to his office I found representatives from the Bulgarian national television and major newspapers set up and ready. The hour-long interview primarily focused on my perspective about drug trafficking through the Balkan region and the world in general. I complimented the countries in the region, including Bulgaria, for their efforts on Operation Containment and the regional sharing of information initiatives I had developed. The media delayed the release of their newspapers and television news broadcasts until they could incorporate my interview. As a side note, Condoleezza Rice was also in Bulgaria at the time, and the following morning, I appeared on the front page of the national newspapers, and they relegated Rice to page thirty-two.

Another memorable visit was to Romania for a meeting with the police generals at an internal conference. I was driven to a small village two hours outside of Bucharest to meet with the minister of interior, who presented me a small, black case with a hatchet, knife, and other sharp weapons. It resembled the kit of an old-time assassin. After delivering a speech to all of the regional police commanders, I was taken to a beautiful restaurant with old-world charm. The meal started with caviar and other delicacies, and it continued for an hour. The feast was fit for a king, and after we ate and drank, I was asked to step outside, where they stood with a beautiful white stallion. With a small entourage, we followed it up a steep hill. At the top, the police commanders had set bonfires, and a small group of musicians played folk music. They made a short speech and presented me with the horse, a gift for supporting Romania and the entire region with Operation Containment. I graciously thanked them, said it was a great honor, but didn't have a place to keep it. Fortunately, they understood, and we all had a great time at an evening with such a dramatic ending.

Chapter 20

I Did It My Way

*Dynamic leader, brilliant tactician, fearless warrior—
these are but a few terms that describe Michael Vigil. He
never followed the easy, less-effective path in his relentless
pursuit of criminals, terrorists, and organized crime groups;
rather he blazed his own trail for others to follow. In the fine
tradition of the most notable leaders and crime fighters of
our time, Mike's command presence, courage, compassion,
mentoring skills, and strategic abilities inspired others to
pursue his lead in achieving excellence and mission success.
In the annals of DEA history Mike will be listed as a true
legend and master of his craft.*

—Michael Todd
DEA Assistant Special Agent in Charge (Ret.)

After two years in headquarters, I was transferred to the San Diego
Division as the special agent in charge (SAC), a coveted position because
San Diego is a great area with some of the best weather in the world. I
was looking forward to the new challenge and working once again on
the Mexican border. The division had its main office on the outskirts of
the city, with satellite offices in Carlsbad, San Ysidro, and the Imperial
Valley. The area between Tijuana, Baja California North, and San Diego,
California, has three large border ports of entry, Otay Mesa, Tecate, and

San Ysidro, with the latter being the busiest land-border crossing in the world. There are over three hundred thousand daily commuters crossing between Tijuana and San Diego. With the millions of pedestrians and vehicular traffic crossing from Tijuana, it is a drug smuggler's dream and a nightmare for the immigration and customs officials unable to contend with the volume of traffic. They do an incredible job, but it's humanly impossible to search each individual and vehicle, despite state-of-the-art technology. Even so, the traffickers build sophisticated tunnels between both countries, equipped with lighting, ventilation systems, and rails to move the drugs across the border in subterranean secrecy. They also use light aircraft to transport large quantities of drugs and vehicles, crossing into the US in isolated areas along the border.

Just before reporting to San Diego, I asked Jack Hook, one of the assistant special agents in charge, to establish meetings with all the significant US law-enforcement agencies in the area, and more important, with the MFJP in Tijuana. When I arrived in San Diego several days later, Jack met me at the airport, and the way into the office, I asked him if meetings had been solidified. He said they were with the exception of the federal police in Tijuana. He had contacted the DEA office there, and they indicated it would take two weeks to arrange.

I called Genaro García Luna, a close friend of mine, who at the time was in charge of the Federal Investigative Agency (AFI). Genaro had done incredible work building the capabilities of the AFI. Genaro was literally the right hand of Felipe Calderón when he was president of Mexico and made huge sacrifices for his country. He told me Francisco Garduño was in charge of the federal police in Tijuana and gave me his cell number.

I knew Francisco. We had become great friends when I was assigned to Mexico City. I called him, and he immediately made an appointment to meet the following day. I was of the opinion that if you have an office along the border, it was imperative to create strategies that encompassed both sides. Most of the significant traffickers were in Mexico, and therefore, it was crucial to have a strong relationship with Mexican authorities. The following day we met, which resulted in an agreement to share information and coordinate investigations. He introduced me to the Mexican federal prosecutor, who also pledged to work with the DEA. I made it a point to have regular meetings with the Mexican officials at my offices or theirs. Again, personal relationships get results, not a rank. Within the San Diego Division, I had hundreds of hardworking agents to work with including David Surh, John Rende, Brian Collier, and Jack Hook, who were my ASACs (assistant special agents in charge). Others that come to mind were Ralph García, Pedro Pena, Abe Perez, Ron Aldridge, Don Thornhill, Misha Piastro, and so many others it is impossible to name them all.

The dominant drug-trafficking organization operating in the Tijuana area was the Arellano Félix family, which was initially composed of seven brothers and four sisters. The organization had an iron grip on drug-trafficking activities in the most lucrative area along the US–Mexico area. They were extremely violent, and some members killed just for the enjoyment. Coldblooded, with no regard for human life, their sole objective was to make millions of dollars distributing drugs, primarily cocaine, in the US, The organization adhered to the silver-or-lead tactic, where Mexican officials either took bribes or were riddled with bullets.

Since operations have always been my forte, I began to innovate strategies to impact the drug trade in San Diego and Mexico. One of my initial ideas was to have a large MFJP group based in the United States and functioning as an agile and well-trained reactionary force. It was important to have this component in the US, because the Arellano Félix organization knew when military and police units were in Tijuana. They had an expansive network of sources keeping them apprised of anything that moved in the area. By basing a large force of MFJP in the US, it would prevent the Mexican police from being threatened or subjected to bribes.

Not long after conceptualizing this plan, Larry Holifield, the regional director for Mexico and Central America, told me he and José Luis

Santiago Vasconcelos, Mexico's deputy attorney general, were coming to San Diego. Both were close friends of mine, and I realized this was my opportunity to put my plan in motion. I met Larry and Santiago Vasconcelos at the airport late one evening and, on the way to their hotel, began to brief them of my plan. When I told Santiago Vasconcelos I would need at least fifty Mexican federal police, he immediately rejected the idea.

I continued to argue with him, in a friendly manner, for over an hour. It continued in the lobby of the hotel. He went upstairs to leave his suitcase and returned to the lobby so we could have dinner. He looked at me and with a smile said, *"Horale, que es lo que quieres?"* (Okay, what is it that you want?) Ultimately, he agreed to give me the fifty federal police, and at dinner we talked about and toasted the old times. I had the highest respect for Santiago Vasconcelos, who always exemplified the highest integrity and was one of the finest Mexican civil servants of all time. He was later killed, along with the Mexican minister of interior, when his plane crashed in the exclusive Polanco section of Mexico City. The jet wash from another aircraft caused their Learjet to go into a flat spin. It was a tragic loss, not only for Mexico but the United States as well.

I forged ahead and began to plan the entire operation, beginning with finding a place for the reactionary force to stay. Initially, I had explored the possibility of putting them in apartments, but that would have been too expensive. I had a brainstorm one morning to explore the possibility of using Camp Pendleton, the Marine Corps base. It had the capability for billeting eighteen thousand personnel. I called the commanding officer to explain my plan and billeting requirements for the Mexican federal police. He realized this would be the first time foreign police would actually be living on a US military base for a long period of time. He said it required authorization from the secretary of the navy and told me to send him a formal, written request. A few weeks later, I received a call from him telling me the secretary of the navy had approved it. The devil is in the details, and I understood the MFJP members would have considerable downtime, so it was imperative that training be provided to occupy their days. A meeting was later held in Mexico City with representatives from the DEA, ATF, FBI, and the US Marshals Service. We agreed the various agencies would participate and provide different blocks of training, while the Mexican police waited for the opportune time to react to a significant enforcement activity.

The operation was code named United Eagles. When the Mexican federal police arrived at Camp Pendleton, I welcomed them to the US and briefed them on their mission and operational objectives. They completely understood what would be expected of them. The plan later bore fruit, with an impressive show of force, when they moved rapidly into Tijuana, arresting two of the principal lieutenants belonging to the Arellano Félix organization. Arrested without incident were Efrain Perez Pazuengo, a.k.a. El Efra, and Jorge Aureliano Félix, a.k.a. El Macuba, who were responsible for numerous murders and corrupting Mexican officials. They operated with impunity in the Arellano Félix organization and were responsible for nearly 30 percent of the cocaine sold on American soil.

United Eagles was also responsible for the arrests of several other major traffickers in Mexico and showed again what could be accomplished by combined efforts between Mexico and the US. This operation, along with other law-enforcement efforts, spelled the demise of the Arellano Félix network. Their reign of terror would soon be at an end, as most of the brothers were placed in tombs or jail cells. Less than a year later, a joint task force between the DEA and FBI in San Diego resulted in the indictments of twelve individuals representing the upper hierarchy of the Arellano Félix organization. A press conference was held in San Diego, attended by Attorney General Ashcroft and Mexican Attorney General Rafael Macedo de la Concha. The media used one of my quotes, which said it all:

> International cooperation and the exchange of
> information are valuable weapons that law enforcement

at all levels should be using to immobilize drug-trafficking organizations worldwide.

■ ■ ■ ■

One of the most interesting cases in San Diego involved Baron Suarez Rothchild, an international drug trafficker who went by the name of Dr. Wu. He was a slippery criminal, who had eluded the DEA for two decades by remaining in the shadows, his underlings taking the risks. Dr. Wu was the common thread in an organization that for years moved millions of dollars' worth of high-grade marijuana, methamphetamine, and cocaine through California's San Diego and Riverside Counties, Hawaii, Australia, and Singapore. We began to develop information on his organization and coordinated the complex and expansive investigation with authorities from numerous countries. Dr. Wu was eventually arrested after shipping a large quantity of cocaine to Singapore that was intercepted by local customs officials. The police in Singapore detained him when he entered the country to collect the money for the cocaine shipment. The investigation lasted two years, until we arrived at the point when we were ready to eliminate the entire organization.

In the early morning hours, more than 150 law-enforcement officers executed twenty-nine search warrants in San Diego and Riverside Counties and in Hawaii. We arrested thirty individuals and seized $500,000, sixteen weapons, including nine assault rifles, and a significant amount of cocaine. Residents of Tijuana, Canada, and Washington State were also charged in three federal indictments. The San Diego Union Tribune, April 3, 2004, by Shannon Tangonan, mentioned, "'What we have accomplished is the immobilization, from top to bottom, of a very significant drug-trafficking network,' Michael S. Vigil, the Special Agent in Charge of the DEA San Diego's Division, said yesterday." I am positive Dr. Wu sat in a Singapore prison awaiting extradition to the US realizing the long arm of the law had reached out and touched him.

Moving forward, I created the Border Special Agents in Charge Coordination Committee representing the DEA divisions along the Mexico border, including the San Diego, Phoenix, El Paso, and Houston Divisions. Los Angeles was also a participant, since drugs coming from Mexico heavily impacted their area of operations. The purpose of the coordination committee was to discuss strategies and other issues of mutual concern. The first meeting was held in Houston. I recommended regular joint meetings with Mexican counterparts to develop a close working relationship, which would facilitate dismantling drug-trafficking organizations on both sides of the border.

Based on this recommendation, the committee traveled to Mexico City to meet with our Mexican counterparts. We had an initial meeting between ourselves at the US Embassy to discuss the topics most important to us. I wanted to initiate a bilateral process of collectively targeting the largest drug-trafficking networks operating in Mexico and the US. The representatives from Los Angeles, for whatever reason, argued against it, saying they were already doing it. True, some of the DEA divisions were coordinating a few investigations, but not at the level required to have a major impact. The sharing of information was inadequate, and no process for selecting and targeting the top-tier organizations existed. The argument continued with no resolution at the embassy.

We were escorted to a very large conference room at AFI headquarters, where Mexican representatives sat on one side and the Americans on the other. There were simultaneous translators in a booth for those not speaking English or Spanish. The two top-ranking Mexican officials in attendance were Santiago Vasconcelos and Genaro García Luna. The others were police commanders from every region of Mexico. We were all seated when Santiago Vasconcelos arrived. He immediately approached me and gave me the traditional Mexican *abrazo* (hug). He chaired the meeting, with the first agenda item being the establishment of a process for collective targeting between both countries. I rested my case and just smiled.

The Mexican representatives briefed us on several major investigations against significant drug-trafficking organizations. They had collected significant information that could be used to exploit the vulnerabilities of these organizations. One investigation was of particular interest to the Houston Division. The Mexican delegation had virtually identified all the key members, warehouses where drugs were stored, smuggling methods and routes, vehicles belonging to the traffickers, residences, and telephone numbers. The SAC from Houston asked if he could have the information. Santiago Vasconcelos was willing to share but also wanted information from Houston. They weren't asking for sources of information or sensitive intelligence, but making sure the exchange of data was reciprocal—as it should be between countries. The border committee allowed us to establish a closer working relationship with our Mexican counterparts, which led to the dismantling of many significant organizations in Mexico and the US.

■ ■ ■ ■

Drug traffickers in Mexico used many sophisticated methods to smuggle vast quantities of drugs into the US and were willing to pay millions of dollars to make it happen. One method included hiring experts with the ability to build tunnels. Some were rudimentary, but many were sophisticated. Early one day, the Border Patrol responded to a ground sensor that had been activated near the international fence in San Ysidro, California. The sensor was next to a public parking lot where people left their vehicles to walk across the border into Tijuana. On arrival, they observed a large cargo truck near the sensor and detected the smell of marijuana emanating from the inside. A search revealed several hundred kilograms of marijuana, and two occupants were arrested. We were contacted, and my agents responded to the scene. I drove to the site and determined the truck had a modified undercarriage with a trap door, which when opened, could receive drugs from underneath. The truck had parked over a manhole cover that had been removed. The marijuana was passed up to the men in the truck, who neatly stacked it inside. The traffickers had built a tunnel originating in Tijuana that followed the drainage system into the parking lot. Two of my best agents, Pedro Pena and Abe Perez, coordinated with Francisco Garduno in Tijuana.

The Mexican federal police conducted searches and, within a short time, located a house several hundred feet from the international fence. The owners, who lived on the top floor, said two men claiming they were from the Mexican state of Sinaloa had rented the ground floor of the house. In one of the bedrooms, stone tiles covered the tunnel entrance. It was very narrow and went down nearly eighteen feet before it began to move towards the parking lot in the US. Witnesses indicated several individuals dressed in cowboy hats and boots regularly backed up a large truck to the house and loaded large barrels. Undoubtedly, this was the dirt being removed during the tunnel construction. Later, we found a warehouse in the US that had another truck similar to the one seized in the parking lot. Through our investigation, we were able to arrest the men involved in this sophisticated smuggling operation, which appeared to be an escalating trend.

In order to be more proactive, we needed more information on the tunnels that had been located along the southwest border during the past ten years. I tasked one of my intelligence groups to compile a comprehensive report on the number of tunnels discovered, level of sophistication, location, and the organizations involved. The results determined that a total of twenty-one tunnels had been discovered between 1990 and 2003. Seven were in the San Diego County area and fourteen along the Arizona border.

It was apparent that following the terrorist attacks on 9/11, drug traffickers began relying on tunnels to avoid increased security at the US ports of entry. Four of the twenty-one tunnels had cart-and-rail systems. Nine were equipped with lights and sophisticated ventilation, and eleven of the Arizona tunnels were connected to drainage systems that reduced the work of the traffickers. All of them, with the exception of one, were located close to ports of entry, allowing easy access to major highways. The majority of the tunnels cost over a million dollars, which meant only the largest criminal groups, such as the Arrellano Félix brothers and Ismael "Mayo" Zambada, could afford them. Apart from the smuggling of drugs, the passageways could potentially be used by terrorists for nefarious activities.

Shortly after the discovery of the tunnel in San Ysidro, I created an ad hoc Tunnel Task Force to allow for intelligence-driven operations and to work jointly with private companies in developing and testing tunnel-detection technology. I had meetings with all federal, state, and local law-enforcement agencies operating on the California–Mexico border. Also included were tunnel experts and first responders. I briefed them on my strategy, and all readily agreed to work together and pool needed resources and subject-matter expertise. A protocol was developed with Mexican officials for the sharing of information and coordination of investigations involving subterranean smuggling. The task force was later formalized and became very effective, leading to the detection of some of the largest and most sophisticated cross-border tunnels.

Its work on tunnel detection and related investigations garnered international attention, and the US Department of Defense requested assistance from the DEA and task force to provide training to the government of Egypt in dealing with clandestine border tunnels. Senator Dianne Feinstein became aware of the task-force work and the threat posed by this smuggling tactic. She passed the Border Tunnel Prevention Act, which made it a crime to knowingly construct, finance, or allow the construction of an unauthorized tunnel across a US international border. Individuals caught using such a tunnel to smuggle aliens, contraband, drugs, weapons, or terrorists face penalties of more than twenty years.

Another investigation focused on the Hell's Angels outlaw motorcycle club. They are one of the top four motorcycle clubs in the US, which also include the Pagans, Mongols, and the Outlaws. The Hell's Angels are the largest and most feared, and they are not hesitant to use violence to protect their organization. They engage in a multitude of criminal activities, such as weapons and drug trafficking, with over one hundred chapters in over twenty-nine countries.

Despite the group's fame, there is much about the Hell's Angels that remains shrouded in mystery. The history of the gang and its current membership are murky topics, and what goes on inside its secretive clubhouses tends to remain there. They had their beginning in Fontana, California, in 1948, at a time when military surplus made motorcycles affordable. The postwar years left many veterans bored and itching for adventure. Along with other outlaw motorcycle clubs, they began to engage in trafficking of drugs, due in large part to the huge profits derived from this lucrative enterprise.

The investigation against the Hell's Angels chapter in San Diego developed from ongoing cases we had on two drug-trafficking networks having a nexus with members of the gang. They were jointly engaged in the marijuana, cocaine, and methamphetamine distribution throughout the US. The investigation was intense and involved the use of informants who made introductions of undercover agents to members of the two organizations supplying the motorcycle club with drugs. Surveillance and undercover drug purchases led to the development of an affidavit and application for telephone intercepts, which were authorized several weeks later. The interception of telephone conversations tied many of the members to a large, criminal conspiracy. The group was very open with their communications, which led to their demise.

Once the investigation had generated enough evidence to make it a strong conspiracy case, we arrested thirty members from the two drug-trafficking organizations. It was now time to impose the rule of law against the outlaw motorcycle gang. A carefully planned operation involving more than 150 officers from the DEA, El Cajon police, San Diego sheriffs, San Diego police, and the ATF descended on their clubhouse in El Cajon, California. Several "stun grenades" were thrown through the windows, forcing the Hell's Angels out the back door and into the hands of SWAT units.

Seventeen members and associates of the San Diego chapter were arrested, including the chapter president, Guy "Big Daddy" Castiglione. The operation was quick, effective, and caught them by surprise. They surrendered peacefully and were handcuffed on the ground, until they could be transported to jail. They appeared to be shell-shocked for hours and were later arraigned on charges of racketeering and conspiracy. In a press conference with the participating agencies, I said, "We have eliminated a scourge from Southern California that had tentacles into the international community. The Hell's Angels have traded their club colors for jailhouse orange and their motorcycle handlebars for prison bars."

San Diego, in the 1990s, was once regarded as the methamphetamine capital of the world due to its long, tumultuous history with the drug, which began during World War II. Its use was prevalent among US military personnel assigned to the Pacific theater of operations. When they returned, principally through San Diego, they brought their addictions with them, giving rise to a new, illicit drug industry. Taking advantage of the situation, outlaw motorcycle gangs such as the Hell's Angels began producing potent methamphetamine, with precursors provided by Mexican criminals. The collateral damage created by domestic production to people, property, and the environment contributes to the overall threat posed by the drug. First responders, law-enforcement personnel, clandestine laboratory operators, and particularly children often are injured as a result of chemical burns, fires, and explosions. There is also costly environmental damage caused by improper storage and disposal of chemicals and waste products, which seep into the ground and water supply.

During a particularly busy day, one of my ASACs, Dave Surh, came to my office and asked if I would like to accompany him to a multiagency meeting at the County Methamphetamine Strike Force. The objective of the organization is the reduction of the problems associated with the manufacture, distribution, sales, and use of the dangerous stimulant.

The first thing that caught my attention was that representation was limited to local law enforcement, prosecutors, and prevention personnel, but did not include Mexican officials. Without the coordination and assistance of Mexico, it was like bringing down a bull elephant with a slingshot. I briefed them on my ideas and explained it would require a few days to lay the groundwork with officials from Mexico's federal police, customs, health, and federal and state prosecutors.

At the second meeting, the room was packed with Mexican representatives. We had a lively discussion and exchange of valuable information. This forum proved invaluable as we began to plan joint efforts and maximize our bilateral efforts against meth trafficking and prevention. In coordination with several local and Mexican agencies, we initiated a cross-border operation named Speed Bump. We began to identify distributors and develop prosecutable cases in San Diego and the Tijuana area.

The operation involved daily coordination with Mexican authorities and the fluid exchange of information critical to investigative efforts in both countries. When we were ready to launch a major offensive, the planning began to ensure arrests and raids would be conducted simultaneously in the US and Mexico. This was extremely important to guarantee the element of surprise. Both prosecutors and police worked closely together to strike the effective blow. The large crackdown resulted in eight hundred arrests and the dismantling of three clandestine labs. Mexico arrested 164 criminals in Tijuana, where the labs were seized.

The *San Diego Union Tribune, April 10, 2004, by Joe Hughes,* had the following quote:

> Michael S. Vigil, the Special Agent in Charge with the Drug Enforcement Administration, said the effort during February and March involved cooperation from the US and Mexican authorities in a new coalition approach to the problem. "Methamphetamine abuse has become a blizzard of global proportions and has taken the lives of many citizens in myriad countries," Vigil told a news conference at DEA headquarters in Kearny Mesa. "We are working on global strategies and

solutions with both local and international coalitions to
end the storm."

■ ■ ■ ■

One of my last acts in San Diego was to honor the memory of Kiki
Camarena by naming the three-story building housing the division's
central offices after our slain brother. Two hundred family members,
former colleagues, and friends paid tribute. I requested DEA and San
Diego Police helicopters fly overhead, with one falling out of formation,
signifying the loss of one of our own. The renaming of the building would
serve as a reminder of the sacrifices made by Kiki and others who fight
to keep the country free of illegal drugs and acts of terrorism. Inside our
large training room, we permanently placed photographs of him selected
by his family. The Association of Former Federal Narcotics Agents
(AFFNA) graciously commissioned and donated a bronze bust. Kiki's
death brought the struggle against drugs to national consciousness. It
also inspired a movie and the creation of a national drug-prevention
campaign known as Red Ribbon Week.

"Kiki Camarena is a symbolic figure for all narcotic agents who paid
the ultimate price," said Michael Vigil, Special Agent in Charge, who
worked alongside Camarena in Mexico. (*San Diego Union Tribune*)

After two short years in San Diego, I decided to retire and take a
job in the private sector in Washington, DC. It was a tough decision,
but I had known the time would inevitably come. I consider myself very
fortunate to have worked in the early golden years of the DEA, when it
was bold, dynamic, decisive, and not risk-averse. In those early years, we
ventured into extreme danger, many times without anyone to watch our
backs, and did so without hesitation. Greatness consists of many things,
and sacrifice is the one that usually remains in the shadows. This book
is dedicated to the DEA agents and other law enforcement professionals
who operated on the frontlines and never compromised their integrity
to advance their careers.

It is also dedicated to those leaders who were not afraid of making difficult decisions, were decisive in their actions, and did not hide behind *process*. These few pushed politics aside and decisively moved forward to accomplish operational objectives in making this world safe from the scourge of illicit drugs and terrorism. The words of Ferdinand Magellan, the first globetrotting explorer, said it best: "The Sea is dangerous and its storms terrible, but these obstacles have never been sufficient reason to remain ashore. Unlike the mediocre, intrepid spirits seek victory over those things that seem impossible. It is with iron will that they embark on the most daring of all endeavors, to meet the shadowy future without fear and conquer the unknown."